Laurence Sterne

LONGMAN CRITICAL READERS

GENERAL EDITOR

STAN SMITH

Research Professor in Literary Studies, The Nottingham Trent University

TITLES AVAILABLE

MARY EAGLETON, Feminist Literary Criticism
GARY WALLER, Shakespeare's Comedies
JOHN DRAKAKIS, Shakespearean Tragedy
RICHARD WILSON AND RICHARD DUTTON, New Historicism and Renaissance Drama
PETER WIDDOWSON, D. H. Lawrence
PETER BROOKER, Modernism/Postmodernism
RACHEL BOWLBY, Virginia Woolf
FRANCIS MULHERN, Contemporary Marxist Literary Criticism
ANNABEL PATTERSON, John Milton
CYNTHIA CHASE, Romanticism
MICHAEL O'NEILL, Shelley
STEPHANIE TRIGG, Medieval English Poetry
ANTONY EASTHOPE, Contemporary Film Theory
TERRY EAGLETON, Ideology
MAUD ELLMANN, Psychoanalytic Literary Criticism
ANDREW BENNETT, Readers and Reading
MARK CURRIE, Metafiction
BREAN HAMMOND, Pope
STEVEN CONNOR, Charles Dickens
REBECCA STOTT, Tennyson
LYN PYKETT, Reading *Fin de Siècle* Fictions
ANDREW HADFIELD, Edmund Spenser
SUSANA ONEGA AND JOSÉ ANGEL GARCÍA LANDA, Narratology: An Introduction
TESS COSSLETT, Victorian Women Poets
BART MOORE-GILBERT, GARETH STANTON AND WILLY MALEY, Postcolonial Criticism
ANITA PACHECO, Early Women Writers
JOHN DRAKAKIS AND NAOMI CONN LIEBLER, Tragedy
ANDREW MICHAEL ROBERTS, Joseph Conrad
JOHN LUCAS, William Blake
LOIS PARKINSON ZAMORA, Contemporary American Women Writers: Gender, Class, Ethnicity
THOMAS HEALY, Andrew Marvell

MODERN GENRE THEORY

JANE STABLER, Byron
STEVE ELLIS, Chaucer: The Canterbury Tales
RICHARD KROLL, The English Novel, Volume I, 1700 to Fielding
RICHARD KROLL, The English Novel, Volume II, Smollett to Austen
CRISTINA MALCOLMSON, Renaissance Poetry
HARRIET DAVIDSON, T. S. Eliot
JEREMY TAMBLING, Dante
KIERNAN RYAN, Shakespeare: The Last Plays
RICHARD WILSON, Christopher Marlowe
NIGEL WOOD, Jonathan Swift
JENNIFER BIRKETT AND KATE INCE, Samuel Beckett
RICHARD DUTTON, Ben Jonson
DAVID DUFF, Modern Genre Theory

Laurence Sterne

EDITED AND INTRODUCED BY

MARCUS WALSH

An imprint of **Pearson Education**

London · New York · Toronto · Sydney · Tokyo · Singapore · Hong Kong · Cape Town
New Delhi · Madrid · Paris · Amsterdam · Munich · Milan · Stockholm

PEARSON EDUCATION LIMITED

Head Office:
Edinburgh Gate
Harlow CM20 2JE
Tel: +44 (0)1279 623623
Fax: +44 (0)1279 431059

London Office:
128 Long Acre
London WC2E 9AN
Tel: +44 (0)20 7447 2000
Fax: +44 (0)20 7240 5771
Website: www.history-minds.com

First published in Great Britain in 2002

© Pearson Education Limited 2002

ISBN 0 582 36850 2

British Library Cataloguing in Publication Data
A CIP catalogue record for this book can be obtained from the British Library

Library of Congress Cataloging in Publication Data
A CIP catalog record for this book can be obtained from the Library of Congress

10 9 8 7 6 5 4 3 2 1

Designed by Claire Brodmann Book Designs, Lichfield, Staffs
Typeset in Stone Serif 9.5/12.5pt by Graphicraft Limited, Hong Kong
Printed in Malaysia

The Publishers' policy is to use paper manufactured from sustainable forests.

Contents

ℒ

PART FOUR
Sources, Imitation, Plagiarism 119

PART FIVE
Narrative and Form 161

In memory of Kenneth Monkman, Shandean

Acknowledgements

୧

Wwe are grateful to the following for permission to reproduce copyright material:

California University Press for extract from 'Running out of Matter' by Carol Houlihan Flynn, in THE LANGUAGES OF PSYCHE: MIND AND BODY IN ENLIGHTENMENT THOUGHT by G. S. Rousseau © 1991 The Regents of the University of California; University of Iowa Press for 'Sterne, Burton, and Ferriar: Allusions to the ANATOMY OF MELANCHOLY in Volumes Five to Nine of TRISTRAM SHANDY' by H. J. Jackson in PHILOLOGICAL QUARTERLY 1974 pp. 457–470; University of Massachusetts Press for 'Job's Wife and Sterne's other Women' by Melvyn New in OUT OF BOUNDS: MALE WRITERS AND GENDER(ED) CRITICISM edited by Claridge/Langland © 1990 University of Massachusetts Press; McMaster University for '"Uncrystalized Flesh and Blood": The Body in TRISTRAM SHANDY' by Juliet McMaster from EIGHTEENTH CENTURY FICTION 2:3 published April 1990, and 'On Sterne's Page: Spatial Layout, Spatial Form, and Social Spaces in TRISTRAM SHANDY' by Christopher Fanning in EIGHTEENTH CENTURY FICTION 10:4 published July 1998; Modern Humanities Research Association and the author for 'Sterne's System of Imitation' by Jonathan Lamb in MODERN LANGUAGE REVIEW (1981) pp. 794–810; University of North Texas for words from 'Words for Sex: The Verbal-Sexual Continuum in TRISTRAM SHANDY' by Ruth Perry in STUDIES IN THE NOVEL 1988 pp. 27–42; University of Oklahoma Press for text from 'Narrative Middles: a Preliminary Outline' by J. Hillis Miller in GENRE 1978; Oxford University Press for extract from 'Laurence Sterne and the "Sociality" of the Novel' by John Mullan in SENTIMENT AND SOCIALITY: THE LANGUAGE OF FEELING IN THE EIGHTEENTH CENTURY 1988 pp. 158–72 and the author, Eve Kosofsky Sedgwick for extracts from 'Sexualism and the Citizen of the World: Wycherley, Sterne and Male Homosocial Desire' by Eve Kosofsky Sedgwick in CRITICAL INQUIRY 1984 pp. 226–228 and pp. 238–245.

Introduction

⚭

STERNE AND 'THEORY'

As early as 1776, just eight years after the publication of its ninth and ultimate volume, Samuel Johnson notoriously remarked 'Nothing odd will do long. *Tristram Shandy* did not last'. The better part of two centuries later, in 1948, F. R. Leavis dismissed Sterne from his version of the 'great tradition' of the English novel in a footnote which accused him of 'irresponsible (and nasty) trifling'. These briefly dismissive and apparently personal and offhand remarks both nevertheless arose out of their authors' theoretical positions: in Johnson's case, in part out of a preference for formal coherence, more substantially out of his regular demand for a credible mimesis based on shared human experience; in Leavis's case, out of his insistence on a morally serious, and morally committed literature. Like any major piece of writing, *Tristram Shandy*, together with Sterne's other masterpiece, *A Sentimental Journey*, has evoked responses which have always been ideologically conditioned. Those responses have become, no less than for other literary writings which are part of the 'canon' which we study, most explicitly theorized in the last hundred years.

After the *succès d'estime* and *succès de scandale* enjoyed in their own time, Sterne's works, and especially *Tristram*, entered their next major period of vogue only in the opening decades of the twentieth century. Sterne's explorations of time sequence and of the association of ideas, of voice and of metafictionality fascinated such diverse modernist novelists as Woolf, Proust and Joyce, and clearly had some influence on the development of the 'stream of consciousness' novel (although, as Molly Bloom had little influence on Sterne, this phrase does not reliably describe any technique that Sterne himself knew or used).[1] *Tristram* became a model, too, for explicit and self-conscious modernist theorizing, most notoriously and influentially in an essay of 1929 by the Soviet formalist theoretician Viktor Shklovsky. Shklovsky explicitly considers *Tristram* not as a distinctive and individual work, produced in and reflecting a particular historical conjuncture, but – in regard to its time shifts, insertions, discovered manuscripts and multiple narratives – as a model for the narrative procedures of the modernist novel. Shklovsky is avowedly not interested in Sterne's book except as it exemplifies and in his view supports a formalist and anti-mimetic theoretics:

I do not propose to analyze Laurence Sterne's novel; I intend to use it merely as an illustration to the general laws of novelistic form, for Sterne here was an extreme revolutionary. His typical method is to proceed by 'laying bare' the literary device; form exists for itself and has no ulterior motivation. . . . Art forms are to be explained in terms of the laws of their artistic orientation and not in terms of their motivation to exhibit a mode of life.[2]

To say that *Tristram Shandy* cannot be understood in terms of its 'motivation to exhibit a mode of life' is a large, daring and deeply dubious claim, which is modified or contradicted by the great majority of Sterne criticism, including (in different ways and degrees) all the essays selected for this volume. Shklovsky would not of course have been distressed by that. His essay in narrative theory is representative of a larger and characteristically theoretical endeavour, the attempt to find general laws and overarching explanations for cultural productions, an attempt which may be represented as scientistic or as mythopoetic. Such an endeavour always shifts emphasis from the particular to the general, from the text to its representativeness (for Shklovsky, *Tristram* is 'the most typical novel in world literature'[3]), from *parole* to *langue*, from the particular and individual expression to the general explanatory system. Many such systems (or 'myths', or 'hypotheses') have developed currency and acquired explanatory power: psychoanalysis, for example, or structuralism, historical materialism, feminism, deconstruction.

Not all of such theoretical approaches work equally well with all texts. Brean Hammond, in an earlier volume in this series, has pointed out how the methods of deconstruction for example, extensively influential in recent criticism of the Romantic period, prove harder to apply to a satiric poet of the early eighteenth century:

Comparing a typical page of Wordsworth to a typical page of Pope alerts the would-be deconstructor to the formidable problems presented by the latter. Pope is dense with referentiality, embodying a Lockean linguistics that, in spite of many difficulties, considers language to make reference to a really-existing world of extra-linguistic reality. Since the root-assumption of deconstruction is the reverse, an already counter-intuitive hypothesis runs even more against the grain of the text when it is applied to Pope.[4]

Tristram Shandy also presents referential obstructions (of rather more problematized kinds) to the blade of deconstruction. It has, too, inbuilt defences against a wide variety of more generalizing and systematic theoretical approaches. Like most great works of literature – like its antecedents *Don Quixote, Gargantua and Pantagruel, The Anatomy of Melancholy* and *A Tale of a Tub*, and in some of the same ways – *Tristram Shandy* itself is meta-theoretical. It asks throughout questions about the nature of narrative and voice, about knowledge and our uses of knowledge, about the nature of reading, about interpretation and misinterpretation in life and in books. In all these areas, *Tristram* was and remains a ground-breaking text. Yet *Tristram* also interrogates the notion of 'Theory' itself. Theorists of a variety of stripes are represented and enacted in Sterne's book, by the learned Doctors of theology of the Sorbonne and of Strasburg, in the nostrums of physicians, above all and most persistently in the person of Walter Shandy, turning to his folios, to mouldy metaphysics, to the obsolete medical and political systems of Avicenna or Filmer. ('Theory', for Sterne as for Swift, is what becomes outdated.) In Walter above all we see how a flight from the urgencies and hard edges of the real world, the particularities of events and objects, the compromises of day to day understanding, into an exclusive obsession with theory – into the dedicated riding of hobby horses – results in confused names, damaged children and a bloody nose.

Theory, then, may aspire to the status of a system, a myth or a discourse, an attempt to explain phenomena in relation to a dominant narrative, and may reduce (and be happy to reduce) a particular cultural product, as Shklovsky reduces *Tristram*, to an instance in its own support. Such a notion of theory, for all its explanatory power, has historically been vulnerable to just the kinds of satiric attack launched by Swift in *A Tale of a Tub* (where modern individualists are made to leave common sense and reason to ride their individual hobby-horses), and by Sterne in *Tristram Shandy* (where, picking up Swift's metaphor, Toby and Walter are represented as reducing every phenomenon in their world to a sign of their respective hobby-horse).

There are however alternative conceptions of theory and its working. Denis Donoghue speaks of 'theories, which are more modest plays of mind, local notions', which 'do useful work', relatively small-scale explanatory theories that serve to explain by larger or smaller contextual evidence.[5] One such theory, in Donoghue's sense, would be Louis L. Martz's demonstration that the procedures of religious meditation underlie, and substantially illuminate, the religious poetry of John Donne and George Herbert.[6] Another is Northrop Frye's argument (itself part of the altogether larger theoretical structure of his *Anatomy of Criticism*) that, historically, prose fiction has been a shifting genre made up, in varying combinations, of four distinct strands: the romance, the autobiography (or confession), the Menippean satire (or anatomy), and the novel.[7]

Tristram Shandy, one of many works which combine two or more of these strands in different ways, clearly shows features of the anatomy – digressive narrative, symposia, catalogues, stylized characters, ridicule of pedantry – as well as of the novel, and, Frye insists, should not be described or judged as if it belonged solely to the history of the novel.

STERNE AND 'THEORY' IN THE TWENTIETH CENTURY

Historically, until the 1980s and indeed beyond, such applications of theory dominated the study of Sterne, as they dominated most aspects of study of eighteenth-century literature. 'Theory' is certainly a word that can be applied in Donoghue's sense to explanations of *Tristram Shandy* and *A Sentimental Journey* by reference to 'Lockean psychology', or 'learned wit', or 'sensibility', or 'play', or 'the body', or 'the book' or 'gender'. Such are locally theoretical accounts, based on more or less particular and relevant areas of knowledge, which have explanatory power as applied to the writing itself.

To take one such 'local theory', the influence upon *Tristram Shandy* of John Locke's *Essay Concerning Human Understanding* (1690) is evident from the first page of the novel, where it is ostentatiously flagged by Sterne's comic paraphrase of Locke's adumbration of the train of ideas (*Essay*, 4th edition, II. 33. 6). Kenneth MacLean, in his masterful study of *John Locke and English Literature of the Eighteenth Century* (New Haven, CT: Yale University Press, 1936), was the first modern scholar to show that Sterne made extensive though not always straightforward uses of a number of key ideas from Locke's *Essay*: the epistemological distinction between judgement (the faculty which discriminates ideas) and wit (the faculty which combines and at worst may confuse ideas); the dangers of abuses of words in human communication; the subjective and relative perception by the human mind of the passage of time; and, especially, the association of ideas, which 'provided Sterne with an entirely new principle of literary composition'. Since MacLean the Lockean context has been discussed at length, and has proven analytically productive even (perhaps especially) when problematized, as increasingly it has been. John Traugott, in his *Tristram Shandy's World: Sterne's Philosophical Rhetoric*, enormously influential since its 1954 publication, demonstrated (what MacLean had certainly in part understood, but had not developed) that 'the Shandean vision of Locke' is a deliberately perverse one. In particular Traugott showed that 'by burlesquing and subverting the philosophical assumptions of Locke, who believed wit to be a positive evil, Sterne protests the moral value of wit' (p. xv). For Traugott, Sterne's strong reading, or misreading, of Locke, made room for human sensibility: '[*Tristram Shandy*] offers to tell us there is a possibility, through an understanding of mental life in its public signs, of sentimental, public communication and understanding among peculiar personalities – which matter Locke had not considered' (p. 72). Ernest Tuveson, in a hugely persuasive (though surprisingly less well-known) essay argued, by contrast, that *Tristram* is a learned late humanist satire, in the tradition of such writers as Rabelais and Swift, in which Sterne's targets among men's strange opinions are perfectly congruent with Locke's attack in the *Essay* on the 'odd notions' that 'many men's heads are filled with'. For Tuveson, Sterne's relation with Locke did not inevitably license a psychologizing or sentimentalizing reading of *Tristram Shandy*. The Lockean connection has continued to provide a powerful if much interrogated heuristic. Arthur Cash has argued that, though Sterne used the Lockean principle of association at some points, it was the larger Lockean principle of the train of ideas that more fundamentally informed the presentation of mind, character and narrative in *Tristram Shandy*. As late as 1975 Helene Moglen rejected Augustan and satiric understandings of Sterne to insist that *Tristram* is the product of a profound and serious reading of Locke, creating from the Lockean principle of association the stream of consciousness novel. W. G. Day made it difficult to think of Sterne as a reverential follower of Locke by drawing attention to his equivocating and often indecent re-workings of some of the great philosopher's explanatory metaphors (the Lockean distinction of wit and judgement, for instance, is transverted and subverted into the difference of farting and hiccupping).[8]

Similarly, constructions and understandings of eighteenth-century sensibility, sentimentalism and sympathy, from the ideas of eighteenth-century philosophers and from some of the social behaviours and modes of the time, and sometimes in relation to mid- and late eighteenth-century movements towards romanticism in writing and feeling, have been developed by modern critics as further local explanatory theories for both of Sterne's novels. John Traugott insisted that Sterne might be saved from accusations of self-indulgent and disingenuous indulgence in ostentatious pleasures of feeling by defining 'sentimentalism' in Sterne's terms rather than ours: 'by sensory apprehension of the behavior of other persons, and by comparing that behavior by an association of ideas with our own, we conceive a sympathy for other persons' (p. 73). Indeed Traugott argued that the 'real order' of *Tristram Shandy* is the philosophic sentimentalism of David Hume:

For Hume, man is always a social being, neither egoistic nor selfless but always in some sympathetic relation (in normal behavior). Reason, being not an active faculty, becomes the slave of the passions, in the respect that reason can do nothing without passional intuition. (p. 74)

Kenneth MacLean found an alternative source for Sterne's emphasis on sympathy, and particularly on the image-making basis of sympathy so often exploited in the *Sentimental Journey* – Yorick's imaginative construction for instance of a prisoner in the Bastille – in Adam Smith's argument in his *Theory of Moral Sentiments* (1759) that 'it is by the imagination only that we can form any conception of the feelings and sufferings of another.' Frank Brady examined Sterne's use of sexual suggestiveness in relation to sensibility, concluding that 'sensibility is the intermediate term between Augustan wit and romantic imagination, and Sterne's problem was to write a comedy in an emerging age of sensibility which maintained a precarious balance at best between wit and sentiment'. Peter Conrad, in a less historically rooted study, viewed Sterne from a romantic perspective, and explored Sterne's mediation of the ironic and sentimental possibilities of the Shakespearean fusion of tragedy and comedy.[9]

A significant set of critical options, then, has been to read *Tristram Shandy* as a novel of sensibility, concerned at least to some extent with individual feelings and psychology, reflecting social attitudes in its own time, and anticipating attitudes of later writers. Such an approach however has been in contest, only occasionally reaching uneasy accommodations, with a very different explanatory hypothesis: that *Tristram* may best be understood as an Augustan satire, whose targets include pedantry and false learning, self-obsessed system building, the abandonment of reason for feeling. It was Douglas W. Jefferson, in a groundbreaking and influential article published in 1951, who first and most persuasively taught us to recognize Sterne as an exponent of a scholastic and post-scholastic 'tradition of learned wit', the last great writer in a pre-enlightenment lineage which included Rabelais, Cervantes and Burton, as well as Sterne's more immediate predecessors Pope and Swift. Like these distinguished forerunners, Sterne both used and parodied the methods and rhetorics of abstract reasoning, and of resort (in *Tristram*, always on the least appropriate occasions and in the least practical ways) to erudite authorities. Brief but significant essays in the late 1940s by Ernest Dilworth and Rufus Putney provided arguments, based on close and careful reading of the two novels, for the satiric rather than sentimental Sterne. Certainly the most substantial and thoroughgoing case for this position was made in the late 1960s by Melvyn New in his *Laurence Sterne as Satirist*.[10] For New, as for many recent commentators, Sterne is not a modernist prophet but a man of his own century, not a pioneer of the psychological novel but a belated member of a Scriblerian and Augustan company, not a sentimentalist but a defender of the values of reason and of Anglican religion. *Tristram Shandy* points not so much forward to Woolf or Joyce, as back to Swift and Pope. Like a latter-day *Tale of a Tub* or *Dunciad* it offers an ironic celebration of 'chaos and confusion, destruction and death', of men abandoning reason and common sense to ride the hobby-horses of their solipsistic obsessions.

STERNE AND 'THEORY' IN THE 1980s AND 1990s

From a theoretical and methodological point of view, writing on Sterne before the 1980s covered, as might be expected, most available bases: intrinsic interpretative studies, for instance, providing close analyses of the rhetoric and form of his novels; narratological accounts of Sterne's innovative strategies in telling his stories, or in making apparent his refusal to tell a story; 'old historical' enquiries, relating his novels to their own time; 'history of ideas' examinations of the cultural and intellectual worlds constructed in Sterne's novels in the light of the philosophies and systems available to him; reader-response analyses, following Sterne's own lead of explicit intercourse with his readers. After its spectacular emergence into the theoretical spotlight in Shklovsky, Sterne's novel certainly became and remained for many writers a paradigm of the modern or postmodern narrative. Nevertheless, it was not otherwise an early or remarkable subject of self-consciously theoretical writing. In an essay written at the end of the 1970s Melvyn New could complain that Sterne criticism had not fully taken on board the new theories, and especially those adumbrated by Bloom, de Man, Hartman, Jameson and Derrida.[11] Less than a decade later, however, Donald Wehrs was able to write that '*Tristram Shandy* has proved suspiciously congenial to successive twentieth-century perspectives, yielding modernist, metafictional, existential, deconstructive, and Lacanian readings'.[12] Certainly the 1980s and the 1990s, the period covered by this selection, have been distinctively the years in which Sterne's writing, and *Tristram* particularly, has become the focus of a wider variety of critical approaches, and some variety of theoretical methods.

It is nevertheless arguable that Sterne's work has remained relatively resistant to such generalizing and isolating theoretical methods (of any intellectual colour) as Shklovsky's. It is true that very few recent theoretical schools have not been represented in recent decades: phenomenology (Swearingen), deconstruction (Miller, Markley), historical materialism (Markley, Franks, Landry, Gerald Maclean), and Foucauldian and Lacanian approaches (Sedgwick, Perry), among others. In virtually all of these writers, however, theory has been integrated with a more careful examination of the Shandean text than Shklovsky proposed, and with a closer attention to Sterne's historical environment. For most of the modern period most commentary on Sterne, a writer now a quarter of a millennium distant from us in language and reference, has been at least informed by a concern with historical and contextualizing scholarship, attempting to explain Sterne by reference to his own time, to the literature and ideas, to the political, social and religious circumstances, that gave his novels birth. Scarcely any modern theoretically orientated critic has avowed a Shklovskian disregard for the material conditions of Sterne's writings. Equally, 'scholarly' or 'empirical' commentaries on Sterne have characteristically been informed by their own kinds of theoretical awareness. The 'tradition' of historical scholarship is of course itself always inescapably a theoretical position, and always potentially theoretically self-conscious. It need be neither a rejection of the theoretical endeavour as such, nor a naive precursor of the exercise of theory, though it may (like Swift and Sterne) conscientiously avoid system building. Scholarship and theory need not be and ought not to be mutually exclusive, as Joel Weinsheimer powerfully insists in a late 1980s essay on *Tristram Shandy* in the classroom:

Over the last decade or so, we have heard entirely too much about the incompatibility of the historical and theoretical approaches and about the dispensability of one or the other. . . . but now that the battle of ancients and moderns has once again ended in stalemate, now that theory has become historical and history theoretical, it has become more evident that between the two approaches to *Tristram Shandy* there is no dichotomy and, in fact, a good deal of coincidence.[13]

The point is demonstrated everywhere in the most convincing recent writing on Sterne.

A particularly imposing and consequential instance of the marriage of the scholarly and the theoretical is Tom Keymer's recent two-part article, 'Dying by Numbers: *Tristram Shandy* and Serial Fiction'.[14] Here Keymer sets out the historical and bibliographical detail of the volume-by-volume publication of *Tristram* between 1759 and 1767, and relates it to a variety of forms of serial publication in Sterne's own century: such encyclopaedias as those of Bayle and Chambers, Nicholas Tindal's translation and continuation of Rapin de Thoyras's *History of England*, the quasi-fictional narratives of the *Spectator* papers, and novels by Richardson (*Clarissa*, *Sir Charles Grandison*) and Smollett (*Sir Launcelot Greaves*), as well as the serial memoirs *An Apology for the Life of Mrs Teresia*

Constantia Phillips (1748–49) and the *Memoirs of Mrs Laetitia Pilkington* (1748, 1749, 1754). Keymer's long essay is an exercise in close and rigorous textual analysis and scholarly contextual positioning, which establishes that *Tristram* had its serial precedents to use and exploit. It is also, throughout, concerned with genuinely theoretical questions arising out of *Tristram* and the literary culture and modes of production which gave it birth. What were the socio-economic contexts and effects of serial publication? How should we conceive the nature of the Sternean text, which 'now seems not so much a fixed product as the trace of an unstable, ongoing process, orchestrated as such by Sterne, recognized as such by his audience of the 1760s, but necessarily remote to later readers'? What are the possibilities of suspense, anticipation and readerly assumptions in the serial text? What problems of closure (or opportunities of withheld closure) are posed by 'indefinite ongoing production'? Does the serial publication of *Tristram Shandy* help us to consider it in closer generic relation to the 'novel', as well as to the satiric forms, of its own times? What, in the focused light of its serial publication, can we make of *Tristram* as 'a work that responds to its own reception', as a flexible, open-ended and contingent process rather than as planned and perfected product, and as a book that deliberately and playfully exposes to view 'all the technical tricks, obstructions and interferences' of the serial process?

The scholarship of Sterne finds its most extensive expression, naturally enough, in the annotation of the multiple difficulties to be found in *Tristram Shandy*. Here simultaneously is to be found one of the main theoretical battlegrounds, between those who would argue for the possibilities of knowledge-based understanding, and the problematizers of determinacy. There have been a number of particular contributions both to the scholarship and the debate. In 1936, for example, Theodore Baird pointed out the significance of the *History of England* written by Paul Rapin de Thoyras (and published in English translation from 1732 to 1745) to the history-line that underlies the action of *Tristram*.[15] H. J. Jackson, in a 1975 essay re-printed here, explored Sterne's uses of Burton's *Anatomy of Melancholy*. In an article published in 1982 as a contribution to a debate in *Essays in Criticism* on the annotation of the English novel, Pat Rogers not only drew attention to the prevalence of proverbs, catchphrases and cant in *Tristram*, but also showed how the reader's recognition of the use of tags and expressions common in his own time but unfamiliar in ours was vital to the understanding of Sterne's writing.[16] The watershed, however, in the annotation of *Tristram* was the appearance of the Florida edition, whose two-volume text published in 1978 was followed, six years later, by a volume of Notes.[17] In his Introduction to the edition (published, in properly Shandean fashion, with the Notes),

Melvyn New claimed, on behalf of himself and his fellow editors Richard A. Davies and W. G. Day, to have maintained a distinction between elucidation and interpretation, between the identification and citation of source passages on the one hand, and the use of those materials in providing closing interpretation:

Editors . . . want to respond to a text precisely as do other readers, by trying to interpret it, that is, by incorporating it into their own coherent (self-satisfying) systems of order and belief. Moreover, that system is bound to exercise a considerable influence over the questions one asks about a text, so that the process of annotation is intricately linked to the interpretative urge. . . . I say *intricately* and not *inextricably*, however, for a strong measure of self-awareness and a consistent concern with the problem can allow the editor to untangle at least some of the linkages and to establish patterns of annotative commentary that work to keep elucidation and interpretation apart.[18]

Indeed nobody has been more conscious than New himself of the permeability of the boundary between elucidation and interpretation. In an article which particularly addressed the problem of annotating Sterne's sexual suggestiveness, New represents the explicating editor's task as a delicate balancing act, an attempt to 'position the reader on the brink of interpretation, to tease that natural and persistent urge to understand the text we confront'.[19] New's *dicta* on the subject of annotation go to the heart of issues of interpretative determinacy and understanding. Not everyone however has been persuaded of the possibility of separating elucidation and interpretation. Jonathan Lamb bridles at the Florida treatment of Sterne's bawdry but also, and more fundamentally, despite all New's protestations, alleges that the Florida annotations control and limit the reader, tending to 're-position Sterne in a grid of borrowings, quotations and allusions that considerably restricts the freedom to read beyond the annotated pale'.[20] Lamb's argument is for leaving readers their interpretative liberty, untrammelled by an annotator's citations (even by citations printed, as in the Florida edition, in a separate volume). With altogether less sensitivity to readers' freedoms, or altogether more belief in the ability of readers to take care of themselves even in the face of annotation, I have myself argued that (though the distinction between elucidation and interpretation is a necessary and workable editorial strategy) all annotation is inevitably interpretative from the outset, and should be confident enough to claim as much:

the choice of what information is necessary to 'elucidate' the text is itself an interpretative judgement. Knowledge of allusion, reference, context, are conditions that make understanding possible. An interpretation is made (at the least, begun), at the moment the editor judges that one piece of information, one allusion or reference, is more relevant than another. To offer information as interpretatively relevant is to interpret.[21]

From such a theoretical perspective Melvyn New might be thought over-modest. The definitive Florida edition of Sterne is now the great main armoury of our knowledge of 'allusion, reference, context', and, I would argue, is *ipso facto* the main condition of our current understanding.

More ostensibly theorized approaches to Sterne's writings have shown a mirroring awareness of the implications of historical context, and our understanding of it, for theoretical judgement. Two distinguished recent essays, published in a collection of criticism devoted to Sterne in relation to modernism and postmodernism, may serve as model interrogations of generalized applications to Sterne of over-arching, and inadequately historicized, theoretical assumptions.[22] Tim Parnell provides a critical re-assessment of Milan Kundera's take on Sterne. As a practising novelist, more particularly as a novelist to whom the experience of totalitarian-ism has been so central, Kundera has naturally responded to Sterne with that necessary process of creative 'misreading' which Harold Bloom has described as characteristic of the powerful artist in his *Map of Misreading* (1975). Kundera finds in the novel as a genre, especially in the sceptical novelistic tradition of Cervantes, Rabelais, Sterne and Diderot, a narrative form which asks questions rather than provides answers, a form which renounces the 'sacrosanct certainties' of totalitarian systems. Parnell quotes Kundera's account of Sterne's novel writing as a radically sceptical game:

[*Tristram Shandy*] is non-serious *throughout*; it doesn't make us believe in any-thing: neither in the truth of the characters, the truth of the author, nor the truth of the novel as a literary genre: *everything* is put in question, *everything* is put in doubt, *everything* is a game.

This, as Parnell points out, is a version of a reading of *Tristram* which has been common in the theoretics of modernism and postmodernism: 'the consistency with which *Tristram Shandy* is alluded to as a model for much experiment and postmodernist narrative has conferred upon the apparent linkage the status of received wisdom'. But, as Parnell insists, the linkage between the radical scepticism of modernity, and the moder-ated scepticism of Sterne and his predecessors, is deeply problematic. For Erasmus and Rabelais, Cervantes and Burton, Sterne and Swift, there are certainties beyond the foolishness of human enquiries.[23] The contents and rhetoric of scepticism are used in the service of belief; it is precisely because human knowledge is necessarily imperfect that we must have resort to higher truth. However far Sterne exploits the strategies of scept-ical narrative, he is a writer of his place and time, an Anglican clergyman who reinforces rather than challenges the tenets of Anglicanism, and is heir to a long European tradition of sceptical writing which attacks religious abuse but also endorses the central truths of religion. Sterne's scepticism is not ours; in his different historical and cultural location, he questions other certainties, and to quite other ends.

Carol Watts, equally cogently, argues that we should attribute to *Tristram Shandy* its own distinctive modernity. The book displays, Watts acknowledges, 'many of the formal characteristics associated with post-modernist fiction: its use of parody and pastiche, its problematisation of representation, its absurdist exposure of the limits of referential theories of language, its complex treatment of identity in time and history, its stress on the local rather than the universal, and the consequent pro-visionality of the "I" subject, and so on'. Further, in contrast to the mimetic, and panoramic, novels of Fielding or Smollett, *Tristram*'s refer-entiality is both fragmentary and local, deliberately confined to its own world of a mere four miles diameter. Deconstructing as it does the poss-ibility of realistic depiction of the world, *Tristram* tempts us moderns to appropriate the text, 'to wrest the narrative from its historical determin-ants, to engage in the pleasures of its formal play'. Yet as Watts reminds us, and demonstrates, *Tristram* appeared to be 'an aesthetic anachronism even to Sterne's contemporaries'. It presents problems of understanding and recognition that we need to solve by attempting to recover 'the novel's aesthetic distance, its formal play, as a condition produced *by* and in response *to*' its own particular context. Many aspects of that response are made clear – 'theorized', we would say – in Sterne's fiction. *Tristram* resembles other novels of its time in presenting itself self-consciously, not as mere history, but as historiography; not as truth, but as telling. Like Fielding, for example, though in an altogether more thoroughgoing and provocative fashion, Sterne discussed both the duties and the difficulties of the 'historiographer' as he tells his tale, beset by accounts to reconcile, anecdotes to pick up, inscriptions to make out, stories to weave in. As Watts insists, 'such an incorporation of "theory" into the text was intended to alert the reader to the kind of contract offered by the text, to produce an awareness of the status of its truth-claim'. Such methods define *Tristram* as a text which confronts issues of modernity in its own time, which engages with contemporary issues of thinking, feeling and apprehension. To describe *A Sentimental Journey* (as Virginia Woolf did) as transparently true to our own modern consciousness, or *Tristram Shandy* (in the words of a recent bibliographer) as 'a thoroughly postmodern work in every sense except the period in which it was written', is entirely appropriative, 'a form of narcissistic misrecognition'. To deny or elide its eighteenth-century origins is, in Carol Watts's words, 'an amnesic reaction to the birth and development, the very pre-history, of the modern'.

Keymer and New, Watts and Parnell, all demonstrate the cogency of the informed and self-conscious interaction, and potential identity, of scholarship and theory. And indeed, the rigorous combination of theoretical self-consciousness with a thorough contextualizing scholarship has been the characteristic tendency of writing on Sterne over the last two decades. Donald R. Wehrs, for instance, in an outstanding and much-reprinted essay, follows the lead of Douglas Jefferson in relating *Tristram Shandy* to its post-Renaissance intellectual context, and in particular the Christian scepticisms of Erasmus, Cervantes and Montaigne; sets the narratology and epistemology of *Tristram* over against that of his more straightforwardly mimetic near-contemporaries Henry Fielding and Samuel Richardson; and fluently discusses these issues of knowledge and understanding in the languages of Barthesian plurality, Bakhtinian polyphony and Lacanian desire.[24] Jonathan Lamb, in a series of articles and in one of the most significant books of recent years, addresses Sterne's problematic uses of rhetoric, intertextuality, imitation and polysemy both within the context of eighteenth-century theorists (notably Addison, Hartley, Hume, Lowth and Burke), and from the perspective of modern theoretical discussions (Freud, de Man, Derrida, Bakhtin).[25] Robert Markley, one of the most theoretically focused modern Sternean commentators, discusses the uses of sentimentality in *A Sentimental Journey* against the background of Shaftesbury's *Inquiry Concerning Virtue*, and in the unremitting light of materialist and gender theories, concluding that 'however much [Sterne] would like to distance himself from his hero's naïve benevolence, he can suggest no alternative to an ideology that can neither interrogate nor change the socio-economic injustices that its "virtues" promote'.[26] Markley's marxizing insistence that sensibility is not merely personal, but a feature of mid-eighteenth-century class and gender structural relations, echoes the concerns of the essay by Eve Kosofsky Sedgwick printed in part in this volume, and of Judith Frank in her late-1980s study of character and class in *A Sentimental Journey*.[27] Markedly similar in methodological and ideological direction, though distinct in subject matter, is an important and subtle study by Donna Landry and Gerald Maclean of birth and obstetrics, male discourse and women's bodies in *Tristram Shandy*, in the light of both high (Whigs and Jacobites) and low (obstetrics, surgeons and midwives) politics in the eighteenth century, which concludes both by acknowledging 'coincidences between Sterne's preoccupations with materializing writing and the histories of individual subjects, and those of our own theoretical moment', and by hoping 'to have opened both his text and our own to the multiple resistances to fixed gender identities and the bourgeois subject's historical forgetfulness made thinkable by such textual processes'.[28] Thoroughgoing deconstructionist approaches to

Sterne's writing have been relatively few, confronting as they do the issues of referentiality noted above. Notable are not only J. Hillis Miller's essay on 'Narrative Middles', printed in this volume, but also Ralph Flores's critique of humanistic tradition and inheritance in *Tristram Shandy* in the course of a determinedly Derridean study of western narratives from Augustine onwards, and John Vignaux Smyth's deconstructive analysis of Sternean rhetorical suggestiveness. Yet more focused and distinctive, and just anticipating the 1980s, is James Swearingen's application of Husserlian phenomenology to *Tristram*, whose small hero's 'whole enterprise is a hermeneutics, a process of self interpretation'.[29]

If there has been one direction more extensively explored than any other in recent theoretical analysis of *Tristram*, it has been gender-based and feminist work, whose products have been almost universally characterized both by carefully nuanced accounts of that text's social and cultural history, and by a serious and engaged attempt to deal with the 'unpleasantness' (to use T. S. Eliot's word) or 'otherness' (to use one of ours) of a major text of an earlier century. Modern readers have repeatedly found a tension, if very often a creative tension, between recognition of the 'canonic' status of Sterne's published fictions, and awareness of the real or apparent sexism and misogyny to be found in them. In a brief but telling essay in Melvyn New's collection on the teaching of *Tristram Shandy*, Elizabeth W. Harries provides a personal account of 'the conflict between my growing commitment to feminist analysis and my abiding belief that *Tristram Shandy* is a book that everyone should read, one of the most important novels ever written'. As Harries convincingly argues, *Tristram* is a particularly rich and provocative instance of an obstacle posed by many canonic texts, the gulf between their gender assumptions and sensibilities and ours. The large-scale issue, as it is defined by Harries – and, for example, by Wayne Booth, in a classic early 1980s essay – is 'how our reeducated imaginations will ultimately reread, reconstruct, or reinvent the works we have been taught to consider classics'.[30] The particular interpretative issue, set out more fully in the introductory note to Part 2 of this anthology and addressed by many essays in the field, including the two by Perry and New offered here, is the extent to which *Tristram* itself delineates, problematizes and undercuts the patriarchalism of the Shandy men.

THIS SELECTION

The ten essays which make up this selection were first published during the 1980s and 1990s, with the exceptions of those by Heather Jackson

(1975) and J. Hillis Miller (1978). They are arranged here in pairs, on five major themes of Sterne criticism in those two decades: the operations of 'sociality' and 'sensibility'; feminism and gender; constructions and representations of the body; Sterne's exploitations of imitation and intertextuality; and two rather different kinds of formalism, the deconstructive narratology of Hillis Miller and Christopher Fanning's study of the implications of book form in *Tristram*. Where possible, I have chosen essays which provide a contrast of theoretical approaches (Kosofsky Sedgwick's feminist materialist approach, and Mullan's older historicism, on sensibility), or answer to each other more directly as part of a particular debate (Perry and New on gender and the 'patriarchal' in Sterne). I have throughout chosen essays which seem to me to combine, to differing degrees across a wide possible spectrum (in which Jackson and Sedgwick no doubt occupy the extremes) the self-consciously theoretical with the historical/contextual. Some of the finest essays of recent years sadly have been too long for inclusion; I think particularly of Thomas Keymer's 'Dying by Numbers: *Tristram Shandy* and Serial Fiction', Melinda Alliker Rabb's 'Engendering Accounts in Sterne's *A Sentimental Journey*' and J. Paul Hunter's 'From Typology to Type: Agents of Change in Eighteenth-Century English Texts'.

NOTES

1. See, notably, Woolf's Introduction to the 1928 World's Classics edition of *A Sentimental Journey* (reprinted in her *The Common Reader. Second Series* (London: Hogarth Press, 1932), pp. 78–85).
2. 'A Parodying Novel: Sterne's *Tristram Shandy*', in *Sterne: A Collection of Critical Essays*, ed. John Traugott (Englewood Cliffs, NJ: Prentice Hall, 1968), pp. 66–89 (p. 66). First published in Shklovsky's *O Teorii Prozy* (Moscow, 1929).
3. Shklovsky, p. 89.
4. *Longman Critical Readers: Pope* (London and New York: Longman, 1996), p. 10.
5. *The Practice of Reading* (New Haven, CT and London: Yale University Press, 1998), p. 21.
6. *The Poetry of Meditation: A Study in English Religious Literature of the Seventeenth Century* (New Haven, CT: Yale University Press, 1954).
7. *The Anatomy of Criticism* (Princeton, NJ: Princeton University Press, 1957), pp. 303–14.
8. Traugott, *Tristram Shandy's World: Sterne's Philosophical Rhetoric* (Berkeley, CA: University of California Press, 1954); Cash, 'The Lockean Psychology of *Tristram Shandy*', ELH 22 (1955): 125–35; Tuveson, 'Locke and Sterne', in J. A. Mazzeo (ed.), *Reason and Imagination: Studies in the History of Ideas, 1600–1800* (New York:

Columbia University Press, 1962), pp. 255–77; Moglen, *The Philosophical Irony of Laurence Sterne* (Gainesville, FLA: University Presses of Florida, 1975); Day, '*Tristram Shandy*: Locke may not be the key', in Valerie Myer (ed.), *Lawrence Sterne: Riddles and Mysteries* (London and Totowa, NJ: Vision and Barnes Noble, 1984), pp. 99–112.

9. MacLean, 'Imagination and Sympathy: Sterne and Adam Smith', *Journal of the History of Ideas* 10 (1949): 399–410; Brady, '*Tristram Shandy*: Sexuality, Morality, and Sensibility', *Eighteenth-Century Studies* 4 (1970): 41–56; Conrad, *Shandyism: the Character of Romantic Irony* (Oxford: Basil Blackwell, 1978).

10. Jefferson, '*Tristram Shandy* and the Tradition of Learned Wit', *Essays in Criticism* 1 (1951): 225–48; Dilworth, *The Unsentimental Journey of Laurence Sterne* (New York: King's Crown Press, 1948); Putney, 'Sterne, Apostle of Laughter', in *The Age of Johnson: Essays Presented to Chauncey Brewster Tinker* (New Haven, CT: Yale University Press, 1949), pp. 158–70; New, *Laurence Sterne as Satirist: a Reading of Tristram Shandy* (Gainesville, FLA: University of Florida Press, 1969).

11. 'Surviving the Seventies: Sterne, Collins, and their Recent Critics', *Eighteenth-Century: Theory and Interpretation* 25 (1984): 3–24.

12. 'Sterne, Cervantes, Montaigne: Fideistic Skepticism and the Rhetoric of Desire', *Comparative Literature Studies* 25 (1988): 127–51 (p. 127).

13. Joel Weinsheimer, 'History and Theory, Literature and Criticism: The Two Knobs of Teaching *Tristram Shandy*', in Melvyn New (ed.), *Approaches to Teaching Sterne's Tristram Shandy* (New York: MLA, 1989), pp. 152–6 (p. 152).

14. Part 1, *The Shandean* 8 (1996): 41–67; Part 2, *The Shandean* 9 (1997): 34–69.

15. 'The Time Scheme of *Tristram Shandy* and a Source', *PMLA* 51 (1936): 803–20.

16. '*Tristram Shandy*'s Polite Conversation', *Essays in Criticism* 32 (1982): 305–20.

17. *The Life and Opinions of Tristram Shandy, Gentleman: The Text*, ed. Melvyn New and Joan New (Gainesville, FLA: University of Florida Press, 1978 (volumes 1 and 2)); *The Notes*, ed. Melvyn New, with Richard A. Davies and W. G. Day (Gainesville, FLA: University of Florida Press, 1984 (volume 3)).

18. *The Life and Opinions of Tristram Shandy, Gentleman: The Notes*, p. 5.

19. ' "At the backside of the door of purgatory": A Note on Annotating *Tristram Shandy*', in Myer (ed.), *Riddles and Mysteries*, pp. 15–23 (p. 21).

20. Jonathan Lamb, *Sterne's Fiction and the Double Principle* (Cambridge: Cambridge University Press, 1989), p. 2.

21. In my *Shakespeare, Milton, and Eighteenth-Century Literary Editing* (Cambridge: Cambridge University Press, 1997), pp. 27–8.

22. Carol Watts, 'The Modernity of Sterne'; Tim Parnell, 'Sterne and Kundera: The Novel of Variations and the "noisy foolishness of human certainty" ', in David Pierce and David de Voogd (eds), *Laurence Sterne in Modernism and Postmodernism* (Amsterdam: Rodopi, 1993), pp. 19–38, 147–55 (my quotations are from pp. 19–21, 26, 27, 147, 151).

23. Parnell's own 'Swift, Sterne, and the Skeptical Tradition', *Studies in Eighteenth-Century Culture* 23 (1994): 221–42 is an equally convincing account of Sterne's inextricable connections with seventeenth- and eighteenth-century scepticism.

24. See note 12 above.

25. 'The Comic Sublime and Sterne's Fiction', *ELH* 48 (1981): 110–43; 'The Job Controversy, Sterne, and the Question of Allegory', *Eighteenth-Century Studies* 24 (1990): 1–19; 'Sterne's System of Imitation', *Modern Language Review* 76 (1981): 794–810, reprinted in this volume; *Sterne's Fiction and the Double Principle*.

26. 'Sentimentality as Performance: Shaftesbury, Sterne, and the Theatrics of Virtue', in Felicity Nussbaum and Laura Brown (eds), *The New Eighteenth Century: Theory, Politics, English Literature* (New York and London: Methuen, 1987), pp. 210–30 (p. 230).

27. '"A Man Who Laughs is Never Dangerous": Character and Class in Sterne's *A Sentimental Journey*', *ELH* 56 (1989): 97–124.

28. 'Of Forceps, Patents, and Paternity: *Tristram Shandy*', *Eighteenth-Century Studies* 23 (1989–90): 522–43 (p. 543).

29. Flores, 'Changeling Fathering: *Tristram Shandy*', in his *The Rhetoric of Doubtful Authority: Deconstructive Readings of Self-Questioning Narratives, St. Augustine to Faulkner* (Ithaca, NY and London: Cornell University Press, 1984), pp. 116–44; Smyth, 'Sterne: Rhetoric and Representation' and 'Philosophy of the Nose', in his *A Question of Eros: Irony in Sterne, Kierkegaard, and Barthes* (Tallahassee, FLA: Florida State University Press, 1986), pp. 13–98; James E. Swearingen, *Reflexivity in Tristram Shandy: an Essay in Phenomenological Criticism* (New Haven, CT: Yale University Press, 1977).

30. Harries, 'Confessions of a Cross-Eyed "Female-Reader" of Sterne', in New (ed.), *Approaches to Teaching Sterne's Tristram Shandy*, pp. 111–17; Wayne C. Booth, 'Freedom of Interpretation: Bakhtin and the Challenge of Feminist Criticism', *Critical Inquiry* 9 (1982): 45–76.

PART ONE

Sociality and Sensibility

From their first appearance Sterne's two fictions, *Tristram Shandy* and *A Sentimental Journey*, have been perceived as having a close, and deeply problematic, relation to 'sensibility' and the 'sentimental'. Readers in Sterne's time regularly understood or estimated Sterne's writing in relation to this influential contemporary cultural fashion, appreciating the fine strokes of human feeling apparent in Uncle Toby's relation with Le Fever or Yorick's with Maria, at the same time as they deplored the contamination of some of Sterne's most pathetic scenes by earthier passions. Sensibility has been a rather less dominant theme in twentieth-century discussion of Sterne; many critics have credibly represented Sterne as a sceptical and satiric intelligence who never willingly or unironically embraced sensibility or sentiment. Some more recent commentators however have re-opened the issue of Sterne's sensibility, moving beyond some of the too-readily homogenized outlines of an extended and diverse eighteenth-century cultural mode to concern themselves, in more pre-cisely theorized or historically contextualized ways, with the presentation in Sterne's novels of what he himself called (in *A Sentimental Journey*) the 'progress of sociality', the intimate specifics of human social interactions, linguistic and non-linguistic, in matters of the head, the heart and other parts of the Sternean anatomy. Notable among such critics are David Fairer, in his essay on 'Sentimental Translation in Mackenzie and Sterne' (1999), and John Mullan and Eve Kosofsky Sedgwick, in the two essays included here.

Sedgwick and Mullan present a striking theoretical, and methodo-logical, contrast. Sedgwick's essay is concerned with an aspect of his-torical masculinity, 'the changing meanings of the bonds between men' – 'homosocial' bonds, as she calls them – and the articulation of those bonds 'through various forms of the conquest and exchange of women', in a Restoration comedy, William Wycherley's *The Country Wife*, and in Sterne's *Sentimental Journey*.[1] Sedgwick finds in *The Country Wife* an essentially 'horizontal' depiction of 'a mainly aristocratic society', emphasizing 'heterosexual love chiefly as a strategy of male homosocial desire' within a rather restricted class field. Here Sedgwick discusses (in the half of her essay not reprinted here) cuckoldry as an institution, the 'rules' of exchange within the symbolic sexual economy of aristocratic society, and the function of wit as a 'mechanism for moving from an ostensible heterosexual object of desire to a true homosocial one'. In Sterne by contrast she finds a more 'vertical' narrative of class relations, belonging to a very different phase of English social history, making sense of the relation of the middle class, and 'the "private" bourgeois family', both to the aristocracy and to working people. The vertical operations of male bonding are illustrated particularly in Sedgwick's examination of the relation of Yorick – parson, narrator, Sternean alter ego – to his French valet La Fleur and, more briefly, to the French aristocrats, and aristocratic and working women, whom Yorick meets in the course of his journey.

Sedgwick's is one of the most explicitly theorized essays in this collection, evidently influenced by Foucault and Freud, and making use throughout of a paradigm, the 'exchange of women', taken from Lévi-Strauss. As such it exemplifies the tendency of theoretically determined writing to elide or blur the particularities of the texts it discusses. Certainly Sedgwick's account of Sterne begs questions: who and what is the person referred to as 'my gentleman', in the quotation from *A Sentimental Journey* which is Sedgwick's epigraph? can La Fleur be simply described as a 'peasant'? Is Yorick a purely social or secular figure? does not the absence of family – and the way Yorick defines family in his meeting with Maria – have something to do with his status and perceived duty as a priest, and his conviction as a Christian? Is Yorick simply a 'gentleman'? to describe him as representative, as '*the* leisured gentleman', offers a less nuanced version of eighteenth-century class stratifications and varieties – and of Sterne/Yorick's own place within them – than most commentators would now be happy to accept.

Above all, Sedgwick is resistant, even obtuse, to issues of irony and voice. This is, however, as she cheerfully acknowledges, deliberate, even inevitable, and amounts to an unwillingness to be seduced by the aesthetic pleasures, and wit, which are themselves, she argues, part of this novel's ideology (as they are part of *The Country Wife*). This is an essay which exposes uncomfortable ideological assumptions, and asks disturbing and inescapable interpretative questions.

Mullan's understanding and exposition of Sternean sensibility is by contrast more fully and subtly informed by the contexts of Sterne's literary environment, and by his relation to eighteenth-century readers. Through the lengthy chapter from which the following extract is taken Mullan examines intertexts philosophical (Locke, Hume, Adam Smith), and aesthetic (Hogarth, Reynolds), and provides a careful account of reviews and pamphlet reactions to Sterne, for 'if we are to recover Sterne's "sentimentalism" we should look at the reception and circulation of his writings'. Mullan documents the extent to which Sterne's contemporaries valued him for his pathos, and saw him as the originator of the late-century vogue for sentimental writing, while questioning the improprieties so inextricably entangled even in his most affecting passages. What troubled his critics however was, as Mullan shows, an essential part of Sterne's purpose and method. The workings of both sentimentalism and suggestiveness 'depended upon that relationship which Sterne elevated above any duty to literature or criticism – the relationship between a text and a private reader flattered to be segregated from "the *herd* of the *world*" '. 'Sociality' is a process of mutual understanding, by which we attempt to 'translate' the whole gestural as well as verbal language of our fellow men and women; but for Sterne this 'progress of sociality' stands above all for 'the relationship between the narrator and those who read', or rather a self-choosing subset of those who read. Social understanding is refined to 'the pact between a knowing narrator and a knowing consumer of novels'. Sedgwick distrusts and deconstructs Sterne's wit, understanding its function in the creation of a reading coterie, or defined and privileged social group; Mullan elaborates Sterne's rhetorical privileging of readers who can think and, more especially, feel; readers who are 'posited as the "few", the exceptional. . . . To feel is to enter into a special relationship with a narrative – to be a special kind of reader.'

NOTE

1. Sedgwick pursues this theoretical approach more fully in *Between Men: English Literature and Male Homosocial Desire* (Columbia University Press, New York: 1985). An important (if entirely bogus) theoretical contribution to the discussion of homosociality in relation to sentimentalism in the eighteenth-century novel was made by Manfred Mickelson, a (fictitious) young academic job applicant well-versed in theory, whose dossier includes this judgement: 'literary sentimentalism – I have in mind not only such major writers as Charlotte Lennox and Mrs Inchbald, but such male writers as Henry Mackenzie and Laurence Sterne – operates as a compensatory mechanism for the "violated" homosociality of the shipboard crew assaulted by pirates. Far from representing an empowering domesticity, as Nancy Armstrong and other leading eighteenth-century scholars have argued, literary sentimentalism demands to be viewed as the representational equivalent of "the lower deck in drag," striving through a reassertion of "feminine" sensitivity to reassert the equilibrium of an "onshore" heterosexuality symbolically and practically suspended when the ship leaves shore with an all-male crew' (http://www.rci.rutgers.edu/~wcd/manfred2.htm).

CHAPTER ONE

'Sexualism and the Citizen of the World: Wycherley, Sterne and Male Homosocial Desire'*

EVE KOSOFSKY SEDGWICK

—They order, said I, this matter better in France—

—You have been in France? said my gentleman,

turning quick upon me with the most civil triumph in the world.

LAURENCE STERNE, A Sentimental Journey through France and Italy

Surprisingly, when Laurence Sterne's Yorick sets his head toward Dover, it is with no developed motive of connoisseurship or curiosity: the gentleman dandy ups with his portmanteau at the merest glance of 'civil triumph' from a male servant. Perhaps we are in the world of P. G. Wodehouse, with a gentleman's gentleman who happens, like Jeeves, to be the embodiment of all the prescriptive and opportunistic shrewdness necessary to maintain his master's innocent privileges – but it is impossible to tell; the servant utters his five words, glances his glance, and disappears from the novel. The prestige that has lent force to his misprision – or is it a sneer? – seems to belong not to a particular personality but to a position, a function (or lack of it), a bond between gentleman and gentleman's gentleman that, throughout this novel, makes up in affective and class significance what it lacks in utilitarian sense. Yorick's

* Extracted from *Critical Inquiry*, 11 (December 1984), pp. 226–45

The writing of this study was supported by a Carnegie Foundation Fellowship from the Mary Ingraham Bunting Institute of Radcliffe College. I am especially indebted to Laura Brown, in addition, for discussing William Wycherley's economic context with me.

bond to another valet is the most sustained and one of the fondest in the novel; and, for most of the novel, the bond is articulated through various forms of the conquest and exchange of women.

In the discussion ahead, I will be using the 'exchange of women' paradigm taken from Claude Lévi-Strauss and, for example, René Girard and Gayle Rubin, to focus on the changing meanings of the bonds between men in a seventeenth-century play and an eighteenth-century novel.[1] These dis-cussions are part of a book-length study of what I am call-ing 'male homosocial desire' – the whole spectrum of bonds between men, including friendship, mentorship, rivalry, institutional subordination, homosexual genitality, and economic exchange – within which the various forms of the traffic in women take place.

What is most foreign to the twentieth-century American reader, in *A Sentimental Journey*, is the relatively crisp and differentiated treatment of class stratification. What is most familiar to us, and also newest in the period under discussion, is the automatic availability and salience, for the description of many different power transactions, of the image of the family – the family as psychoanalysis conceives it, comprising one parent of each gender and, as subject, a single, male child. I have chosen *A Sentimental Journey* as the *end point* of this discussion in order to emphas-ize the relative newness of this particular salience of the nuclear family, which we as post-Freudian readers take for granted, and in order to point to some of its political implications and groundings. The fantasy polarities of omnipotence and utter powerlessness, of castration and phallic entitle-ment, of maternal nurturance and deprivation form in *A Sentimental Journey*, as in more recent thought, the ground onto which other power transactions are mapped. As Michel Foucault suggests, the meaning of sexuality itself is new under this regime, as well . . .

Part of my contention in these readings will be that this modern narrative of the male homosocial subject was first and most influentially elaborated *as part of* a broad and very specific reading of class: that the crispness and breadth of class differentiation in Sterne is most important to the emerging family narrative. To say that this narrative has (or originally had) a strong, conscious content about class is not exactly to celebrate it, however. The class awareness, acute and crucial as it is, *is* not only bourgeois-centered but based on an aggressive pastoralization of working people and an expropriation of the aristocracy, too, for the cognitive needs of elements of the middle class. In short, the struggle to control the newly potent terms of the male homosocial spectrum depended on mobilizing a new narrative of the 'private', bourgeois family – a narrative that was socially powerful because it seemed itself able to make descriptive sense of relations across class.[2]

The Country Wife, on the other hand, is socially rather horizontal. It depicts a mainly aristocratic society, of which cuckoldry is the main social engine. 'To cuckold' is by definition a sexual act, performed on a man, by another man. Its central position means that the play emphasizes hetero-sexual love chiefly as a strategy of homosocial desire. In the title of a study of the play, David Vieth acutely calls it an 'anatomy of masculinity'.[3] Specify-ing further, I will discuss it as an analysis of several different paths by which men may attempt to arrive at satisfying relationships with other men . . .

What changes do we find in moving up a century to the more ver-tical but equally intense male homosocial bond between Yorick and his French valet La Fleur in *A Sentimental Journey*? The underlying terms of Yorick's involvement with La Fleur are conventional in a way that the degree of his involvement is not. An unquestioning paternalism – an assumption that his own welfare is also La Fleur's; that La Fleur's urgent, personal desire to be of service both goes with the terms of employment and at the same time testifies to a special, personal rapport between them; that La Fleur's cares and involvements can be nothing but a miniaturized, comic version of his own – lies behind the condescension of the recurrent epithets, 'honest' and 'poor' La Fleur. La Fleur, like all the peasants Yorick encounters across the Channel, is seen as childlike – unqualified for any serious work but ready for music, dance, and frolic at any hour of the day. Like the peasantry in general, La Fleur has a natural, untutored talent for music and a natural joyousness of temper. On the other hand, he must, like a child, be protected from worry.[4] In short, La Fleur is ruefully acknowledged to be an encumbrance, though a cheering one – a child himself, in relation to whom Yorick can seem a merely attractively childlike adult. Yorick is unusual in acknowledging how fluctuant and uncertain his own grasp is on 'adult' responsibilities. He is entirely conventional, though, in assigning La Fleur an *un*changingly childlike relation to them. The resulting imbalance is structured like the gender roles in *The Country Wife*: Yorick, like Horner, has a free and potentially manipulative choice of roles, which is displayed as both attractive and somehow renunciatory in relation to the more rigid role assignments of others. Working people in Sterne, like the women in Wycherley, are offered no such flexibility, however. A difference is that Horner's personal control – even his compulsiveness about it – is visible to the play's audi-ence, while the manipulative potential of Yorick's position, even when he exerts and profits by it, is presented to the reader as well as to the other characters as a form of vulnerability and helplessness.

Yorick's articulateness about the way he thinks of La Fleur – his need to describe and justify, under the guise of celebrating, the particular, paternalistic shape of the bond between them – is, like the very degree of his emotional investment in La Fleur, a sign not of a stable, hereditary, traditional bond to a servant but of an anxious and ideologically threatened one. Or more precisely: rather than being a sign of a traditional bond, it is an explicit, ideologizing narrative *about* such a bond and, hence, suggests Yorick's belated and anxious relation to the earlier, stabler relationship. One useful view of ideology is precisely as a narrative that makes explicit, in idealizing and apparently contemporaneous terms, the outdated or obsolescent values of an earlier system in the service of a newer system that in practice undermines the basis of those values. Thus, Yorick not only is not used to but is acutely anxious about this master–servant bond whose 'naturalness' he is so busy justifying. For instance, when La Fleur asks for a day off '*pour faire le galant vis-à-vis de sa maîtresse*', Yorick is highly discommoded ('Now it was the very thing I intended to do myself'); appealing to his own feelings, his reservoir of received ideas, however, he finds there a modern, capitalist version of nature and the social contract that actually undermines his ability to exact service from his own servant:

– The sons and daughters of service part with liberty, but not with nature in their contracts; they are flesh and blood, and have their little vanities and wishes in the midst of the house of bondage, as well as their task-masters – no doubt they have set their self-denials at a price – and their expectations are so unreasonable, that I would often disappoint them, but that their condition puts it so much in my power to do it.
    Behold – Behold, I am thy servant – disarms me at once of the powers of a master – (pp. 339–40)

In his Enlightenment ethos it is necessary for Yorick, as it had not been for the employers of personal servants in *The Country Wife*, to make explicit to himself the countervailing, 'natural' grounds that make it appropriate for one person to surrender liberty to another – and to couch them not in the crudely rationalistic, potentially egalitarian modern terms of economic power and want but in the reassuringly backward-looking ones of quasi-familial obligation. If La Fleur is like a child, he belongs (not *to*, but) *with* someone who is a little like an adult: his employer.

The area in which La Fleur is more or other than a child is, again, nothing new in the annals of paternalism: it is the sexual. For a servant to have the assignment of sexual knowing and acting-out in relation to a more refined, inhibited, or inexperienced master is a usual topos. Again, all that is perhaps unusual here are the emotional intensity and the dense, novelistic texture and specificity with which this part of the servant–master bond is rendered and rationalized. The free crossing, too, between *propria persona* conquests and triangulated conquests between the two men is a bit dizzying. La Fleur is seen as busy *both* in making his own conquests – which are always effortless and multiple and most often aimed at the servants of the women in whom Yorick is interested, *ad majorem Yorick gloriam* – *and* in prospecting and courting on behalf of his master. For instance, La Fleur's puppyish eagerness to show Yorick in his best light to an aristocratic woman, a potential patroness (or lover?), creates a situation where Yorick needs to produce an instant billet-doux to her. Yorick finds himself pen-tied, but – no problem: La Fleur, having created the opportunistic space, then fills it by offering with 'a thousand apologies for the liberty he was going to take . . . a letter in his pocket wrote by a drummer in his regiment to a corporal's wife, which, he durst say, would suit the occasion'.

'I had a mind to let the poor fellow have his humour' (p. 161), Yorick says, and reads the tawdry document:

It was but changing the Corporal into the Count – and saying nothing about mounting guard on Wednesday – and the letter was neither right or wrong – so to gratify the poor fellow, who stood trembling, for my honour, his own, and the honour of his letter – I took the cream gently off it, and whipping it up in my own way – I seal'd it up and sent him with it to Madame de L*** – (p. 166)

With this characteristically insouciant move, Yorick is playing the peasant man and the aristocratic woman off against one another through a powerful set of 'fanciful' identifications. Without releasing La Fleur from his infantilized role of 'poor' incompetent, Yorick is nevertheless at the same time submitting to his erotic advisement, making La Fleur his mentor/father in a conspiracy to capture the desired woman. By involving La Fleur in the plot, emphasizing and insisting on his lower class, Yorick is also implicitly reducing – even insulting – Madame de L***, of whom he has till now been rather frightened. Toward La Fleur, then, Yorick's bourgeois and male homosocial needs lead him to adopt a pastoral, split view: La Fleur can be cast as both a feckless, dependent child and a sexually expert father/advisor. (Neither of these can be mistaken for an equal; the pastoralizing split might be compared to the one in white Southern ideology between negro viewed as child and negro viewed as Mammy.) The masculine complicities built into this split relationship, then, permit Yorick to make double use of Madame de L***: Yorick's bond to her is a guarantee of his right to condescend to 'poor' La Fleur, but the locker-room, lower-class nature of his confidential bond with La Fleur, and their ability to relegate Madame de L∗∗∗ between them through 'universal' male wisdom about how to deal with women, lets Yorick place her, too, firmly in the category of those whom he deserves to master.

This incident is only one example of Yorick's facility for creating instant, supportive, apparently egalitarian 'families' around himself by his deftness in playing gender and class attribution off against one another. How thoroughly gender divides the pie of class – how thoroughly class divides the pie of gender – our hero is aware, and the new male type he personifies is a deft broker of these differences. Not the least deft of his strategies, as I have suggested, is the casting of a veil of nostalgic pathos, linked to the traffic in women within an idealized 'classless' nuclear family, over his power negotiations with men.[5] Rather than read Yorick psychoanalytically, that is, I would like to read him as pioneering in the ideological use of male 'androgyny' and of ostensibly universal psychoanalytic perceptions to express and assuage the specific homosocial anxieties of the male middle-class intellectual.

What features of the social landscape in *A Sentimental Journey* facilitate Yorick's manipulations? To begin with, class difference, although one of the main dimensions along which the social landscape is mapped, is described in particularly stylized terms. I am not referring here merely to the pastoralization of the servant/peasant class but to the absence of any working class (especially of men) *except* for servants and peasants. Servants are personally responsible to, and in the paternalistic care of, persons of Yorick's class or higher; while peasants, in the novel's pastoral, distant view, are easily perceived as decorative, animating projections on a distant prospect of the picturesque. Each group is viewed in a way that makes it singularly susceptible to being read through a fantasy of the personal, a fantasy of the middle-class male person. Women of the working classes are even more available for this imaginative expropriation: if not personal servants, they are vendors of personal linen, or of gloves, or precisely of sexual services. Thus, far from presenting a cross-grained world of work that might occasionally frustrate, be indifferent to, or even fundamentally oppose the desires of the leisured gentleman, the novel edits and amends the working classes in the image of the gentleman and his desires. Similarly, the powers of the aristocracy and even of royalty do not, in this novel, seem either to arise from or to result in interests that are fundamentally different from those of

the novel edits and amends the working classes in the image of the gentleman and his desires

the middle-class intellectual. The difference between Yorick and his aristocratic patrons is causeless, a given, a difference as vast as species difference
but as easily sublimated as mercury. It is pure mystique; any material differences are expressive of the true difference but not causally involved with
it. Accordingly, familial-style techniques of ingratiation, personal sub-
mission, swagger, sweetness, seductiveness – techniques that are purely
individualistic, based on no explicit perception of class or group interest
– are the appropriate ones for dealing upward across class difference, as well.

The fact that *A Sentimental Journey* is, by definition, a novel of travel,
is probably important in permitting it to present such a wishful, seductive, impoverished social map with such an influential degree of conviction.
For an Englishman (or in our century, an American) to travel for pleasure
– especially to poor areas or countries – is to requisition whole societies
in the service of fantasy needs. This is perhaps especially true of sexual
fantasy. A present-day traveler I know reports that among the English-
language T-shirts that are popular in Japan (for example, 'Let's Sports
Furiously All Day and Sweat'), by far the most common is one that says
simply 'SEXUALISM'. This insinuating use of a literary reification of sexual
desire, in the service of mobility and cosmopolitanism, is close to the
strategy that appears in Sterne.

In our discussion of Wycherley, we isolated 'wit' as a seventeenth-
century name for the circulable social solvent, the sign that both represented political power in the male homosocial framework and could,
through sublimation (through shedding its relation as sign to a material
signified), come to be a supposedly classless commodity in its own right.
In Sterne, 'wit' continues to be a name for that solvent. For instance,
Yorick finally equips himself with a passport by (inadvertently) convincing a complete stranger, the Count de B****, that he is *the* Yorick, the one
in *Hamlet*: '*Un homme qui rit . . . ne sera jamais dangereux*. – Had it been for
anyone but the king's jester, added the Count, I could not have got it
these two hours' (p. 293). In addition to wit, however, sex itself, sexual
desire, in this late eighteenth-century psychological novel, takes on the
same representational volatility, the same readiness to represent every form
of mobility and claim to power. Where in *The Country Wife*, sex, however
commodified and circulable, was still implicit in only one kind of situation
– that of cuckoldry – in *A Sentimental Journey*, every touch, every relationship, every exchange, seems to beg to be translated into sexual language
– into the language of blood engorgement, of pulsing dilation, of the sexual
fungibility of women. The predictability of this translation is, needless to
say, one of the things that makes the novel sound so 'psychoanalytic'.

To anyone who has an appreciation of the astonishing plangency
and elasticity of the narrative voice and form in *A Sentimental Journey*,

descriptions like the ones above will sound plonking, churlish, literal-minded, irrelevant to the special pleasures of this book. In fact, it is one of the distinctions of the book – and one of its main ideological techniques, as well – that to say anything about it is necessarily to plonk; so protean, so mercurial are its tones and generic choices that the critic finds it more than usually impossible to paraphrase, to isolate 'representative' incidents, or to make assumptions about a 'normative' readerly response.

What makes it worth plonking ahead with this book – not leaving it untouched as an article of aesthetic appreciation, of sheer seductive virtuosity – is, I think, that the techniques by which it disarms analysis are themselves in the very closest relation to its sexual–political meaning. The creation of a warm, pseudo-egalitarian space of familial pathos, for instance, is not the work merely of the novel's thematics: the insinuating nervous interruptive style tugs the reader into a complex, mirrorlike play of identifications in her or his very effort to lend continuity to the successive sentences. An apparently trivial matter of punctuation, the lack of any system to signal the frequent change of speakers, is, I think, particularly important. Appearing to open up the narrative, as it were, democratically to the permeation of different voices from the society, it also assimilates those voices to elements of Yorick's consciousness – and, at the same time, gives the same kind of 'reality' to his fantasy interlocutors, his fantasy foils, his slightest mental projections, that it gives to the people around him. The project of mapping a large-scale sociology of class and gender onto a private narrative of individual development within 'the' family becomes easier – becomes invisible, a matter of course – through such techniques, which render the intersubjective transparent to the intrapsychic.

In a sense, the lambency of Yorick's eros makes it especially difficult to isolate homosocial elements as distinct from heterosexual ones. Again, however, this perceptual difficulty, this transparency of the subject, is not a sign so much of a particular author's skill as it is of a newly emerging 'universal' literary consensus based on the normative figure of the pseudo-androgynous, sexually highly valent male intellectual within the context of an increasingly eroticized and family-dominated public discourse.

I suggested earlier that Yorick's insistent explanations of the 'naturalness' of the servant–master relation gave support in backward-looking, ideological terms to a relation that was really more modern and less stable than the rationalizations would suggest. Similarly, the centrality of the image of the family in *A Sentimental Journey* coincides with a loss in the material stability of the families themselves. The image of the family that is most explicitly valorized is the reactionary one of the patriarchal peasant family that he sees in his rural travels. The idyllic, the idealized and scenic, family described there seems to recede when Yorick's own life and concerns loom larger in the novel, however. This image of the family is not dissipated, then – in fact, it is far more powerful – but it is, so to speak, diffused. In place of the clear, literal generational layers of grandparents, children, and grandchildren, Yorick uses the charged image of the patriarchal family as a ready and enabling, but unspecifiable, image of 'consanguinity' to legitimate his sexual exploitation of the *fille de chambre* (see p. 226). Similarly, in his fantasies about the mad, betrayed peasant Maria, Yorick does not distinguish between the relations of mistress and of daughter:

Affliction had touch'd her looks with something that was scarce earthly – still she was feminine – and so much was there about her of all that the heart wishes, or the eye looks for in woman, that could the traces be ever worn out of her brain, and those of Eliza out of mine, she should *not only eat of my bread and drink of my own cup*, but Maria should lie in my bosom, and be unto me as a daughter.

(p. 391)

What remains to be made explicit is perhaps chiefly the simple absence from the novel of any shred of a literal family for Yorick. As in modern European thought on the larger scale, the ideological force of the concept of 'the family' strengthens as the jurisdiction and the private material basis of the family itself become weaker and more internally contradictory, under the atomizing effects of early capitalism. That the blossoming – or at least, the broadcast pollination – of a lambent and abstractable consciousness of sexuality itself was also concomitant with the ideological sublation of the family, is one of the points of Foucault's *History of Sexuality*.

The claim for universality made by Yorick's plural, inviting narrative voice is not exactly belied by the precision with which the novel shows him to be a male, unpropertied, English, valetudinarian intellectual of middle age. Instead, the claim seems to be that *only* the person so specified *can* achieve a universal consciousness. Perhaps, also, as we have seen in Wycherley, it is the unpropertied intellectual male who has the most to gain during this century from the literary assertion of any 'universal' value. At any rate, like Horner's power, Yorick's is presented in the form of noncommutative equations of 'identification' and 'desire' that are specified by both gender and class: he is mobile, encompassing, universal; others are fixed, static, limited. That these *are* forms of power, Horner conceals from others; Yorick, through the image of the family, mystifies it to himself and to us as his progeny.

NOTES

1. The best summary of this paradigm, including the importance of Claude Lévi-Strauss, is in Gayle Rubin, 'The Traffic in Women: Notes toward a "Political Economy" of Sex', in *Toward an Anthropology of Women*, ed. Rayna R. Reiter (New York, 1975), pp. 157–210. René Girard's *Deceit, Desire, and the Novel: Self and Other in Literary Structure*, trans. Yvonne Freccero (Baltimore, MD, 1965), fits nicely into this schema, though it does not itself explicitly advance it.
2. See Alan Bray, *Homosexuality in Renaissance England* (London, 1982), and my forthcoming *Between Men: English Literature and Male Homosocial Desire*.
3. See David M. Vieth, 'Wycherley's *The Country Wife*: An Anatomy of Masculinity', *Papers on Language and Literature* 2 (Fall 1966): 335–50.
4. See Laurence Sterne, *A Sentimental Journey through France and Italy*, ed. Wilbur L. Cross (New York, 1906), pp. 227–8; all further references to this work will be included in the text.
5. To describe the modern psychoanalytic family as 'apparently egalitarian' or 'classless' is a condensed formulation of its very complicated relation to the forms of hierarchy in the world around it. Hierarchically organized as this family is by both age and gender, it is 'classless' in the obvious sense that its members share a social class rather than competing for one. (This is not true of the preindustrial, extended, cohabitant family of, for instance, the Poysers in *Adam Bede*; and of course modern nonfamily groups are ideologically supposed to be distinct from the family precisely because they are organized around individual competition for social advancement.) Again, while social and political paternalism take their very name from the family, the paternalism of the family is, by contrast, 'apparently egalitarian' because sons *are* to grow into the status of fathers, daughters of mothers – as workers are not to grow up into the status of owners (nor, to complicate the matter, daughters of fathers). The view of the nuclear family as a haven in the heartless world of capitalist competition seems to be as ineradicable as it is riddled with contradiction. Good discussions can be found in Michèle Barrett, *Women's Oppression Today: Problems in Marxist Feminist Analysis* (London, 1980); Frances E. Olsen, 'The Family and the Market: A Study of Ideology and Legal Reform', *Harvard Law Review* 96 (May 1983): 1497–1578; and Zaretsky, *Capitalism*.

CHAPTER TWO

'Laurence Sterne and the "Sociality" of the Novel'*

JOHN MULLAN

There is so little true feeling in the *herd* of the *world*, that I wish
I could have got an act of parliament, when the books first
appear'd, that none but wise men should look into them.

(Sterne to John Eustace, February 1768)[1]

For Yorick in the *Sentimental Journey* perfectly intelligible conversation depends on gestures rather than words, on sensitivity to the non-verbal rather than confidence in what can be said:

There is not a secret so aiding to the progress of sociality, as to get master of this *short hand*, and be quick in rendering the several turns of looks and limbs, with all their inflections and delineations, into plain words. For my own part, by long habitude, I do it so mechanically, that when I walk the streets of London, I go translating all the way; and have more than once stood behind in the circle, where not three words have been said, and have brought off twenty different dialogues with me, which I could have fairly wrote down and sworn to. (*Sentimental Journey*, ed. Gardner Stout (Los Angeles, 1967), p. 172)

In the end all becomes 'plain words' – the transcriptions and inferences of a narrative. The 'progress of sociality' is the progress of this narrative: 'sociality' stands not so much for the relationship between the narrator

* Extracted from John Mullan, *Sentiment and Sociability: the Language of Feeling in the Eighteenth Century* (Oxford: Oxford University Press, 1988), pp. 158–72

'Sociality' is what we are to enter into when we read Sterne's text

and those whose 'looks and limbs' he describes (he is a distanced connoisseur, an amused translator), as for the relationship between the narrator and those who read, those who are to benefit by the habit and art of his translation. Yorick stands 'behind in the circle', not participant but transcriber. Out of his observations of gesture comes 'sociality': the sociality of the text. Sterne's coinage refines social understanding to the pact between a knowing narrator and a knowing consumer of novels. 'Sociality' is what we are to enter into when we read Sterne's text.

Sterne's fiction is notoriously self-conscious about the modes of a novel's coherence – about the powers of a narrator to convince, to beguile and to satisfy. It is attentive to its 'sociality'. Sterne may have made new capital, and a new kind of instant literary fame, out of this self-consciousness, but he was exploiting conventional expectations. In an age in which narrative fiction was suspected by many, even of its more enthusiastic consumers, of being suggestive, improper, promiscuous, novels were thick with descriptions of how narratives should be attended to and interpreted. They constantly concerned themselves, technically and moralistically, with the effects of telling stories. As we have seen, novels of sentiment keenly rehearsed the art of comprehending the pathos of narratives; the capacity to respond with tremulous sensibility to a tale of misfortune was represented as a sufficient sign of virtue. The use of 'the story of Le Fever' in Volume VI of *Tristram Shandy* is a clear enough indication of Sterne's awareness of this genre of the internalized tale, included to demonstrate the sympathies of its auditors. It is a story that comes to us freighted with the responsiveness of Toby and Trim to another's misfortunes; its point is the sympathy of which they are capable. But then sympathy is most graphic when it is not spoken, Toby and Trim not being the most competent handlers of words. It takes Tristram's narrative to describe 'the several turns of looks and limbs' that accompany the telling and reception of Le Fever's story: 'fool that I was! nor can I recollect, (nor perhaps you) without turning back to the place, what it was that hindered me from letting the corporal tell it in his own words; – but the occasion is lost, – I must tell it now in my own' VI. v: 415–16). Narrative has to translate, has to make 'plain words' mediate the natural articulacy of feeling. And translation (a metaphor invoked throughout *Tristram Shandy*) is a matter of inference and induction – a freedom that comes with the acceptance of error. There is the understanding of which the likes of Toby and Trim are capable, signified in their gestures, their sighs, their looks, and there is the sociality of the text – the relationship between narrator and reader – through which that understanding is represented. Richardson attempted to produce the poignancy of sentiment in 'writing to the moment', which became writing which threatened to evade moralistic control. Sterne concedes that sentiment can only be glimpsed across the distance between a translator and an 'original'; that while feeling is supposed to transcend words, it takes words (at once judicious and inaccurate) to translate sentiment. *Tristram Shandy* is writing away from the moment.

There have grown up literary-critical versions of *Tristram Shandy* as an anachronism, a modern novel before its time. To represent it as such, however, is to ignore the ways in which the novel's field of play and manœuvre might have been fitted to the competence of its admiring eighteenth-century readers. 'I know there are readers in the world, as well as many other good people in it, who are no readers at all, – who find themselves ill at ease, unless they are let into the whole secret from first to last, of every thing which concerns you' (*Tristram Shandy*, I. iv: 7): *Tristram Shandy* is always admonishing incompetent or intemperate readers, but that does not mean that it is not colluding with those who are more deft. All those moralisms about the dangers of novels which get repeated through the eighteenth century take reading only for the 'story' as the trap into which the unwary fall. Sterne's satire on story-lovers exploits such rhetoric, and presumes a reader who will know better. It is this implied reader with whom *Tristram Shandy* establishes its sociality, a reader privileged to look down on the possibilities of misinter-pretation which the novel invokes. So the misunderstandings and non-communications shown in *Tristram Shandy* are only apparent. Walter and Toby Shandy shake their heads over the behaviour of women in pregnancy,

but certainly since shaking of heads came into fashion, never did two heads shake together, in concert, from two such different springs.

God bless ⎱ 'em all – said my uncle *Toby* and my
Duce take ⎰ father, each to himself. (IV. xii: 285)

Unknowing disagreement is resolved into intelligible gesture. Eccentric differences of perception are only eccentric – the accidental crossings of Walter's and Toby's reasonings are comic because the novel can trace the different paths by which they appear to arrive at the same point: 'He was a very great man! added my uncle *Toby*; (meaning *Stevinus*) – He was so, brother *Toby*, said my father, (meaning *Piereskius*)' (VI. ii: 410). Difference is referred to from a vantage-point from which it can be perfectly comprehended. 'There is nothing shews the characters of my father and my uncle *Toby*, in a more entertaining light, than their different manner of deportment, under the same accident' (VIII. xxvi: 578). Helene Moglen is typical of many modern critics in seeing in this play of differences, this entertainment, an admirable pluralism: 'there is never an absolute truth (only a number of possible points of view which must be balanced against one another)'.[2] But although the novel does offer 'opinions' rather than truths, most of these come from Toby, Trim and Walter and are the products of obsession. They are not offered to the reader as if they were adoptable perceptions. What is offered as exemplary, in the usual manner of sentimentalism, is the sympathy that can bridge the gulf between perceptions.

'The truest respect which you can pay to the reader's understanding, is to halve this matter amicably, and leave him something to imagine' (*Tristram Shandy*, II. xi: 109): whatever its promises of pluralism, Sterne's novel can only propose a sympathy which overrides monomania because it is authoritative enough to trace obsessions like Walter's and Toby's through their bizarre and specific involutions. The certainty of this legibility allows the narrator of *Tristram Shandy* ironically to project precisely the promise of pluralism to which I have just referred. For 'so long as a man rides his HOBBY-HORSE peaceably and quietly along the Kings highway, and neither compels you or me to get up behind him, – pray, Sir, what have either you or I to do with it?' (I. vii: 13). The text makes much of accepting privatized fixation as an inevitable condition, but the reader of this is safe in the knowledge that obsessions are just private. They are self-containing ('there is no disputing against HOBBY-HORSES'), and, in this novel, they are brought into the light of day by a narrative which sees them, follows them, socializes them. Sterne pilfered the singular vocabularies which possess members of the Shandy household from encyclopedias and reference books;[3] they were intended to be recondite, deracinated, impractical. 'It is the nature of an hypothesis, when once a man has conceived it, that it assimilates every thing to itself as a proper nourishment; and, from the first moment of your begetting it, it generally grows the stronger by every thing you see, hear, read, or understand. This is of great use' (II. xix: 151). The naturalization of monomania here involves the shift from 'a man' to 'you', a claim for the universality, and thus intelligibility, of obsession. Yet the 'great use' to which this form is put in *Tristram Shandy* necessarily involves the assurance of a distance between reading and the blindness of such obsession. For reading must be allowed to make sense of the differences and limited conflicts which are represented, and those in recent years who have detected the spectre of madness in this novel have failed to recognize how obsession is only introduced with a narrative which absolutely comprehends it, which plays upon it.[4] The Hobby-Horse is an impediment to identification: we are to understand, not to share, the odd commitments of characters in *Tristram Shandy*. And we are to understand, too, that these characters are not quite the slaves of their vocabularies because they are bound together by more than words.

Tristram declares that he believes that

the hand of the supreme Maker and first Designer of all things, never made or put a family together . . . where the characters of it were cast or contrasted with so dramatic a felicity as ours was, for this end; or in which the capacities of affording such exquisite scenes, and the powers of shifting them perpetually from morning to night, were lodged and intrusted with so unlimited a confidence, as in the SHANDY FAMILY. (III. xxxix: 236)

In this family is found the 'felicity' of contrast, of comprehensible difference. Scenes in this 'whimsical theatre of ours' are 'exquisite', a word meaning, in the eighteenth century, esoteric or finely wrought or sensibly felt. Sterne means all these: we are given, as if spectators, the fastidiously drawn drama of inclinations at once ludicrously eccentric and keenly felt. Walter has 'exquisite feelings' about noses and names; while these prompt him to reasonings incomprehensible except to him and the reader, they also provoke (with his son's name and nose both botched) the benign sympathy of Uncle Toby for his distress. In this world of obsessions, intense feeling is both ludicrous and admirable.

This is the trick of Sterne's sentimentalism. As the writer of *Yorick's Skull* (1777) had it, *Tristram Shandy* should be considered 'rather as an admirable caricature of history, than an exact portrait of private life' – as a text which works by 'alluring mankind with flattering deceptions, beyond the bounds of probability'.[5] The fellow-feeling of which Walter, Toby and Trim are capable does redeem the influence of obsession, leading R. F. Brissenden to write that against 'the isolating and socially disruptive force of the hobby-horse and the ruling passion Sterne sets the power of sympathy'.[6] But then monomania and sympathy are also inextricable; as exercised in *Tristram Shandy*, they are equally 'beyond the bounds of probability'. As *Yorick's Skull* goes on to say, the bonds of sympathy, like the influences of each hobby-horse, are extrapolated past the 'usual': 'By carrying us beyond our usual feelings, he has taught us, that the human heart is capable of the greatest improvement; and that nature never feels herself more noble and exalted, than in the exercise of benevolence and humanity'.[7] The finer feelings illustrated in *Tristram Shandy* – the tears of Toby or Trim; Walter at his most eloquent when words are not enough – are as whimsical as what passes for conversation or argument in Shandy Hall. Sterne privileges the truths of gesture over those of words, but it is wryly done; characters reveal their better instincts, their 'benevolence and humanity', in moments of innocence which are to be approved by a reader who is anything but innocent – a reader tutored enough in the ways of narrative to recognize the untutored 'human heart'.

Thus the use of Locke in *Tristram Shandy* – referring us to the mingled misunderstandings and sympathies of the Shandy household, but also to the understanding, the contract, between reader and narrator. The 'sagacious Locke' is mobilized to draw attention to that 'fertile source of obscurity' in Shandy Hall: 'the unsteady uses of words which have perplexed the clearest and most exalted understandings' (II. ii: 86). But Locke's concern with the ways in which words can fail, communication go awry, is appropriated by a narrative which can reveal obscurities, explain misunderstandings, show the sympathy that is supposed to transcend speech. References to Lockian epistemology are provided as only sham explanations of the eccentric preoccupations which Sterne describes. It is not necessary to possess a great deal of scholarly knowledge to have doubts about the seriousness with which Sterne does exploit Locke; the very tag 'sagacious' should be enough to arouse suspicions when it appears in a text which so satirizes deference to learning and literary precedent. The resources of scholarship can, however, confirm such suspicions. Melvyn New sees the question of the relation between 'philosophy and literature' as particularly problematic: 'That we cannot even settle the most basic problem of whether Sterne agrees or disagrees with Locke is perhaps a strong indication that the question has not yet been asked in a manner that could produce a satisfying answer'.[8] As he and Geoff Day have argued, there is little reason to believe that Sterne read Locke diligently; the evidence of specific borrowings suggests that Sterne might have arrived at his knowledge of the philosopher's writings through second-hand sources.[9] Tristram, indeed, warns us of the easy availability of Locke's *Essay concerning Human Understanding* (misnaming the title in the process): 'many, I know, quote the book, who have not read it' (*Tristram Shandy*, II. ii: 85). Perhaps too few modern commentators have attended to Ferriar's dry remark of the 1790s: 'It was not the business of Sterne to undeceive those, who considered his Tristram a work of unfathomable knowledge'.[10] As Ferriar began to show, *Tristram Shandy* is full of mangled erudition – plagiarisms calculated to make a virtue of the fragmentation of that 'literature' defined by Johnson in his *Dictionary* as 'learning; skill in letters'. If *Tristram Shandy* was a newly opportunistic kind of literary commodity whose ideal was fashion, it was appropriate that it should play fast and loose with literary precedents, and improbable that Locke could ever be absolved from this process. Locke is not Sterne's intellectual mentor. His writings are invoked in order to show the superiority to such specialized philosophy of the descriptions that narrative can provide. And Locke is a particularly useful measure of the capacities of Sterne's narrative because, while he theorized the inconsistencies of thought and language, *Tristram Shandy* sets out to demonstrate how understanding can surmount private fixation and misapplied vocabulary.

Tristram Shandy first refers us to Locke for the description of 'an unhappy association of ideas which have no connection in nature' (I. iv: 9); in this case it is Mrs Shandy's association of the winding of the clock with 'some other little family concernments'. Any editor of the novel will direct the reader to Locke's discussion of the 'wrong Connexion in our Minds of *Ideas* in themselves, loose and independent one of another'.[11] Locke seems to describe exactly the fixating form of association to which Toby, Walter and the rest are prey:

Some of our *Ideas* have a natural Correspondence. . . . Besides this there is another Connexion of *Ideas* wholly owing to Chance or Custom; *Ideas* that in themselves are not at all of kin, come to be so united in some Mens Minds, that 'tis very hard to separate them, they always keep in company, and the one no sooner at any time comes into the Understanding but its Associate appears with it.[12]

Yet Locke characterizes the resultant 'Unreasonableness' as a 'Madness' which always threatens discourse, and which, if it prevails, will make 'a Man . . . fitter for *Bedlam*, than Civil Conversation'. There is some kind of distance between this and the hobby-horses harmlessly ridden through the pages of Sterne's novel. What an editorial direction to the relevant passage from Locke's *Essay* can actually obscure is the bathos of the allusion.

This famous joke about the winding of the clock and the associated sex life of Tristram's parents is less at the expense of Mrs Shandy, who after a while cannot dissociate the one from the other, than of her husband, whose 'extreme exactness . . . to which he was in truth a slave' leads to the connection of the two incongruous activities. And what is Walter Shandy but the book's very own 'philosopher'? Always desiring 'exactness', he had 'an itch in common with all philosophers, of reasoning upon every thing which happened, and accounting for it too' (III. xviii: 189). It is into his mouth that Sterne puts the book's 'most extensive borrowing from Locke',[13] the discussion of *duration and its simple modes* begun in Volume III, chapter XVIII. But we can scarcely take too seriously any explanation that *he* would repeat so religiously. And the narrative does not allow us to follow it seriously: his argument terminates only in Toby's complete failure to understand him. Though Walter is 'in one of his best explanatory moods', nothing is explained. He is brought up short in his 'eager pursuit of a metaphysic point into the very regions where clouds and thick darkness would soon have encompassed it about'; Toby associates his brother's words with the military terminology on which he so often relies. The very process of habitual association on which Locke has commented has been set in motion to interrupt the paraphrase of Locke which Walter is producing. Not just bathos, but the matter of philosophical explanation made to frustrate its style. But then the authority of the philosophical text is constantly undermined by being tested against the special propensities of the members of the Shandy household. Locke's analysis of 'the great and principal act of ratiocination in man' is brought forward to explain Toby's strange 'deportment' as he listens to Walter's lecture on 'his systems of noses' (III. xl: 237–8). In fact, it can explain no such thing. Toby's 'fancy' is in excess of any thesis offered by the 'great reasoner'. In a parody of Locke's warnings about the dangers of metaphorical language, Toby is shown transforming Walter's figures of speech according to the dictates of his own obsessions. The customary errors against which Locke so seriously warned intervene to upset the application of his analysis of measurement and judgement. Examples of how parts of Locke's *Essay* are deflated by their introduction into *Tristram Shandy* are many and various, and almost all of them (as above) refer the reader to the explanation of misunderstanding and miscommunication. The *Essay concerning Human Understanding* is used as if it will clarify failed acts of speech or interpretation; in fact, it falters before them.

There is one point at which the rejection of Locke as a proper guide to thought and language is made quite explicit. The 'Author's Preface' which appears half-way through Volume III of *Tristram Shandy* promises that the book will provide 'all the wit and judgment (be it more or less) which the great author and bestower of them had thought it fit originally to give me' (III. xx: 193): 'wit and judgment in this world never go together; inasmuch as they are two operations differing from each other as wide as east is from west. – So, says *Locke*, – so are farting and hickuping, say I.' Locke had argued that 'judgment', which involved the careful discrimination of ideas, was incompatible with 'wit', which was defined as 'lying most in the assemblage of *Ideas*, and putting those together with quickness and variety, wherein can be found any resemblance or congruity, thereby to make up pleasant Pictures, and agreeable Visions in the Fancy'.[14] 'Wit' should be dissociated from 'judgment' because the former involved 'Metaphor and Allusion' which might provide 'entertainment and pleasantry' but which were not 'conformable' to the 'Rules of Truth, and good Reason'.[15] Locke characterized 'Figurative Speech' as 'an Abuse of Language',[16] a succumbing to opportunistic association which could only corrupt proper communication. In order to assert that 'wit and judgment' are 'indubitably both made and fitted to go together', *Tristram Shandy* contradicts Locke in the manner of its explanation, reflecting at inordinate length on an improbable analogy between these faculties and the 'curious' but symmetrical 'ornaments' on the back of the chair 'I am this moment sitting upon' (III. xx: 200–1). As it pursues the metaphor over several paragraphs, the text does not just contradict Locke, it also refuses to obey the Lockian stipulations for a reasonable discourse. This over-insistent pursuit, like most of the text's engagements with Locke, directs us to an anxiety which runs through Book III of the *Essay concerning Human Understanding*. Whimsically applied metaphor is one example of the unreasonable or eccentric association of ideas against which Locke wished to guard. For him, words should be tethered to the privately conceived ideas that they were to recreate in the mind of another:

To make Words serviceable to the end of Communication, it is necessary . . . that they excite, in the Hearer, exactly the same *Idea*, they stand for in the Mind of the Speaker. Without this, Men fill one another's Heads with noise and sounds; but convey not thereby their Thoughts, and lay not before one another their *Ideas*, which is the end of Discourse and Language.[17]

Of course, inappropriate ideas are always being excited in each other's minds by the inhabitants of Shandy Hall. But this is demonstrated not to confirm but to relieve Locke's worries about the inconsistencies of words. Sterne's characters can rely on bonds of unspeakable sympathy; the reader of *Tristram Shandy* can rely on the ability of the narrative to reveal the pressures of fixation and the paths of misunderstanding which are special to the enclosed world of 'Shandyism'.

Walter, Toby and Trim are not inhabiting some Lockian nightmare of unmeaning 'noise and sounds'. In their odd, but intelligibly consistent, customs of conversation they point up the incapacities of Locke's theory of language. A contemporary philosopher puts the obvious objection to Locke like this:

Since thoughts cannot be formulated whether inwardly or outwardly unless there are ways of formulating them, that is, unless a language is already presupposed, it follows that Locke's epistemological units must already be functioning as crypto-linguistic units before he comes formally to consider language at all. His official account of language is thus in a way redundant.[18]

Sterne's characters are indeed incapable of thoughts which are not fixed to particular, if strange, vocabularies. They are attached to the world by the metaphors and allusions on which they rely, and which protect them against death, discord and disaster. They are not mad, first because they are attached to each other by sympathy, and second because they are innocents whose limited ways with words are displayed to a reader who has to be sophisticated to comprehend their transparent instincts.

The reader is constituted as knowledgeable not by any deep familiarity with learned texts, but simply by complicity with the narrative's confidences – by the sociality of the novel. One of the effects, in fact, of the rhetoric of the narrative is to subvert pretensions to the knowledge that is erudition:

You see as plain as can be, that I write as a man of erudition; – that even my similes, my allusions, my illustrations, my metaphors, are erudite, – and that I must sustain my character properly, and contrast it properly too, – else what would become of me? Why, Sir, I should be undone; – at this very moment that I am going here to fill up one place against a critick, – I should have made an opening for a couple. (*Tristram Shandy*, II. ii: 85)

The irony is signalled by having this addressed to 'Sir Critick', for the understanding reader is anybody but one of the pedants whom the text treats with mock deference: 'Gentlemen, I kiss your hands' (p. 84). It is the 'Critick' who is invited to consider the relevance of Locke's *Essay*, and given enough to compose a pretence of erudition: 'It is a history-book, Sir, (which may possibly recommend it to the world) of what passes in a man's own mind; and if you will say so much of the book, and no more, believe me, you will cut no contemptible figure in a metaphysic circle.' It is the 'Gentle critick' who is told of Locke in order to be shown what 'the confusion in my uncle *Toby*'s discourse . . . did *not* arise from' (p. 86):

THERE is nothing so foolish, when you are at the expence of making an enter-tainment of this kind, as to order things so badly, as to let your criticks and gentry of refined taste run it down: Nor is there any thing so likely to make them do it, as that of leaving them out of the party, or, what is full as offensive, of bestowing your attention upon the rest of your guests in so particular a way, as if there was no such thing as a critick (by occupation) at table. (p. 84)

The 'critick' is the representative of pedantic (and probably scanty) learn-ing, and the moralizer on narrative impropriety; in later volumes 'he' is also to be quite specifically the hostile reviewer or lampooner of *Tristram Shandy*. The knowledgeable reader has to be somebody else.

Locke put into the hands of the 'critick' is never going to reveal much. But then it takes the critick to believe that Locke could be a sufficient guide. The reader who is not the critick will trust more to Tristram's ability to demonstrate the commitment to saving metaphors which qualifies the inhabitants of Shandy Hall as innocents. This nar-rator tells us of a world in which confusion reigns but is also contained.

Locke's scheme is implied when we are told of Uncle Toby's problem – ''Twas not by ideas, – by heaven! his life was put in jeopardy by words' (II. ii: 87) – but the hyperbole of this signals the reader's inoculation against the same confusions. The cadence of mock-concern defuses Lockian regrets because it is a reminder of the distance between Toby's simple, ingenuous 'perplexities' and the knowing confidences and nudges which pass from narrator to reader. It is this distance which allows another rebuff to Locke, the production of feeling, sentiment, that which can hardly be spoken, as a criterion of unanimity. For it is unworldliness, artlessness, that gives rise to overflowing sentiments, eloquent gestures, fraternal sympathy. Walter scorns Toby's hobby-horse, his innocent obsession, only to succumb to fellow feeling:

[Uncle Toby] look'd up into my father's face, with a countenance spread over with so much good nature; – so placid; – so fraternal; – so inexpressibly tender towards him; – it penetrated my father to his heart: He rose up hastily from his chair, and seizing hold of both my uncle *Toby*'s hands as he spoke: – brother *Toby*, said he, – I beg thy pardon; – forgive, I pray thee, this rash humour which my mother gave me. (II. xii: 115)

Walter's association of his 'rash humour' with his mother is not arbitrary: fellow-feeling is largely a male prerogative in this novel. *Tristram Shandy* is punctuated by these rushes of sentiment, re-

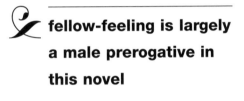

fellow-feeling is largely a male prerogative in this novel

storing a harmony which words have supposedly unsettled; the harmony is of a rather special kind – men neutered, segregated from women, the door closed behind them.

They depend on words, of course, but also on the meaningful look or the eloquent tear: the currency of sentimentalism. It is when they are silent that they best communicate. Trim, in his attempt to read out a sermon, is drawn into the story of his brother's fate at the hands of the Inquisition: '– The tears trickled down *Trim*'s cheeks faster than he could well wipe them away. – A dead silence in the room ensued for some minutes. – Certain proof of pity!' (II. xvii: 125). Stricken by the disaster of the crushing of his son's nose, which is also an irony at the expense of his 'philosophy' of noses, Walter eventually looks up from the bed where he has lain 'as if the hand of death had pushed him down', to see the silent Toby: 'My father, in turning his eyes, was struck with such a gleam of sun-shine in his face, as melted down the sullenness of his grief in a moment' (IV. ii: 274). Toby's vocabulary may be restricted, but he does not have to rely on words:

There was a frankness in my uncle *Toby*, – not the *effect* of familiarity, – but the *cause* of it, – which let you at once into his soul, and shewed you the goodness of his nature; to this, there was something in his looks, and voice, and manner, superadded, which eternally beckoned to the unfortunate to come and take shelter under him. (VI. x: 426)

The very impediments to speech, Toby's lack of talents 'that way', allow, so the story goes, for a more fundamental communication. And that communication is ever-visible: 'My uncle *Toby* stole his hand unperceived behind his chair, to give my fathers a squeeze' (VII. xxxiii: 586). The benevolent gaze, the clasping hand, the moistening eye: these are not just ready defences when words fail; they are more poignant communications than words can possibly manage.

But then there is an irony in this, which can be stated with reference to Yorick's characterization, in *A Sentimental Journey*, of a communication deeper than can be accomplished by speech:

There are certain combined looks of simple subtlety – where whim, and sense, and seriousness, and nonsense, are so blended, that all the language of Babel set loose together could not express them – they are communicated and caught so instantaneously, that you can scarce say which party is the infecter. I leave it to your men of words to swell pages about it. (p. 168)

The rhetorical suggestion is that the signifier (the look, the gesture) can exist in all innocence, detached, for a special moment, from the words which hamper expression. An irony of *Tristram Shandy* is that Tristram is one of these 'men of words' (though the words are often jolted from other contexts, other commentators). Much in *Tristram Shandy*, like the uncomprehending gesture which Toby offers Mrs Wadman when she asks about the location of his wound, 'requires a second translation', showing 'what little knowledge is got by mere words – we must go up to the first springs' (IX. xx: 624). Sterne's narrator provides translations, decoding obsessions and gestures. His narrative, his garrulous commentary, lets the reader into the secret of expressions which defy words, and can do so because these expressions are the prerogative of those who are (admirably and ludicrously) innocent. The text eludes questions about whether its sentimentalism is 'sincere' or not by exploiting (and not, like Richardson, agonizing over) the distance between the reader it presumes and the paragons of feeling it describes. This means that Sterne has shrugged off the usual duty of sentimentalism: the teaching of virtue. 'Nasty trifling', F. R. Leavis called it;[19] given his belief in the moral duties of literature, the description is not so far from the mark.

NOTES

1. Letter from Sterne to Dr John Eustace, Feb. 1768 (*Letters*, 411).

2. H. Moglen, *The Philosophical Irony of Laurence Sterne* (Gainesville, FLA, 1975), 5.

3. See New's Introduction in Laurence Sterne, *The Life and Opinions of Tristram Shandy, Gentleman*, ed. M. New, R. A. Davies, and W. G. Day (3 vols, Gainesville, FLA, 1984), vol. iii, 'the Notes', 24–9. This edition is henceforth referred to as *Florida Edition*.

4. Max Byrd, *Visits to Bedlam: Madness and Literature in the Eighteenth Century* (Columbia, SC, 1974), 114, and Michael DePorte, *Nightmares and Hobby-horses: Swift, Sterne, and Augustan Ideas of Madness* (San Marino, Calif., 1974), 116.

5. *Yorick's Skull or College Oscitations* (London, 1777), 34–5.

6. R. F. Brissenden, *Virtue in Distress: Studies in the Novel of Sentiment from Richardson to Sade* (London, 1974), 194.

7. *Yorick's Skull*, 35–6.

8. *Florida Edition*, Introduction, iii: 17.

9. Ibid. iii: 16–17, and see W. G. Day, '*Tristram Shandy*: Locke May Not Be the Key', in V. G. Myer (ed.), *Laurence Sterne: Riddles and Mysteries* (London, 1984), 75–83.

10. John Ferriar, *Illustrations of Sterne* (London, 1798), 5.

11. John Locke, *An Essay concerning Human Understanding*, ed. P. H. Nidditch (1975; rpt. Oxford, 1979), II. xxx: 397.

12. Ibid. II. xxxiii: 395.

13. See Day, 'Locke May Not Be the Key'.

14. Locke, *Essay*, II. xi: 156.

15. Ibid. 156–7.

16. Ibid. III. x: 508.

17. Locke, *Essay*, III. ix: 478.

18. R. F. Holland, 'Epistemology and Education', in *Against Empiricism: On Education, Epistemology and Value* (Oxford, 1980), 15.

19. F. R. Leavis, *The Great Tradition* (1948; rpt. Harmondsworth, 1977), 10.

PART TWO

Feminism/Gender/Sexualities

A rguably the most prolific and productive modern debate about Sterne has arisen from gender-based and more particularly from feminist theoretical directions. *Tristram Shandy* has from its first appearance been accused, and repeatedly convicted, of being a 'man's book': of using a male sexual language, of privileging 'masculine' wit over 'feminine' sentiment, of portraying friendships, relationships and discourses among men to the exclusion, both verbal and physical, of women. In recent years a stout and sophisticated defence has been mounted, with some theoretical and interpretative variety and considerable cogency, by a series of critics themselves writing from predominantly feminist positions. The main line of argument has been that, though Walter Shandy – exponent of a patriarchal family politics which owes much to Robert Filmer, the leading seventeenth-century apologist of patriarchalism in the state – and even Tristram may be guilty of misogyny, Sterne himself is another voice, and of another mind. Leigh Ehlers examines the aftermath of Tristram's disabling accident with the sash window, and points out that, while Mrs Shandy turns to the practical restoratives lint and basilicon, Walter Shandy resorts less usefully, and more quixotically, to 'a couple of folios'. Ehlers concludes that Sterne's novel 'envisions the possibility, though not the actuality, of a truly humanistic household . . . in which men and women co-exist in harmony, love and respect' ('Mrs Shandy's "Lint and Basilicon": The Importance of Women in Tristram Shandy', 1981). Juliet McMaster argues that *Tristram Shandy* is '*about* misogyny, and against it', and that Sterne 'wrote about an ongoing war of the sexes, and even suggested the possibility of truce and peaceful cooperation' ('Walter Shandy, Sterne, and Gender: a

Feminist Foray', 1989). Helen Ostovich, in an essay drawing on reader-response as well as feminist theory, provides a nuanced account of Sterne's 'literary intercourse with the reader', including, and especially, the female reader ('Reader as Hobby-Horse in *Tristram Shandy*', 1989). In an essay informed by a particularly sophisticated feminist theoretics, Paula Loscocco concludes that '*Tristram Shandy* insists intransigently on the fact of the antifeminist error' (' "Can't Live without 'em": Walter Shandy and the Woman Within', 1991).

An altogether harder line is taken by Ruth Perry, in the first of the two essays I reprint here. Beginning with the Freudian and Lacanian position that 'our culture and the language that models and mirrors it are phallocentric', Perry goes on to dismiss the 'humanist' reading of Ehlers and others. Miscommunication between men and women 'is at the centre of the comedy, not a by-product of it'. Mrs Shandy is not, comfortably, 'a vivid presence and beneficent antidote to the obsessive Shandy men'. Rather, 'the talk in the book, the verbal play, is co-extensive with the sexual relations of the "story", and . . . both are rooted in the primacy of male friendship and in a subliminal distrust of women'. It might very well be argued that Perry's detailed interpretation of the textual data is often enough forced to fit her argument. 'Women's desire is helpless and amusing, like the unproductive cow at the end of volume 9'; but in this episode are we not more likely meant to think, with Obadiah, that the fault (and the comedy) lies with Walter Shandy's grave-faced but infertile bull? Does such use of evidence quite justify Perry's assertion that 'Mrs Shandy . . . and the other women barely exist in the narrative except in their concern for the phallus'?

Yet there is much in the argument Perry advances that carries conviction, in relation both to *Tristram Shandy* and its eighteenth-century context. Concerned or not with the phallus, women are substantially excluded from domestic relations: 'it is men who make family in *Tristram Shandy*'. Sterne makes a comedy (though much else) of childbirth, but obstetrics were no joke before anaesthetics and asepsis, and Caesarean section (which Walter proposes to his wife) was always fatal to the mother in Sterne's time. And if women in the novel are wise, and often wiser than the men, they are wise in silence: 'in this phallocentric world women have no language', Perry argues, 'to call their own'.

My second chosen essay presents itself as a direct answer to Perry. Melvyn New's response insists that Sterne's language is as little phallocentric as it possibly can be and, paradoxically, less phallocentric than Perry's own, preferring a sceptical openness (which had been characteristic before Sterne of Michel de Montaigne and Thomas Browne, among others), whereas Perry speaks in the familiar voice of modern critical authority. Mrs Shandy's questioning and noncommittal silence identifies her as a sceptical satirist, like Sterne himself. In attempting to demonstrate this, New 'follows the clue of Sterne's own fictions', including his sermons. He begins with Sterne's sermon 'Job's Expostulation with his Wife', an illustration, for New, of how meaning in Sterne's fiction 'is shown to inhere in the space between speaker(s) and auditor(s), a mutual and balanced exchange between two or more voices', in which mastery is at least as likely to lie with Mrs Shandy, the wiser and more humane partner, as with her theory-obsessed husband. The emphasis is on affectionate domestic relations, reflecting a view of eighteenth-century life often enough valued and depicted in Sterne's time (affectingly and representatively in the family groups of the painter Arthur Devis) if not in some retrospective analyses. Throughout his essay New emphasizes the interwoven relation in Sterne's writing of sensibility and desire: 'the awareness of the whole of the human experience, including both the exchange of sexual roles, aggressor and recipient, active and passive, and the knowledge that sensibility is not limited to those stirrings we can accept with clean hands and uplifted hearts'. That awareness, New insists, must override the limiting – phallocentric? – terminologies of theory. Even in the last moment of the *Sentimental Journey*, where Yorick's hand reaches into the space between two beds, we may find 'the portrait of a person', like ourselves, 'forever reaching across the void for the person (the knowledge) on the other side'. And in this, New suggests, Sterne may teach us that 'both "feminist" and "phallocentric" are already words so loaded with human passions that they recall nothing so much as Walter's faith in names and Tristram's insistence that "noses" only mean "noses"'.

This telling remark comes late in New's essay; that 'feminist' and 'phallocentric' are two terms with determined senses is a commonplace assumption underlying Perry's essay, and it's an assumption which badly needs deconstruction. The theoretical discourse in which the parallel term 'patriarchal' is taken to have a single and agreed value, and a consistent and overwhelming historical force, already seems precarious in the face of more nuanced, particularized, and historically contextualized studies of family and social relations in the eighteenth century. In a short time Perry's assumption might well look both dated and simplifying, and essays like hers will then become (indeed, are already becoming) compelling objects of intellectual history. New's reply, for all its virtues, arguably does not offer a full version of that deconstructive analysis, or ultimately challenge Perry's on its own ground; but its concluding sentences, a plea for intellectual tolerance by Sterne's leading modern critic – a post-holocaust Jewish scholar commenting on eighteenth-century England's most charitable sceptical intelligence – offers a direction that any civilized or civilizing theoretically informed modern literary writing might take.

CHAPTER THREE

'Words for Sex: The Verbal-Sexual Continuum in *Tristram Shandy*'*

RUTH PERRY

N o one who has read *Tristram Shandy* can doubt its double obsession with sex and with language. To explore the connection
between these elements is to uncover a connection more profound than the double entendres, the dirty jokes, the suggestiveness in
every detail, the obscenity in the sentimentality and the sentimentality
in the obscenity.[1] In its extreme verbal and sexual self-consciousness,
Tristram Shandy allegorizes the continuity and interchangeability of these
two realms in a manner at once descriptive and diagnostic. Language in
Sterne's hands is not merely a coy medium for representing the sexual –
although it is that – nor a simple substitute for it, a manifestation of
the sublimatory remains of repression. As Freud suggested and Lacan
developed the idea, language is coextensive with sexuality.

For Sterne as for the rest of us, although perhaps more exaggeratedly,
sex was just another language and language just another form of sex. One
notes that in his own life, Sterne
sought highly verbal courtship
romances in which the possibility of physical consummation
was elusive. His own wife had
been consumptive when he met
and courted her. As his bio-
grapher Arthur Cash remarks:

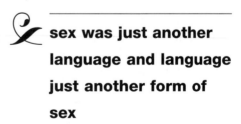

sex was just another language and language just another form of sex

* Reprinted from *Studies in the Novel*, 20 (University of North Texas, 1988), 27–42

'Sterne made sentimental love to women who were sickly – his wife in 1740–41, the woman he courted in Paris in 1764, and Sarah Tuting.'[2] In his famous book too, passionate contact between people is enacted verbally; all the conversations in *Tristram Shandy* are sexual.

Melvyn New has suggested that sexuality and speech are connected in Sterne's novel insofar as both are mastertropes for creativity which, in his reading, is the central theme of *Tristram Shandy*. Sexual anxiety thus becomes a metaphor for linguistic uncertainty and both reflect the desire to keep going – to perpetuate the self – and the fear that one will not be able to do so.[3] Helene Moglen makes the connection through the concept of need: both language or communication and sexuality are basic needs of the human organism.[4] Neither of these formulations addresses the question of the gender loadings of the particular cultural constructs they invoke – 'creativity' and 'basic needs'.[5] Yet feminists and Freudians alike agree that our culture and the language that molds and mirrors it are phallocentric.

Ernest Jones noted with astonishment the overwhelming preponderance of phallic imagery in western culture, although he subsequently normalized his observation to refer to sexual symbols in general.[6] Freud's observations of this phallocentricity in the symbolic realm of culture led him to assume that it was the remarkable anatomical difference between the sexes, instantly and universally interpreted by boys and girls in the identical manner, that was the originary cause that set in train the developmental dynamic that created adult men on the one hand and adult women on the other. The phallus named them, both men and women. According to his scenario, the young of both sexes instantly perceive male anatomy as normative and female anatomy as deficient – as lack or absence. Mutual inspection inevitably entails castration fear in little boys and penis envy in little girls. So literally did Freud cling to this formulation that he used this same anatomical metaphor – penis envy – to describe the responses of adult female powerlessness to patriarchal culture.

Jacques Lacan reinterpreted Freud's assertion symbolically and metaphorically as part of his larger argument that sexuality, as a primary aspect of identity, is structured by language and constructed in language. He theorized that the unconscious, created by an individual's entry into a symbolic order (language), consisted of those elements denied or repressed by the conscious formulations of the evolving organism. To say it another way: the consequence of mediating lived experience with language, according to Lacan, is the evolution of an unconscious structured like language and with the logic of a language. This linguistically structured unconscious represents the repressed content of experience, that which has been excluded by conscious use of this symbolic system. As the developing human being is increasingly alienated from desire by social interdictions, mediated by language, the repressed content of that desire structures itself below the surface of consciousness. The symbolic systems of language and of the unconscious thus develop simultaneously and interdependently, like a weaving in which what appears on one side of the cloth determines the pattern on the other side. Seen this way, language acquisition is the process which distances, mediates and contains original desire; the unconscious is the repository of that which is distanced, mediated and contained by the individual's entry into the symbolic order.

Lacan retained the Freudian terms 'phallus' and 'castration' as he retained their central importance in his account of psychosexual development, although he defined them more abstractly than had Freud. The phallus became for Lacan that-which-satisfies-the-mother, equally yearned for by boys and girls; and castration fear became a new way of symbolizing the impossibility of ever so satisfying her. 'Castration' thus became for Lacan anything which interceded between the child and his mother. As Juliet Mitchell and Jane Gallop have noted, both these accounts, the Freudian and the Lacanian, privilege the male term so completely and automatically that they reveal a male-centered conception of reality which simultaneously inscribes both sexual and verbal dominance.[7]

Not that it needed a French psychoanalyst come from Paris to tell us that our language – and the reality it conveys – is androcentric. For years feminists have protested the generic 'he' which conflates the universal with the masculine. It is a commonplace to note that the male is the normative, unmarked term whereas the female must be marked – as in 'female doctor', or 'woman lawyer', or in suffixes such as in the word 'poetess'. There are more words for 'man' in the language, and far more positive ones. Words for women often evolve sexual overtones: compare courtier to courtesan, sir to madam, master to mistress, even king to queen. Women are labelled as fruit or animals, goods to exchange.[8]

The Lacanian account emphasizes the specifically anatomical character of this cultural androcentricism. The implications of this definition for women's relation to language, to culture, to the structure of the unconscious, and to a culturally determined sexuality are catastrophic. A number of French feminists – Luce Irigaray, Julia Kristeva, and Hélène Cixous preeminently – convinced of this aspect of Lacanian thought, have claimed that the entire symbolic, verbal order is male, no matter who holds the pen. This is how the culture maintains and upholds male privilege at the profoundest level of thought, and disenfranchises female reality. Even when the literal social relations of patriarchy are not present, the very laws of grammar, syntax, and semantics reproduce the patriarchal order. So phallocentric are the origins, constructions, and conventions of the written language, they claim, that it cannot be used in its present form for describing women's reality. It is bound to misrepresent them, and implicitly to define them only as absence or silence.[9] Again, the issue is the simultaneous exclusion of women from the linguistic and sexual order through the symbolizing of anatomical difference.

Nowhere is the continuity between these exclusions clearer than in *Tristram Shandy*, a man's book if ever there was one. Even in its own day it appealed less to women than to men: in the records of a large provincial bookseller it was the only book bought and borrowed exclusively by male customers.[10] *Tristram Shandy* might also be read as if it were invented by some Lacanian disciple to demonstrate the fragility of the self, the obsessional yet precarious preoccupation with the phallus, the problematic nature of sexuality itself – and the important absence of women from a constitutively verbal world. From the very first scene of the book, when Walter Shandy exclaims 'Did ever woman, since the creation of the world, *interrupt* a man with such a silly question?' women figure only as foils for male actions, and are essentially *hors de combat*. What I want to suggest is that the talk in the book, its verbal play, is co-extensive with the sexual relations of the 'story', and that both are rooted in the primacy of male friendship and in a subliminal distrust of women.

*

Some critics, maintaining that the humanism of the book has a universal appeal, have argued that the tragedy lies precisely in the incapacity of the narrator to imagine and represent wholesome heterosexual relationships. The widow Wadman and Jenny offer the Shandy men their best chance for salvation in this view, but Uncle Toby and Tristram are unable to avail themselves of it, to our collective, cosmic, sadness.[11] This argument, however, ignores the economy of desire in the book, the love between men, the rueful attitude towards heterosexuality, the marital mismatch of the Shandys and its implied inevitability in Walter Shandy's lamentation that nature, so exact in most things, eternally bungles 'in making so simple a thing as a married man' (p. 776). The miscommunication between men and women is at the center of the comedy, not a by-product of it. The famous 'beds of justice' scene in which Mr and Mrs Shandy discuss putting Tristram in breeches, is a case in point. Here, as elsewhere, Mrs Shandy's 'participation' is marked by an absence so profound as to frustrate any hope of contact.

– We should begin to think, Mrs *Shandy*, of putting this boy into breeches. – We should so, – said my mother. – We defer it, my dear, quoth my father, shamefully.

– I think we do, Mr *Shandy*, – said my mother. – Not but the child looks extremely well, said my father, in his vest and tunicks. – He does look very well in them,—replied my mother. – (p. 526)

They talk at cross purposes, Mrs Shandy's blankness and opacity at its most eloquent. They do not speak the same language; they could talk until doomsday without ever arriving at anything other than their usual stalemate. How different is this parodic echo from the true accord shared by Toby and Trim as they discuss, say, the news of Le Fever's appearance at the inn. Their sentiments, their assessment of the situation, and their impulse to action in that scene, are so similar as to be practically unspoken. But how different the not-speaking from that which exists between the Shandys.

Within this tradition of humanist interpretation, Leigh Ehlers reads the novel as a warning about the folly of rationalistic, male-centered – not to say phallocentric – modes of being.[12] Reading as a feminist, determined to value rather than devalue the work that women do, she describes eloquently what the Shandean view misses. Although Tristram sneers at Mrs Shandy when she stays home to finish knitting Walter Shandy's 'pair of large worsted breeches' rather than take part in the expedition to the continent, her knitting, Ehler says, 'indicates not indifference, but love and care; she at least attempts to restore order and creativity to a house visited by death (Bobby's) and plagued by declining potency (Walter's and later Tristram's). In such a context, Elizabeth's knitting represents neither triviality nor stupidity, as Tristram seems to think: it represents an act of life, the very answer to his flight from death, an answer lying unrecognized at home.'[13] The progressive repression and symbolization of the sexual in the course of the narrative, Ehlers argues, corresponds to the increasing alienation of the Shandy men from love, from normality, and from life. Relations with women – with Jenny, with Mrs Shandy, and with the widow Wadman – are the interpersonal dimension, as it were, of the ever-widening gap between the mind and body, intellect and procreation. Tristram's failure with Jenny and Toby's failure with the widow Wadman symbolize men's failure in the novel to connect with women and with nature. Stuck in a world of words, intellectualizations, and compulsive ratiocination, their rationalistic, patriarchal will-to-power leads them to misuse reason in a manner that alienates them from life and the female principle. It goes without saying that impotence is the price of this vain attempt to transcend the body with the mind.

This formulation, however helpful, does not explain why impotence operates in *Tristram Shandy* more often to thwart women – all of whom desire the phallus – than to symbolize male frustration. Walter Shandy's arcane scholarship and his sterile intellectualizing protect him from his wife's sexual demands as much as they insulate him from all other unwelcome facts. As critics have often noted, he responds to crisis – from Bobby's death to Tristram's accident with the window sash – by spinning theories and burrowing ever deeper into recondite texts. When required to pay a large jointure to his grandmother to compensate her for his grandfather's small nose, he takes to his room with a treatise on noses, to recover the financial (sexual) blow. 'He solaced himself with *Bruscambille* after the manner, in which, 'tis ten to one, your worship solaced yourself with your first mistress' (p. 266), observes the narrator, emphasizing the Shandean equivalence between the verbal and the sexual.

However self-defeating this style of coping might seem, the way it works in the narrative penalizes women more than men, and leaves them out in the cold. The widow Wadman is but a 'tenant for life' unless she can beget a (male) child (p. 759). The way she stalks Uncle Toby, the way Mrs Shandy sighs about the rigid regularity of Walter Shandy's connubial performance on the first Sunday of the month, the way the women of Strasburg chase Slawkenbergius to touch his nose – these are the comic objects of a Restoration bawdiness rather than agents of any tragic discovery about failed manhood or humanity. Women's desire is helpless and amusing, like the unproductive cow at the end of Volume IX. The fact that men are unable to satisfy such desire is symptomatic of the cosmic irony of human life, but the overtones are comic rather than tragic, and women are the butts of the joke.

At a theoretical level, the traditional humanistic reading of the novel opposes the verbal to the sexual and assumes – with a heterosexual bias – that where interactions with women are inhibited, the cause must lie in repression and sublimation. But if Freud and Lacan are right, the verbal and erotic realms are continuous rather than antithetic, and sublimation is expressive: verbal behavior manifests while it symbolizes repressed erotic behavior. Therapists seeking clues to repressed content in the unconscious trace its lineaments not only in the body and in early memories, but in the individual verbal style as well as the unconscious intrusions – the slips and puns – that distort and disrupt it.[14] In other words, conscious linguistic behavior points, like a complex set of directional signals, to those experiences and desires which for whatever reason cannot be articulated within the socio-linguistic system of a given culture. This behavior constitutes, as it were, the terms of repression. To speak therefore of the dissociation of mind and body, of the intellectual and the physical, is misleading; for they are always mutually dependent, co-extensive, and together constitute a whole. If the hyperverbal activity in which the Shandy men engage one another is a form of sublimation, the homosocial bond strengthened by that activity is what is being repressed and sublimated.

One is tempted to examine, as biographical ballast for this reading, Sterne's lifelong friendship with Hall-Stevenson, begun during their under-graduate days at Cambridge. Indeed, the verbal fireworks of *Tristram Shandy* suggest the tomfoolery of sophomoric youth, undergraduates drunk on a little learning, simultaneously impressed by pedantry and scorning it – and egging one another on to show off. In the novel, this undergraduate sensibility is overlaid with the deepening understanding of a grown man, sustained in life's disappointments by an old friendship.

Sterne's friendship with Hall-Stevenson, probably the deepest human relationship of his life, infuses *Tristram Shandy* with its own particular warmth, their mutual affection immortalized in the strength of feeling that exists between Eugenius and Yorick. The arcane books into which both Tristram and Walter Shandy dip with such delight apparently furnished Sterne and Hall-Stevenson with similar amusement, when they were first discovered on the shelves of Hall-Stevenson's library at his ancestral seat, dubbed by him 'Crazy Castle'. Sterne spent much time there over the years, carousing bachelor-style with Hall-Stevenson and his cohorts, a group of rapscallions who called themselves the Demoniacs in imitation of Sir Francis Dashwood's Hell-Fire Club at West Wycombe, Buckinghamshire (also known as the Rabelaisian Monks of Medmenham Abbey).[15] If ever there was an ideal reader for *Tristram Shandy*, Hall-Stevenson was that reader. No other non-fictional writing of Sterne's resembles the tone of *Tristram Shandy* so much as his letters to Hall-Stevenson, whom he even addresses occasionally as 'Anthony Shandy'.

Lodwick Hartley's fine article, 'Sterne's Eugenius as Indiscreet Author', explores the relationship of these two men and the parallels between Hall-Stevenson's tasteless and ribald writing, published in the years following Sterne's success, and Sterne's own dazzling book. He writes:

In fact, the often fantastic quality of Hall-Stevenson's *Crazy Tales* should not obscure their remarkable thematic relationship to *Tristram Shandy* in both implied and overt anti-Catholicism, anti-feminism, and misogamy, as it also should, even more importantly, not obscure a brotherhood of sexual frustration of two men who were, as Sterne put it in his sermon called 'The History of Jacob Considered', 'disappointed in marriage . . . (because) they were mistaken in the person'. As superior as the first two books of *Tristram Shandy* most assuredly are to *Crazy Tales*, the latter volume suggests with important cogency some of the atmosphere and some of the frames of reference out of which the work of genius developed.[16]

*

Without speculating about the personal and psychological sources of the Shandean sensibility, the phallocentricism in this novel is clear enough, even if the preoccupation is fearful, protective and concerned, rather than exuberant, sensuous, or aggressive.[17] Every volume has its jokes about penises and noses, about castration and impotence, from the threat posed by the forceps to the infant member, to the widow Wadman kicking out her corking pin. Genital pain is more present than genital pleasure, as in the episodes of the hot chestnut in Phutatorius's breeches (soothed by a damp page from the printing press), the window sash falling without its counterweight on Tristram's penis, and the flying piece of rock which struck uncle Toby's groin at the battle of Namur. Nor is heterosexuality associated with genital pleasure. Heterosexual sex is just something that happens to you, like Trim's erection on the last night with the fair Beguine. The sex scenes in Kafka's *The Castle* have this same quality of being overtaken willy-nilly by the somewhat bewildering instincts of the body. A man may be set on fire at either end, we are told, 'provided there is sufficient wick standing out' (p. 674).

Of course *Tristram Shandy* also demonstrates the impossibility of adequately representing sexual reality – or any other experience – and the absurdity of trying. At every turn the narrator undercuts both his own seriousness and the possibility of any coherent existential meaning, whether ethical, historical, or any other way of knowing 'ending, as these do, in *ical*' (p. 72). The book emphasizes rather the difficulties of communication – hence the irritations of family life – and the inevitable inaccuracy of any literary rendition of human experience. 'Unhappy *Tristram*!' Walter Shandy apostrophizes at Toby after telling of the destruction of the infant nose; 'nothing left to found thy stamina in, but negations . . .' (p. 354). Sterne's continuous dramatization of the difficulties of representation lend *Tristram Shandy* the experimental and avant garde qualities that have made it such an attractive text to modernist critics.[18] Within the narrative itself, the fluid boundaries between the 'real' and its representation keep fluctuating. Sterne's paean to 'Freudian' symbolism, perhaps the most enthusiastic in our language, is itself infused with libidinous energy: 'The word in course became indecent, and (after a few efforts) absolutely unfit for use. . . . The evil indeed spread no further then –, but have not beds and bolsters, and night-caps and chamber-pots stood upon the brink of destruction ever since? Are not trouse, and placket-holes, and pump-handles – and spigots and faucets, in danger still, from the same association? – Chastity, by nature the gentlest of all affections – give it but its head – 'tis like a ramping and roaring lion' (p. 414). As Moglen remarked, language masters man in this novel, and dominates and directs his imagination.[19] Innuendo always works both ways. So pornographic is Tristram's imagination that he can stimulate himself with the metaphor of sticking his finger in a pie (p. 670).

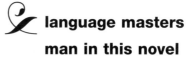

language masters man in this novel

Uncle Toby's representation of the battle of Namur is a case in point. Both a recreation and a celebration of the decisive events of his life, his game soon takes on its own expressive life. From the moment he discovers that 'the history of a soldier's wound beguiles the pain of it' (p. 88), he begins to build his defenses – and his bridges – to compensate for the injury. His fortifications model his sexual reality: in the excitement of firing the cannon, his partnership with Trim, and in the creation of a womanless world. The widow Wadman's confusion is very much to the point when Toby offers to show her where the rock hit him, for his wound is inscribed both on his body where he first suffered it, and on the map where he represented and learned to live with it.

If Uncle Toby's story and its representation figure the deliberate mimetic inversions of the novel, they also bring into focus the absence of women. Despite the valiant attempts of Ruth Faurot and Leigh Ehlers to demonstrate Mrs Shandy as a vivid presence and beneficent antidote to the obsessive Shandy men, she and the other women barely exist in the narrative except in their concern for the phallus.[20] As Tristram himself avers, 'all the SHANDY FAMILY were of an original character throughout; – I mean the males, – the females had no character at all . . .' (p. 73). From Walter Shandy's point of view, Mrs Shandy is merely in the way. Not only does she not have the good grace to enter properly into the spirit of the thing in that first hilarious scene, but she is a spoilsport later too, for refusing to let him try out his theory of genius birth with a caesarian – although, to be fair, we sympathize with her when she turns pale at the suggestion.

All the comic business about childbirth demonstrates the author's failure to take seriously the woman's point of view. Childbirth was a dangerous business in Sterne's day; one out of every ten married, fertile, child-bearing women in England died of complications.[21] A few expert physicians in London, Sir Richard Manningham among them, bettered those odds somewhat, but dangerous man-midwives in the country worsened them; they had neither medical education, nor the traditional midwife's long apprenticeship, nor much practiced knowledge of female anatomy. Their stock in trade were the instruments which traditional midwives eschewed – the 'tire tête' which punctured the fetal head for extraction, the forceps, and the 'crotchet', a blunt hook for pulling out the mangled fetus. Dr Slop, whose green baize bag jangled so terribly as to frighten away Hymen, is representative of the type.[22] Hester Thrale, writing to a friend in 1773, said this about these practitioners:

I hate these Country Accoucheurs – these *Demi Savans*: They are so forward to produce their *Instruments*. A London Hospital would have saved this Child I doubt not, tho' the Birth *was* laborious. I find there was no wrong Presentation, only a Lentor in the pains perhaps – With Opium & Encouragement, & not putting her too soon upon Labour, I verily do think that a skilful Practitioner might have brought the Baby forward with the *Forceps* at worst – but they are so plaguy hasty. – Either Doctor Denman or an old Woman would have waited – but since the horrid death-doing Crotchet had been found out, & its use permitted – Oh! many & many a Life has been flung away.[23]

As Arthur Cash has informed us, Sterne was well aware of the controversy over man-midwives, and the life-threatening dangers for women of lying in. The decade preceding the publication of *Tristram Shandy* had seen a number of important tracts published on both sides of the question, arguing the pros and cons of 'scientific obstetrics' versus the old-fashioned tried and true midwifery of the village matrons.[24] All the same, we are meant to be amused at Walter Shandy's outwitting his wife of her London lying-in, and his attempt to convince her of his 'rational' theories of childbirth. We recognize that Walter is a hopeless intellectualizer, and that he takes refuge from life in endless theorizing, but it is a loved, familiar foible, and we do not read it as callousness about her pain and danger. The narrator trivializes Mrs Shandy's final insistence upon the woman midwife, by likening it to the way his 'dear, dear Jenny' capriciously chooses the bargain cloth when the bolt of silk was out of the question.

This attitude is all the more striking because of the tone taken elsewhere in the novel towards physical danger and death.[25] So central to Sterne's imagination were the twin spectres of illness and death that the three deathbed scenes are among the most dramatic moments of the novel: Eugenius sitting up with Yorick during his last moments (pp. 33–5); Trim silently following Toby's coffin (p. 545), and Toby gallantly promising Le Fever that he will take care of his son, pledging his word as a fellow soldier and a man of honor (pp. 511–12). Indeed, one suspects from the way Sterne is repeatedly drawn to them, that he may have indulged himself in deliciously sentimental daydreams of his own demise, friends gathered at the bedside with much weeping and wringing of hands, while he chattered on bravely.

Each of these scenes conjures up a different configuration of love. Yorick's dying, which comes early in the first volume, introduces the presiding genius of the book and sets an affectionate, fraternal tone. Toby's funeral – a flash forward which interrupts the description of how sucking and puffing on the Turkish pipes will fire the cannon on Trim's dandy new rig – reminds us how important Toby is to Trim and to his brother Walter. Trim's ashen face and trembling hand tell us how badly Toby will be missed, which renders him doubly precious when he reappears.

So outrageously melodramatic is the scene of Le Fever's death at the inn, with Toby warmly and generously pressing his hand and relieving the good man's anxieties about his son, that Sterne feels obliged to mock his own sentimentality: 'the pulse fluttered – stopp'd – went on – throb'd – stopp'd again – moved – stopp'd – shall I go on? – No' (p. 513). But the self-parody does not cancel the emotional effects of Toby's frank kindness or Le Fever's boy's distress – all intensified by the presence of death.

Unlike these scenes, Mrs Shandy's risk is played for its comic relief rather than for its sentimental possibilities. Not having a presence, how could her absence be tragic? The scenes which feature women in this novel are always slapstick; they hardly ever call up feelings of love – in a text in which lovableness is the central redemptive virtue. The only exception to this pattern, the only woman who arouses the narrator's sentimental feelings, is the crazy, mute Maria, who plays upon a pipe so sweetly in Moulins.

*

In this phallocentric world, women have no language to call their own. To begin with, they have no access to the exclusively male institutions (the army and the university) which furnish the conversational gambits and metaphysical metaphors for the Shandy brothers. What they know, they know with their bodies – 'My mother . . . knew no more than her backside what my father meant' (p. 4) – not through language. As demonstrated in the Shandys' interchange about putting Tristram into breeches, in which Mrs Shandy stubbornly echoes Mr Shandy's words, women have no range, no play, no flair. They can resist language, but not initiate or command it.[26]

Sterne jokes about this discrepancy in their fluency right at the beginning:

What could my father do? He was almost at his wit's end; – talked it over with her in all moods; – placed his arguments in all lights; – argued the matter with her like a christian, – like a heathen, – like a husband, – like a father, – like a patriot, – like a man: – My mother answered every thing only like a woman; which was a little hard upon her; – for as she could not assume and fight it out behind such a variety of characters, – 'twas no fair match; – 'twas seven to one.

(p. 55)

The comical juxtaposition of the bovine blankness of a female with the overabundance, the leaping and frisking facility of a male, is one of the narrator's standard tropes. Susannah, that leaky vessel, cannot remember the four-syllable name Trismegistus long enough to get it to the baptismal chamber. The Frenchwoman's only use for Yorick's sermon is to curl her hair with the pages. The entire anecdote of the Abbess of Andouillets and her little novice Margarita, funnels down to the single slapstick scene in which the two of them, spluttering and intimidated, have to collaborate – each pronouncing a syllable – to produce a single word. And Maria, who pipes so sweetly in Moulins, is mute.

Excluded from both the verbal and erotic relations in this novel, women are excluded from the domestic relations as well; it is men who make family in *Tristram Shandy*. The love they bear one another is not primarily sexual but familial – tolerant, comfortable, and habitual.[27] Toby boasts of Trim's loyalty to his mother and father. The brotherly love between Walter and Toby is seconded in Trim's devotion to his brother Tom, remembered every time he wagers his Montero cap. Yorick confides his troubles to a deeply sympathetic Eugenius. Toby could have treated Le Fever no better if he were kin. And Le Fever's son, raised as Sterne himself was, in the army, with an entire company of troopers as his family, bursts into tears when Toby offers to toast his father as 'an old soldier' for the name 'sounded in his ears like the name of a friend' (p. 504).

The marriage between Toby and Trim is the emotional center of the book – by far a truer, more successful marriage than the wary heterosexual misalliance between Walter Shandy and his wife. All day long they play at guns and forts in their prepubescent Paradise, the toy towns they build the only social entities they need deal with.

Making war for them is like making love: 'Never did lover post down to a belov'd mistress with more heat and expectation, than my uncle *Toby* did, to enjoy this self-same thing in private' (p. 113), writes the narrator. He recalls how Toby blushed scarlet with pleasure at the thought of enjoying the privacy of their rood-and-a-half of land for their toy fortifications, when Trim first suggested it.

Sterne marvelously conveys their mutual enjoyment in the way they catch fire from one another as they go at it, delighted to be playing their favorite game again. Chapter xviii, Vol. IV is a veritable love duet, in which though they begin by talking at cross purposes, their natural accord brings them into tune with one another until they come into perfect harmony and end with a grand finale.

– And for my own part, said my uncle *Toby*, though I should blush to boast of myself, *Trim*, – yet had my name been *Alexander*, I could have done no more at *Namur* than my duty – Bless your honour! cried *Trim*, advancing three steps as he spoke, does a man think of his christian name when he goes upon the attack? – Or when he stands in the trench, *Trim*? cried my uncle *Toby*, looking firm – Or when he enters a breach? said *Trim*, pushing in between two chairs – Or forces the lines? cried my uncle, rising up and pushing his crutch like a pike – Or facing a platoon, cried *Trim*, presenting his stick like a fire-lock – Or when he marches up the glacis, cried my uncle *Toby*, looking warm and setting his foot upon his stool. – (p. 352)

He repeats it again later, this little dance they do, only this time he leaves out the content, so as to render the sense of escalating excitement in its purest form.

– There is no way but to march cooly up to them, – receive their fire, and fall in upon them, pell-mell – Ding dong, added *Trim*. – Horse and foot, said my uncle *Toby*. – Helter skelter, said *Trim*. – Right and left, cried my uncle *Toby*. – Blood an' ounds, shouted the corporal; – the battle raged, – *Yorick* drew his chair a little to one side for safety. . . . (pp. 454–5)

Language manages for them a visceral, almost non-verbal, contact.

Language manages for them a visceral, almost non-verbal, contact

These two share not only high romance, but a domesticity as comfortable as an old shoe – like the jackboots that Trim, in his ingenious way, manages to convert into toy cannon. His use of everyday household objects sanctifies their partnership. The fortifications which they build extend into the rows of cabbages and cauliflowers of the kitchen garden. We find them standing together in the most marital of poses, Toby apostrophizing Trim, 'resting with his hand upon the corporal's shoulder, as they both stood surveying their works . . .' (p. 450) and engaging in that most marital of combats, a squabble they have had for the last twenty-five years: whether or not Trim should be allowed to stand behind his master's chair when Toby dines alone. Their union is even blessed by a child, Le Fever's son, whom Toby educates as if he were his own. And when Le Fever's son goes off to join the army – and where else could he go? – we are told by the narrator that he parted from Toby 'as the best of sons from the best of fathers', with kisses and tears (p. 519).

All of Nature participates in their union. The very soil of their estate, perfect for their purposes, has just enough clay in it 'to retain the form of the angles and indentings' of their model towns and fortifications, but not so much that it clings to the spade (p. 534). Walter Shandy on the other hand, with a spouse much less compatible and certainly less tractable than his brother's mate, keenly feels the force of the world against him, thwarting his dearest wishes.

As if to illustrate the assertion that when discourse has a phallic focus, women can never be speaking subjects, this novel is structured as a series of all-male conversations: Eugenius lecturing Yorick on sobriety and decorum; Toby and Trim conferring about their fortifications; Walter Shandy orating to Toby about the consolations philosophy can offer to the bereaved; the dinner of the learned greybeards, called together to determine whether or not the name Tristram, once conferred in baptism, can be rescinded. Walter Shandy, Dr Slop, Toby, Trim, Yorick, Eugenius, and the other speakers march past one's eyes talking, reading, gesticulating, posing. Our loquacious narrator tells us that his father 'was a born orator . . . Persuasion hung upon his lips' (p. 59). Corporal Trim loves the sound of his own voice. The narrator himself is a literary man, and does not so much think of himself as narrating events in a realistic fashion as fictionalizing his experience, spinning tales, telling stories, self-consciously and explicitly imitating the whimsy of Cervantes or the bawdy of Rabelais, dancing and prancing, digressing and zigzagging his way through the volume. If there is anything that he prides himself on, it is his brilliant, extravagant, verbal cavorting. He has a virtuosity gone slightly haywire, primed with jokes, scraps of information, puns, double entendres, absurd quotations, ready to fire off in any direction at the slightest startle. Cherished characters, like Toby or Yorick, rise like Neptune from a sea of words.

From this point of view, the actual scene of Tristram's birth can be seen as an emblem of the novel. Walter Shandy is comfortably ensconced in the downstairs parlor with his immortal brother uncle Toby, while on the floor over their heads, they hear the sounds of a great deal of running back and forth. 'What can they be doing brother? quoth my father, – we can scarce hear ourselves talk' (p. 70). Walter Shandy's words are accurate to the mood of the novel beyond the particular occasion, and they highlight an interesting truth. For, although *Tristram Shandy* is ostensibly about birth and death, sexuality and generation, these things are perceived muffled through several walls, and the narrative spotlight comes to rest most often and most continually upon men alone, talking. In its very form, *Tristram Shandy* shows how the eroticized verbal functions in the bonding between men. And its plot, its story, is about the birth of a son into a family of men: Walter Shandy, Uncle Toby, Corporal Trim – and that reluctant vessel, Mrs Shandy.

NOTES

1. All page numbers cited in the primary text will refer to the Florida edition of *The Life and Opinions of Tristram Shandy, Gentleman*, 2 vols, paginated as one, eds Melvyn New and Joan New (Gainesville, FLA: University of Florida Press, 1978). Two classic articles about the sexual and scatological jokes in *Tristram Shandy* are Robert Alter, 'Tristram Shandy and the Game of Love', *American Scholar* 37 (1968): 316–23, and Frank Brady, 'Tristram Shandy: Sexuality, Morality, and Sensibility', *Eighteenth-Century Studies* 4 (1970): 41–56.
2. Arthur H. Cash, *Laurence Sterne, The Later Years* (London and New York: Methuen, 1986), p. 221. Earlier in this volume Cash explains that Sterne 'invented his own sort of sentimental love' (p. 183).
3. Melvyn New, *Laurence Sterne as Satirist* (Gainesville, FLA: University of Florida Press, 1969), pp. 82–3, 178.
4. Helene Moglen, *The Philosophical Irony of Laurence Sterne* (Gainesville, FLA: The University Presses of Florida, 1975), p. 113.
5. By the end of her argument, Moglen suggestively states that 'the phallus comes to stand for man's alienation from himself and from his environment', although she never directly confronts the implications of this symbolism for women. Ibid., p. 143.
6. The paper by Ernest Jones is 'The Early Development of Female Sexuality'. For a discussion of the early observation and the later revision see Jane Gallop, *The Daughter's Seduction* (Ithaca, NY: Cornell University Press, 1982), pp. 15–19.
7. Juliet Mitchell, 'On Freud and the Distinction Between the Sexes', from *The Longest Revolution* (New York: Pantheon, 1984), pp. 221–32 and Jane Gallop, *The Daughter's Seduction, passim*. Gallop analyzes Mitchell's earlier treatment of the psychogenic basis of sexuality in *Psychoanalysis and Feminism* (New York: Pantheon, 1974) and applauds her insistence on Freud's nonbiologism, his treatment of sexuality as *created* – for all intents and purposes – by social relations in a particular cultural context. But she also states that by imagining a political solution to the problem of patriarchy, Mitchell implicitly denies the culturally structured unconscious that she had previously been at such pains to establish. *The Daughter's Seduction*, pp. 1–14.
8. Three excellent books dealing with sexism and language are Dale Spender, *Man Made Language* (London and Boston, MA: Routledge & Kegan Paul, 1980); *Women and Language in Literature and Society*, eds Sally McConnell-Ginet, Ruth Borker and Nelly Furman (New York: Praeger, 1980); and *Language, Gender, and Society*, eds Barrie Thorne, Cheris Kramarae and Nancy Henley (Rowley, MA: Newbury House Publishers, 1983). This last volume has an annotated bibliography on the subject.

9. The clearest expositor of this position is Luce Irigaray in 'This Sex Which Is Not One', 'The Power of Discourse and the Subordination of the Feminine', and 'Così Fan Tutti,' all in *This Sex Which Is Not One*, trans. by Catherine Porter (Ithaca, NY: Cornell University Press, 1985). See also Hélène Cixous's 'Laugh of the Medusa' in which she tries to write in a new female mode, trans. in *New French Feminisms*, eds Isabelle de Courtivron and Elaine Marks (Amherst, MA: University of Massachusetts Press, 1980), pp. 245–64. For a lucid discussion of the similarities and differences among Irigaray, Cixous, Kristeva, and Monique Wittig, see Ann Rosalind Jones, 'Inscribing Feminity: French Theories of the Feminine' in *Making A Difference: Feminist Literary Criticism*, eds Gayle Greene and Coppelia Kahn (New York: Methuen, 1985), pp. 80–112.

10. I am grateful to Jan Fergus for making available to me her unpublished paper 'Provincial Readers of the Major Eighteenth-Century Novelists', in which she notes Clara Reeve's distaste for *Tristram Shandy* and reproduces the figures for its circulation in the provinces. It apparently appealed predominantly to educated male professionals.

11. See, for example, Jean-Jacques Mayoux, 'Variations on the Time-Sense in *Tristram Shandy*' in *The Winged Skull: Papers from the Laurence Sterne Bicentenary Conference*, eds Arthur Cash and John Stedmond (Kent, OH: Kent University State Press, 1971), pp. 3–18 and James E. Swearingen, *Reflexivity in Tristram Shandy* (New Haven, CT and London: Yale University Press, 1977), pp. 196–257.

12. Leigh A. Ehlers, 'Mrs Shandy's "Lint and Basilicon": The Importance of Women in *Tristram Shandy*', *South Atlantic Review* 46 (1981): 61–73.

13. Ibid., 64.

14. David W. Stewart, 'Jacques Lacan and the Language of the Unconscious', *Bulletin of the Menninger Clinic* 47 (1983): 53–70.

15. Arthur Cash, *Laurence Sterne: The Early and Middle Years* (London: Methuen, 1975), p. 193.

16. Lodwick Hartley, 'Sterne's Eugenius as Indiscreet Author: The Literary Career of John Hall-Stevenson', *PMLA* 86 (1971): 434.

17. See Patricia Meyer Spacks's discussion of this obsession in 'Early Fiction and the Frightened Male', *Novel* 4 (1970): 14; and *Imagining a Self* (Cambridge, MA: Harvard University Press, 1976), pp. 127–58. See also Morris Golden, 'Sterne's Journeys and Sallies', *Studies in Burke and His Time* 16 (1974): 60–1.

18. See, for example, 'Sternian Realities – Excerpts from Seminars Chaired by John Traugott: "New Directions in Sterne Criticism" and Gardner D. Stout Jr, "Sterne and Swift"' in *The Winged Skull*, pp. 76–93; Cyrus Hamlin, 'The Conscience of Narrative: Towards a Hermeneutics of Transcendence', *New Literary History* 13 (1982): 205–30; and Shari Benstock, 'At the Margin of Discourse: Footnotes in the Fictional Text', *PMLA* 98 (1983): 204–25.

19. *The Philosophical Irony of Laurence Sterne*, p. III.

20. See n. 12 and n. 13. Ruth Faurot, 'Mrs Shandy Observed', *Studies in English Literature* 10 (1970): 579–89.

21. Ruth Perry, 'The Veil of Chastity: Mary Astell's Feminism', *Studies in Eighteenth-Century Culture* 9 (1979): 25–43.

22. The relation between Sterne's literary caricature and the reality of male-midwives has been beautifully documented by Arthur Cash, 'The Birth of Tristram Shandy: Sterne and Dr Burton', in *Studies in the Eighteenth Century*, ed. R. F. Brissenden (Canberra: Australian National University Press, 1968), pp. 133–55.

23. *Thraliana: The Diary of Mrs Hester Lynch Thrale, 1776–1809*, ed. Katharine Balderston, 2 vols (Oxford: The Clarendon Press, 1942), 2: 974–5.

     The best short history of midwifery in this period is by Barbara Schnorrenberg, 'Is Childbirth Any Place For A Woman? The Decline of Midwifery in Eighteenth-Century England', *Studies in Eighteenth-Century Culture* 10 (1981): 393–409.

     The following is a contemporary description of the male-midwife written by a woman-midwife in 1737, alarmed at the rate at which man-midwives (whether scarcely trained quack physicians or members of the Barber-Surgeons' Guild) were encroaching on a traditionally female profession, and at the dangerous technology they were bringing with them.

     I have made it my Observation within these few years that more Women and Children have died by the hands of such Professors, than by the greatest imbecility and ignorance of some Women-Midwives, who never went thro', or so much as heard of, a Course in Anatomy. For, give me leave to tell those young Gentlemen pretenders, who undertaked the Practice of Midwifery with only the knowledge of dissecting the Dead, that all the Living who have or shall come under their care, in any difficulty, may severely pay for what knowledge thay attain to in the Art of Midwifery; especially such young ones as now pretend to practice: by whom (I am well assured) there are many sufferers both Mothers and Children; yea, Infants have been born alive, with their Brains working out of their heads; occasion'd by the too common use of Instruments: which I never found but little use to be made of, in all my practice (Sarah Stone, *A Complete Practice Of Midwifery* [London, 1737], Preface, pp. xii–xiii).

24. William Smellie, a very influential and distinguished Scottish physician who practiced in London, published his *Treatise on the Theory and Practice of Midwifery* in 1751. That same year Dr Frank Nicholls, a Fellow of the College of Physicians, published *A Petition of the Unborn-Babes* in which he accused careless and ignorant man-midwives of killing mothers by the misuse of instruments. In 1752 he proposed that the College of Physicians offer lectures for midwives. In 1760, Elizabeth Nihell, a French-trained midwife, published a diatribe against man-midwives called *A Treatise On the Art of Midwifery. Setting forth Various Abuses therein, Especially as to the Practice with Instruments: the Whole Serving to put all Rational Inquiries in a fair Way of very safely forming their own Judgment upon the Question; Which it is best to*

employ, In Cases of Pregnancy and Lying-in, a Man-Midwife; or a Midwife – and in which she had the unfortunate judgment to attack Smellie.

25. The best treatment of this theme is still by W. B. C. Watkins, *Perilous Balance* (Princeton, NJ: Princeton University Press, 1939).

26. Sterne identifies women with nature and men with culture as this ideological construct in Western culture is explored by Sherry Ortner in 'Is Female to Male as Nature Is to Culture?', *Women, Culture and Society*, eds Michelle Zimbalist Rosaldo and Louise Lamphere (Stanford, CA: Stanford University Press, 1974), pp. 67–87. Note also Walter Shandy's advice to Toby (p. 727) to prevent the woman in his life from reading Rabelais, Scarron, or Don Quixote, the literary sources of *Tristram Shandy*. Melvyn New subscribes to these equivalences uncritically when he interprets the widow Wadman as 'the flesh that man is heir to; the flesh that the sentimentalist would like to ignore, and indeed does ignore. Toby has it forced upon him' in *Laurence Sterne as Satirist*, p. 197.

27. This is not to say that family feeling is not sexualized. 'You, my dear brother *Shandy*, who have sucked the same breasts with me' (p. 555), is how Toby affirms his bond to Walter.

CHAPTER FOUR

'Job's Wife and Sterne's other Women'*

MELVYN NEW

Those who hold the pen – write. Moses was a man. That's why
he wrote that a man could have ten wives, but if a woman
looked at another man she had to be stoned. If a woman had
held the pen she would have written the exact opposite.

I. B. SINGER, *The Magician of Lublin*

In a recent article on Sterne's handling of sexual relations in *Tristram Shandy*, Ruth Perry suggests one way in which some 'French feminists – Luce Irigaray, Julia Kristeva, and Hélène Cixous preeminently –' would have discounted Singer's wry, seemingly evenhanded comment: Convinced by Lacan, they would argue 'that the entire symbolic, verbal order is male, no matter who holds the pen. This is how the culture maintains and upholds male privilege at the profoundest level of thought, and disenfranchises female reality.' With this conviction in mind, Perry goes on to find *Tristram Shandy* to be 'a man's book if ever there was one', which is not too surprising given the fact that Sterne's culture and language ('the very laws of grammar, syntax, and semantics reproduce the patriarchal order') are the same as our own and hence phallocentric.[1]

* Reprinted from Laura Claridge and Elizabeth Langland (eds), *Out of Bounds: Male Writers and Gender (ed) Criticism* (Amherst, MA: University of Massachusetts Press, 1990), pp. 55–74

I would like to disagree with this reading but have difficulty locating a language that is not 'phallocentric' and hence not guilty of reproducing those patriarchal (or colonizing) tendencies that Perry so deplores. What I will suggest in this essay, therefore, is simply that when such a new language does come about, Sterne's writings will, I suspect, seem closer to it than will Perry's – or Irigaray's, or Kristeva's. I am not at all certain what literary criticism will sound like in its new language, but here is a typical passage in the old that might serve as a touchstone: 'We recognize that Walter is a hopeless intellectualizer, and that he takes refuge from life in endless theorizing, but it is a loved, familiar foible, and we do not read it as callousness about her pain and danger' (Perry, 'Words for Sex', 35). What I most respond to in this passage is the voice of authority, telling me what 'we recognize', what we 'love', and what 'we do not read'; it is, in that important sense, a patriarchal reading despite its content.

But Sterne, I suggest, teaches us to read differently. For example, since there is no disputing tastes, and since everything has two handles, a less patriarchal writing of Perry's observations might read: 'I think that Walter is a hopeless intellectualizer and resent his taking refuge from life in endless theorizing; nonetheless, I love this familiar foible (though other readers do not and find him both ludicrous and culpable), and I do not think he is callous about her pain and danger (although other readers have taken many pains to demonstrate just how callous he is).' That is to say, I do not so much want to oppose Perry as to suggest a criticism perhaps closer to Sterne's own insights, a criticism that hovers among the alternative readings that books and life and love (the particular subject of the discourse) seem always to offer. More particularly, I would like to read Sterne with two quotations firmly in mind from a book I begin to suspect was as close to his heart as any other, Pierre Charron's *Of Wisdome*.[2] The first sets out the problem: Wisdom consists, Charron writes, of being 'free from presumption and obstinacy in opinion; vices very familiar with those that have any extraordinary force and vigor of spirit; and rather to continue in doubt and suspense, especially in things that are doubtfull, and capable of oppositions and reasons on both parts, not easily digested and determined. It is an excellent thing, and the securest way, well to know how to doubt, and to be ignorant' (453). And the second offers a solution, which I take to be the beginning of a nonphallocentric discourse: 'Peremptorie affirmation and obstinacie in opinion, are ordinary signes of senslesnesse and ignorance. . . . It were good to learne to use such words as may sweeten and moderate the temeritie of our propositions, as, It may be, It is said, I thinke, It seemeth, and the like' (335).

Sterne was, of course, an astute observer of 'obstinacie in opinion', which he often labels 'hobby-horsical' behavior; he was also, I would like to suggest, an ardent explorer of alternatives to it, ever resistant to the temptations of absolutism, ever aware as well of the human proclivity to both dominate and succumb. Moreover, as numerous readers have noted, Sterne's exploration most often followed the byways of human sexuality, particularly, as is readily apparent in *Tristram Shandy* and *A Sentimental Journey*, within the institutions of marriage and courtship. In reversing the common sequence of the two (that is, courtship *followed* by marriage), I follow the clue of Sterne's own fictions, which begin in the Shandys' marital bed but end, despite his clerical robes, his enervated condition, and, I suspect, even his own deepest inclinations, with the grotesque *Journal to Eliza* and, at the very last, his hand stretched across the space between two beds, reaching for the end that remains out of sight. I cannot here follow all the stations of Sterne's exploration but will make four separate excursions, each marked by a single exchange of dialogue between a male and female. My aim is not so much to rescue Sterne from Perry's charge of phallocentrism as to suggest he already understood its

> he . . . was, in his life and writings, exploring ways to rescue himself

dangers and was, in his life and writings, exploring ways to rescue himself.

The first exchange, significantly, is one Sterne borrowed from Scripture; it appears in his sermon 'Job's Expostulation with His Wife' (2.15) and is taken from Job 2:9–10: 'Then said his wife unto him, Dost thou still retain thine integrity? curse God, and die. But he said unto her, Thou speakest as one of the foolish women speaketh. What? Shall we receive good at the hand of God, and shall we not receive evil? In all this did not Job sin with his lips.' Insofar as there is any significance to the ordering of Sterne's sermons, 'Job's Expostulation' may have an influential place – the final sermon of his first collection, published in two volumes in 1760, just after the overwhelming success of the first two volumes of *Tristram Shandy*. Sterne's thesis is a commonplace one in eighteenth-century Christian apologetics: The Stoic (classical) philosophy fails to answer human needs; only Christianity, in its acceptance of human weakness and in its consolations, is capable of doing so. But what interests me particularly in the exchange between Job and his wife is Sterne's interest in the meanings and motivations behind the exchange – the manner in which meaning eludes the commentator, in which the text, far from imposing an authoritative interpretation, becomes a field for potentialities: 'Though it is not very evident, what was particularly meant and implied in the words' of Job's wife, he writes, we can ascertain something from Job's reply to them.[3] The strategy of interpretation is significant, placing the sentence into a dialogue, judging its meaning from the response it elicits. It is, for Sterne, a key to understanding human communication, for always in his fiction meaning is shown to inhere in the space between speaker(s) and auditor(s), a mutual and balanced exchange between two or more voices.

Moreover, the key word in her sentence is thrown into the deepest possible doubt: 'On the other hand, some interpreters tell us, – that the word *curse*, in the original, is equivocal, and does more literally signify here, to bless, than to blaspheme' (215). This is not, to be sure, Sterne's own quibble but a commonplace in Scripture commentary, as for example in Matthew Poole's *Annotations upon the Holy Bible*: 'But although this word sometimes signifies *cursing* . . . yet most properly and generally it signifies *blessing*, and so it may very well be understood here as a Sarcastical or Ironical Expression.'[4] Sterne had read Poole or a similar commentator, for he too talks of considering the sentence 'a sarcastical scoff at Job's piety' (216). And once the possibility of interpretation is opened, new alternatives suggest themselves; Sterne, 'without disputing the merits of these two interpretations', offers a third, 'still different from what is expressed in either of them': 'instead of supposing them as an incitement to blaspheme God, – which was madness, – or that they were intended as an insult, – which was unnatural; – that her advice to curse God and die, was meant here, that he should resolve upon a voluntary death himself [that is, suicide]' (216–17). Behind this suggestion, Sterne argues, is the wife's 'concern and affection' for Job, her knowledge that 'he was a virtuous and an upright man, and deserved a better fate'; indeed, 'her heart bled the more for him' (217–18). In short, without forcing one view over another (although his rhetoric cannot help but be swayed by his *new* interpretation), Sterne shifts the moment of scriptural dialogue into a domestic scene, binding husband and wife together in mutual affection and desperation and finding the meaning of their words in the interplay of their feelings. Most particularly, Sterne avoids the temptation to view the wife as a fool ('foolish woman', that is, 'The fool hath said in his heart, There is no God' [Ps. 14:1]) or a shrew (the standard, long-standing interpretations),[5] opting instead for an idealized marital context where 'concern and affection' dominate.

I would also call attention to the aggressive nature of the wife's advice, as paraphrased by Sterne: 'since thou hast met with no justice in this world, – leave it, – die – and force thy passage into a better country' (219). No character in Scripture (excepting Adam and Christ) can be seen as more the innocent victim of brute paternalistic power than Job, whose God allows him to be used as an object in a duel of strength with Satan. Indeed, Job's response to his wife's advice is precisely that of the victim, 'receiving' good, 'receiving' evil. But in the exchange wrought by 'concern and affection' she rejects receptivity for penetration, her 'force thy passage' suggesting an active resistance to omnipotence. Job rejects her advice; and, indeed, earlier commentators had linked such advice to the devil, suggesting in no uncertain terms that Eve and Job's wife be read as analogous figures.[6] It is of particular interest, therefore, that Sterne seeks a sympathetic reading of the sentence, understanding the relationship between Job and his wife in the context of domestic regard and the exchange of traditionally assigned roles; it is a pattern we shall see repeated in the fictions.

We cannot date Sermon 15, but without doubt it was written before *Tristram Shandy*, possibly a decade or more earlier. The story of Job is never too far from Sterne's mind, however, when he portrays the Shandy family,[7] and insofar as Walter Shandy is thwarted and tormented in every plan of his life, we might recognize in Elizabeth Shandy a counterpart to Job's wife. The dialogue between the two is one of Sterne's most consistently brilliant feats in the work. For our purposes, we might as well begin with the first exchange as with any other: '*Pray, my dear*, quoth my mother, *have you not forgot to wind up the clock?——Good G—!* cried my father, making an exclamation, but taking care to moderate his voice at the same time,——*Did ever woman, since the creation of the world, interrupt a man with such a silly question?*' (1:1).[8] Critics have often been harsh with Mrs Shandy, seeing in her portrayal by Sterne a marginalized, dull, and insignificant woman in a fiction about male relations.[9] She is considered, much as Walter considers her, colorless, passive, stupid, long-suffering, and the like. But to consider anyone through Walter's eyes is to consider the world through the eyes of a foolish person, and that itself should alert us to the richer possibilities of Sterne's portrayal. Surely, we need not sympathize with Walter, for example, in his exasperation with Mrs Shandy's question. Consider, again, the situation: Locked in a marital embrace, Walter brings to bear what is left of his sciatica-weakened loins to the task at hand, while Mrs Shandy, physically beneath him, has – as in that wonderful scene in Woody Allen's *Annie Hall* – mentally relocated herself to sit by the side of the bed, observing the scene and thinking of other things to be done on Sunday nights. This is not perhaps her failure of sexual appetite but his of performance, and Sterne is shrewd enough to see the relationship between the two often – if not always – in that light.[10] From the many clues of Tristram's illegitimacy that hover over the text, abetted by Mrs Shandy's own unrelenting hints in that direction,[11] her views of midwives versus Walter's, and her role in child rearing versus the never-to-be-ready *Tristrapaedia*, Sterne seems again and again to give the edge to Mrs Shandy in wit, perception, intelligence – and *mastery* of the situation. In Sterne's satire of the Shandy household, Mrs Shandy represents, as much as Yorick, many of the values Sterne holds most dear.

The exchange tells us something more. Behind Mr Shandy's concern with the interruption is his theory of the Homunculus, a 'phallocentric' theory of generation if ever there was one, namely, that the entire child in miniature is in the sperm.[12] Several of Walter's theories can be dismissed as distinctly ludicrous or purposefully anachronistic, as, for example, his embrace of the long-discredited patriarchal politics of Robert Filmer.[13] The animalculist theory, however, was still credible in the 1760s, although under pressure from an opposing school, the ovulists. What is important, therefore, is Sterne's own (nonscientific) skepticism about a theory that, like the legal judgment in the case of the Duchess of Suffolk (IV. xxix: 391) that 'the mother was not of kin to her child', appears to him patently absurd. What Sterne rejects, I would suggest, is a point of view that argues against his own sense of mutuality in the domestic (procreative but, more significantly, marital) relationship. Walter Shandy's procreating by himself, the image manifest in the opening exchange with Mrs Shandy, finds analogues throughout the fiction, where separation, isolation, impotence, and finally death everywhere threaten the Shandy males; that the work is comic and, finally, affirmative in its belief that communion and love can be found thriving in this world is, I would suggest, the result of the triumph of a feminist view over the phallocentrism of a goodly portion of the world. No person is more important than Elizabeth Shandy in her embodiment of Sterne's argument against the 'singleness' (and 'singlemindedness') of the Shandy males.

Still, Mrs Shandy does not seem to share the affection and care that Sterne sought to find in Job's wife – unless we consider her interest in her children as its manifestation. The marriage itself is, at best, an estranged one, modeled, one is tempted to suggest, upon Sterne's own failed marriage to Elizabeth Lumley.[14] The causes of that failure are captured in this first exchange, which is not an exchange at all; Mrs Shandy is not responding to Mr Shandy, and his retort clearly does not answer her question. More important, his effort to bring the moment to its necessary (for him) conclusion, his desire to impregnate his wife in a powerful and possessive gesture, is defeated on two counts. First, Mrs Shandy's interruption scatters and disperses the animal spirits; and, second, we have at least the suspicion planted that his seed falls not on barren but on occupied ground and hence falls sterile. If Tristram's eight-month birth is in reason as much as any husband can expect (I. v: 8), we nevertheless must leave some room for a nine-month gestation; if Mrs Shandy is already pregnant, Mr Shandy's efforts are obviously as untimely as his later work on the *Tristrapaedia* – and as futile.

I have elsewhere argued that the energy of *Tristram Shandy* lies in its capacity to interrupt itself with additional material, to prevent itself from concluding.[15] Mrs Shandy might be said to embody that spirit of interruption, digression, incompleteness – of suspense, in Charron's sense of the word. Her body in one place, her mind in another, she captures the true Shandy spirit that refuses to reduce oneself or one's world to a

> **Mrs Shandy might be said to embody that spirit of interruption, digression, incompleteness – of suspense**

single hypothesis. Further, as Sterne sought his digressive energy in the work of others – and found as well an anxiety of emulation in his desire to keep up with the digressive likes of Rabelais and Burton, Cervantes and Montaigne – so Mrs Shandy has possibly been preinscribed, though more to Mr Shandy's anxiety than her own. Indeed, she may be said to embody in two distinct ways the digressive spirit of *Tristram Shandy*; and insofar as she does give birth to a son named Tristram in the course of the fiction, she must be said to have generated the work. Or, put another way, Walter's urge to drive toward his conclusion, Tristram's straight line at the end of Volume VI ('The *best line!* say cabbage-planters' [VI. XL: 572]),[16] and Toby's inclination to show Mrs Wadman the very place – on the map – are all projections of male failure in the Shandy household; Mrs Shandy's interruption is the fertile moment out of which Sterne's entire fiction will emerge.

This reading of the opening scene of *Tristram Shandy* is constructed on a fiction I would like to call momentarily into question, namely, that a text trying to close itself is 'male', where a text striving to remain open is 'female'. There is a question of appropriation here that perhaps underlies this entire collection of essays, for one should be wary of a thesis that turns Rabelais, Cervantes, Montaigne, Burton, and Sterne, that is, the entire satiric or Menippean tradition, into 'feminist' writing. What seems to have happened is that we discovered *first* that certain forms of nonnovelistic fiction also had literary interest, indeed, as much interest perhaps as the so-called realistic novel, which modern critics inherited as the *type* against which to measure all long narratives; and, *then*, in a shrewd political gesture, the heretofore marginalized forms were appropriated by the heretofore marginalized readers (women, blacks, postmodernists, lovers of Sterne as opposed to lovers of Fielding) as the genres of their own voices. Such a scheme is bound to be questioned by a rectifying fiction in the near future. In the meantime, however, one clue remains in the opening dialogue of *Tristram* that might enable us to accept our present paradigm for the nonce with only a few additional qualms. *Tristram Shandy* is a book about human truths, and perhaps the single most evident truth of its world is that male and female have different shapes; surely no other work readily comes to mind with more slits, cracks, crevices, buttonholes and keyholes, on the one hand, or more sticks, fingers, noses, and artillery on the other. This, in turn, establishes one clear dichotomy, even in a world that resists the simplicities of dichotomous thinking: The act of penetration differs from the act of reception. But if we return to Job's wife for a moment, recall my suggestion that her advice was to penetrate (to force a passage), Job's response to remain receptive to 'good' and 'evil'. In *Tristram* also, the physical structures seem to be deceptive. Mr Shandy, 'penetrating' his Mrs Shandy, cannot overpower her mind or possess her body; she remains unpossessed, un-'penetrated', by his desires. Conversely, she is clearly not receptive, despite the fact that he is 'in' her. His drive toward completion is met with digression, his theory scattered and dispersed upon the shoals of Mrs Shandy's otherness. What I would like to suggest, most tentatively, is that in this incompatibility might be found the seeds for two of the fictions by which we image forth the world – the one, Walter's fiction, phallocentrism, which overpowers the world with ideas, the other, Elizabeth's fiction, which undercuts ideas with the world. Insofar as *Tristram Shandy* is a work of the second order, Mrs Shandy, a true skeptic (satirist?), is its creator.

But of course Sterne wrote the work, and somewhere in the course of his writing he seems to have become fascinated with the idea that the fundamental incompatibility examined in the Shandy household had to be resolved into a better union of male and female, one that would, after the last volume of *Tristram* appeared, address Sterne's own pressing anxieties: his bad health, his domestic unhappiness, his dubious salvation. His first excursion during the final year of his life was a desperate flirtation with a married woman thirty years younger than he. We know about Eliza Draper primarily through Sterne's letters to her and the portion of his 'Journal to Eliza' that he did not send to her.[17] His second, and far more successful excursion is the aptly named last fiction of his life, *A Sentimental Journey*; in that work, Sterne captures, if only intermittently, a sexual dialogue at one and the same time genderless and procreative and, above all, acceptable to Grace.

The 'Journal to Eliza' is in the shape of a dialogue with one voice: 'wrote the last farewell to Eliza by Mr Wats who sails this day for Bombay – inclosed her likewise the Journal kept from the day we parted, to this – so from hence continue it till the time we meet again – Eliza does the same, so we shall have mutual testimonies to deliver hereafter to each other' (135). The motif of mutual journal keeping is depressingly obsessional as the journal continues; for example:

April 16: I shall read the same affecting Account of many a sad Dinner which Eliza has had no power to taste of. (137)

May 13: Surely 'tis not impossible, but [I] may be made happy as my Eliza, by so[me] transcript from her . . . we taste not of it *now*, my dear Bramine[18] – but we will make full meals upon it hereafter. (152)

June 2: By this time, I trust You have doubled the Cape of good hope – and sat down to your writing Drawer, and look'd in Yoricks face, as you took out your Journal; to tell him so. (157)

June 15: Mark! – you will dream of me this night – and if it is not recorded in your Journal – Ill say, you could not recollect it the day following. (165)

June 21: I long to see [your journal] – I shall read it a thousand times over If I get it before your Arrival – What would I now give for it – tho' I know there are *circumstances* in it, That will make my heart bleed. (168)

And, finally,

July 7: I can see and hear nothing but my Eliza. remember this, when You think my Journal too short, and compare it not with thine, which tho' it will exceed it in length, can do no more than equal it in Love. (179)

We have here a dialogue with an imaginary correspondent, wished into being by the author's own desire. Far more accurate a perception of the relationship is perhaps supplied by Sterne's depressing assessment of June 30:

I have wrote [a mutual friend] a whole Sheet of paper about us – it ought to have been copied into this Journal – but the uncertainty of your ever reading it, makes me omit that . . . which when we meet, shall beguile us of many a long winters night. – *those precious Nights!* – my Eliza! – You rate them as high as I do. . . . They are all that remains to us – except the *Expectation* of their return – the Space between is a dismal Void – full of doubts, and suspence. (173)

The desire for correspondence is double-edged in Sterne's journal. On the one hand, he wants to bridge the empty space between himself and Eliza, between male and female, with a language that nourishes and heals – and we must remember that Sterne's entries are replete with accounts of his decrepitude at this time.[19] On the other hand, the correspondence he seeks has at least as much to do with reflecting himself as with reaching another (or, indeed, being reached by another) – as he writes his journal, he must see Eliza at her desk writing hers. Indeed, the many references to sensibility and sentiment, sympathy and pathos in the 'Journal' all appear to come from this single urge, to find in another human being one's own self:

I want You to be on the other side of my little table, to hear how sweetly your Voice will be in Unison to all this – I want to hear what You have to say to Your Yorick upon this Text. . . . how pathetically you would enforce your Truth and Love upon my heart to free it from every Aching doubt – Doubt! did I say – but I have none – and as soon would I doubt the Scripture I have preach'd on.

The burden of the 'correspondence' then, is enormous: 'for if thou art false, my Bramine – the whole world – and Nature itself are lyars' (175). Sterne has, it seems to me, trapped himself in the very toils he had set for Walter Shandy. Driven by sickness, by a painful estrangement from his wife and daughter, by what he almost certainly feared, his impending death and judgment, the 'Journal to Eliza' is a fabric of lies designed to keep reality at a comfortable distance. And the cornerstone of the fabric is the lie of possession, of knowing – the core of the Shandy males' failure and of Sterne's sad failure here: 'leave [my expressions of doubt] as a part of the picture of a heart that *again* Languishes for Possession – and is disturbed at every Idea of its Uncertainty' (175). Behind the sentimentalism of the 'Journal', behind its language of feeling and sympathy and suffering,[20] behind even its empowering of Eliza as both his God ('all powerful Eliza' [179]) and his alter ego ('I resemble no Being in the world so nearly as I do You' [161]), is a desperate push for power, the need to triumph over, to gain control of, his own sickness and death. The cost – his familial relations, his accurate perception of reality, his inevitable disappointment – is inconsequential in the face of his need to dominate, and the journal plunges blindly forward in its self-deceptions for four months. As the 'space' between them widens, in time and in distance, the idea of possession becomes more and more obsessional: 'and in proportion as I am thus torn from your embraces – *I cling the closer to the Idea of you*', he writes on July 7 (178). It is, I would suggest, Sterne's lowest point.

As with many forms of obsessional behavior, one cure appears to be the granting of what the patient most believes he desires. On July 27 Eliza's 'dear Packets' arrive from over the seas, and Sterne spends the evening and the next day, until dinner, reading 'over and over again the most interesting Account – and the most endearing one, that ever tried the tenderness of man' (185). Five entries later, Sterne ended the 'Journal to Eliza'.[21] Eliza's 'Journal', we must suspect, could not sustain the fiction he had created; whatever else Eliza Draper was, she was not 'up to the ears' in love with Sterne as he had forced himself to believe, was not anguishing over her loss as he had convinced himself he was anguishing (as in a mirror) over his, was not, in short, penetrated by his own desires or possessed by his own imaginings. The silence into which Sterne wrote from April through July was a sustaining space; Eliza's interruption of that silence scatters and disperses Sterne's animal spirits, and he wisely withdraws to a far more fertile field, his own art, in order to complete *A Sentimental Journey*.

One would tend to think rather badly of Sterne for his 'Journal to Eliza' (though not, I hope, for the 'moral' reasons of Thackeray),[22] did we not know he was writing it simultaneously with the *Journey*, a work that seems in important points to reverse the course of his 'dialogue' with Eliza, returning Sterne to the sustainable insights of his view of Job's wife and of Mrs Shandy. The final exchange I will discuss occurs in a chapter appropriately entitled 'The Translation'. Though it is apparent from the chapter and the one following that the title refers to the 'translating' of nonverbal gestures into verbal statements, I would suggest, as well, that Sterne is interested here in 'translating' a discourse of opposition and cross-purpose into one that promises, through correspondence, the creative harmony of a peace that accepts difference. Beyond that, Sterne is also 'translating' sentimental expressions of that harmony (the eighteenth-century gambit he was simultaneously using unsuccessfully in the 'Journal to Eliza') into a language more appropriate to human beings in whom 'nature has so wove her web of kindness, that some threads of love and desire are entangled with the piece'.[23]

'Upon my word, Madame, said I when I had handed her in [to her carriage], I made six different efforts to let you go out – And I made six efforts, replied she, to let you enter' (173). The scene is the doorway to a concert in Milan, where Yorick encounters the Marquesina di F***,[24] as she attempts to exit. The situation is one we have all experienced: 'she was almost upon me before I saw her; so I gave a spring to one side to let her pass – She had done the same, and on the same side too; so we ran our heads together: she instantly got to the other side to get out: I was just as unfortunate as she had been; for I had sprung to that side, and opposed her passage again – We both flew together to the other side, and then back – and so on – it was ridiculous' (172). The beautifully matched dance stops when Yorick stands still and allows the Marquesina to pass, after which he follows her to her carriage to apologize in the exchange quoted above. The dialogue continues: 'I wish to heaven you would make a seventh, said I – With all my heart, said she, making room.' The chapter then concludes with Yorick's assertion that 'the connection which arose out of that translation' afforded him more pleasure than any other he made in Italy.

In a work replete with unrealized flirtations, the 'connection' is a moment of fulfillment unique in the *Journey* in its implicit actualization. It is noteworthy, therefore, that it takes place in a portion of Yorick's journey that remained 'unwritten', namely, the journey to Italy. Perhaps it is a projection of the fulfillment to be achieved at journey's end, after all has been learned and experienced; or perhaps, more subtly, it suggests that 'connection' must always be that portion of our journey that remains unverbalized, unwritten. What is most apparent is that Sterne finds a moment of absolute harmony in the stasis he portrays as a silent dance which brings about the exchange of gender-oriented responses. Yorick, forgoing his attempts to control the exchange, does 'the thing I should have done at first – I stood stock still' (172). The Marquesina, seizing the opportunity, penetrates the space between the two and passes through. Only then does Yorick resume the aggressor role, pursuing her down the passageway, but his pursuit ends in the stasis of the dialogue under discussion, mirroring the earlier static dance in its neatly balanced arrangement of 'six different efforts', and the highly charged play on 'letting in' and 'letting out'. I would like to suggest that in this wonderful dialogue Sterne has found an analogy for Charron's wisdom: 'It were good to learne to use such words as may sweeten and moderate the temeritie of our propositions, as, It may be, It is said, I thinke, It seemeth, and the like' (335).

In the chapter just prior to this one, entitled 'The Gloves', we have a very similar exchange – so similar, indeed, that the juxtaposition of the two chapters, otherwise unrelated, appears to my mind quite purposeful. The scene is one in which Sterne's insistence upon human sexuality undercuts his age's attempt to mask desire with the language of sentiment. In the *grisset*'s shop, Yorick is fitted for a pair of gloves, a scene of the utmost delicacy, the feeling of the *grisset*'s pulse, and of the utmost sexuality, insofar as the fitting of a glove is yet one more trope for sexual union. But this time, Sterne gives us a hint of completion, one that significantly sets language aside:

There are certain combined looks of simple subtlety – where whim, and sense, and seriousness, and nonsense, are so blended, that all the languages of Babel set loose together could not express them – they are communicated and caught so instantaneously, that you can scarce say which party is the infecter.

. . . she had a quick black eye, and shot through two such long and silken eyelashes with such penetration, that she look'd into my very heart and reins.

(168–9)

The nonverbal gesture, which Sterne uses so successfully in *Tristram Shandy* to allow Walter and Toby to bridge some of their mental and emotional gaps, is here made a viable path between the baffling conflicts of the self and the elusive intentions of the other. Most significantly, this movement from self to other is imaged first as a silent sexual balance, much like the stasis before the concert door ('which party is the infecter?'),[25] followed by the male surrender of aggression (pursuit) to the female who 'penetrates' his reins. Perhaps Sterne's major insight into the nature of human desire is the idea that the most satisfying human harmony is achieved when the female penetrates and the male receives. I would prefer to believe that, with the model of Christian love constantly before him in his clerical role, Sterne could perceive the genderless potentiality of this exchange: Christ the incarnate God could enter us, male and female both; and male and female both could receive Christ; and I particularly lean toward this

> 𝒵 **the most satisfying human harmony is achieved when the female penetrates and the male receives**

view because the strong sexuality of the passage is so much more in tune with traditional Christian belief (including the belief that man is born into a body) than with the secular sentimentality that was replacing it.[26] But even if we cannot accept the idea that Christianity provided Sterne's answer to male–female relationships, it does seem evident that sometime during the course of his own married and 'unmarried' life – and perhaps most poignantly in his encounter with Eliza – Sterne came to value both the moments of 'stasis' when male and female 'correspond' fully with one another and the subsequent moments of 'exchange', in which self and other become a creative (procreative) whole.

The problem of entering into, penetrating the other, the problem of knowledge, holds Sterne's attention throughout the middle of *A Sentimental Journey*. Of particular significance for unraveling Sterne's commentary on the Age of Sentimentality are the chapters concerned with a caged starling, a bird the Sterne family used on its coat of arms, identifying its dialectical rendition *starn* with Sterne.[27] Yorick 'translates' the bird's song as 'I can't get out', but for Sterne the exercise of translation, no matter how energetically pursued, is often nothing more than words, 'sentiment . . . sans amour'. Significantly, Yorick replays the encounter with the Marquesina; the bird cannot 'get out', and Yorick, try as he might imaginatively to enter into the bird's captivity, cannot 'get in': 'I could not sustain the picture of confinement which my fancy had drawn' (203). The bird is passed from hand to hand but is never freed, for the roles remain always the same: 'all these [the owners] wanted to *get in* –

and my bird wanted to get out' (205). This failure is more than a failure of imagination; insofar as Yorick's efforts to identify with the starling are conscious and aggressive (filled as they are with English Francophobia), they are diametrically opposed to the exchange of roles that Sterne finds necessary for true penetration and connection. Until the bird is allowed to leave the cage and Yorick can enter it, Sterne sees no communication taking place, despite the emphasis his contemporaries placed on moral sensibility and empathic understanding. There are actions missing here – the freeing of the bird, the entering into captivity – that no intensity of sentiment, no virtuosity of language can replace. Sterne's interest is focused on the nature of that action, the paradoxical passivity that seems its necessary concomitant, and the transfer of (sexual) identity that is achieved at the moment of fulfillment.

A more successful encounter occurs in the closing pages of *A Sentimental Journey*, in Yorick's penultimate encounter with a woman, the lovesick Maria. The scene revisits an earlier portrayal in *Tristram Shandy*, and the gesture of reinvention is an important one. Here, at the end of his life, with his wife and daughter permanently separated from him, with Eliza an ocean apart from him, literally and figuratively, Sterne rewrites male–female relations in a manner at once self-justifying and self-condemning; he writes, in short, as a man about to be held account-able for his conduct before a higher tribunal than this world can offer. Nowhere in his previous writing does Sterne come closer to portraying a workable union of desire and language than in this second encounter with Maria. As he weeps with her in mirrored, balanced actions ('Maria let me wipe them [her tears] away . . . with my handkerchief. – I then steep'd it in my own – and then in hers – and then in mine – and then I wip'd hers again'), he discovers in a convincing manner the strongest sense of identity, not with Maria but with himself: He discovers the existence of his soul.

I felt such undescribable emotions within me, as I am sure could not be accounted for from any combination of matter and motion.

I am positive I have a soul; nor can all the books with which materialists have pester'd the world ever convince me of the contrary. (271)

The feeling, significantly, is not free from sexual desire.[28] Yorick's descrip-tion of Maria is really the first time he 'sees' the woman he is with as a physical being rather than a sentimental construct:

Maria, tho' not tall, was nevertheless of the first order of fine forms – affliction had touch'd her looks with something that was scarce earthly – still she was feminine – and so much was there about her of all that the heart wishes, or the

eye looks for in woman, that could the traces be ever worn out of her brain . . .
she should *not only eat of my bread and drink of my own cup*, but Maria should
lay in my bosom, and be unto me as a daughter. (275)[29]

The last part of the passage paraphrases Nathan's parable of the poor
man's ewe lamb (2 Sam. 12: 3), which is cared for as Yorick vows to
care for Maria; the source alerts us to the fact that not only should we not
burden 'as a daughter' with complex interpretation but also that it is a
moment of legitimate insight on Yorick's part. Nathan uses the parable
to recall to David his sin of taking Bathsheba from Uriah, David being
Sterne's favorite example of the stern moralist who is severe to other
sinners but blind to his own transgressions. As such, the biblical allusion
reminds us again of the question of identity; as David is forced to
acknowledge his desire (and his sinfulness), so Yorick, finally, comes to
an honest acceptance of his own desires – free from sentiment, from
deception, from innuendo, from repression.

It is within this context of a hard-won embrace of the complex
nature of man, a compounded creature, that Yorick's famous apostrophe
to sensibility in the next chapter might best be understood. It has often
marked Sterne as the foremost sentimentalist of a sentimental age, often
been used to suggest Sterne's celebration of the 'heart' over all else. But
coming late as it does in the *Journey*, its context is the exploration that
has preceded it of sensibility's relation to desire, and in this context
we understand 'sensibility' as that particular capacity which makes love
possible: the awareness of the wholeness of the human experience,
including both the exchange of sexual roles, aggressor and recipient,
active and passive, and the knowledge that sensibility is not limited to
those stirrings we can accept with clean hands and uplifted hearts:

– Dear sensibility! source inexhausted of all that's precious in our joys, or costly
in our sorrows! thou chainest thy martyr down upon his bed of straw – and 'tis
thou who lifts him up to HEAVEN – eternal fountain of our feelings! . . . all comes
from thee, great – great SENSORIUM of the world! which vibrates, if a hair of our
heads but falls upon the ground, in the remotest desert of thy creation. (277–8)

Yorick's prayer is an assertion of providence (Matt. 10: 29–31), God's
continuing hand in human affairs despite the Fall, despite the intricate
web of good and evil that human life has become, despite even, perhaps,
the phallocentric nature of postlapsarian language and society. Yorick's
prayer is a *humble* assertion of faith.[30]

And faith is answered by 'Grace', the penultimate chapter of everything Sterne ever wrote. Tristram had found a similar moment of communion in the peasant dance at the end of his tour through France,

although the moment is tainted by repressed desire, Nannette's 'cursed slit' in her petticoat (VII. xLiii: 649–51). Nothing interferes, however, with Yorick's appreciation of this moment. In harmony at last with himself, he is able to be in harmony with others. The beautiful assertion that he beholds '*Religion* mixing in the dance' (284) is an insight gained through travel and loneliness and, perhaps we should add, glancing at Sterne's biography again, the impending threat of death, which renders the need for human connection all the more intense and necessary. Importantly, the 'grace' is not spoken but acted out; but equally import-ant, Yorick is able to find the words to express the joy of the dance without equivocation or innuendo. The distance between Tristram and Yorick at this point is the measure of the spiritual peace Sterne found in *A Sentimental Journey*; and the distance between the Sterne of the *Journey* and of the 'Journal to Eliza' is his awareness and acceptance that the moment of 'Grace', of insight, of possession, of knowing something, anything, for certain, is ultimately no more than a moment in the rush of life. Tristram flees from insight, Walter Shandy chokes it to death; Yorick is simply unable to sustain it, which, in a fallen world, is man's natural relationship to grace.[31] And so the 'Case of Delicacy' is the final chapter, reminding us that the quest is as long as life itself, that however else we may recall Yorick, recall any human life, including our own, it is also the portrait of a person forever reaching across the void for the person (the knowledge) on the other side.[32] Insight, love, wholeness, grace, all are possible for the human being in this model, but none per-manently. What is permanent is the difficulty of living with imperman-ence, the intense desire to possess completely and forever that which we hope will afford a moment's insight or a moment's pleasure; and, insofar as that difficulty and that desire encourage our surrender to the twin aggressions of absolutism and order in the face of life's complexity (and joy), Sterne would seem to be urging us (and himself) to seek a better solution.

It is in this manner that I think Sterne initiates a feminist discourse, if that is what stands in opposition to the phallocentric one. But even in this last moment, Sterne might teach us something more, for both 'feminist' and 'phallocentric' are already words so loaded with human passions that they recall nothing so much as Walter's faith in names and Tristram's insistence that 'noses' mean only 'noses'. One of Sterne's richest insights, I believe, is that only by eschewing naming and the expectations of order and domination that naming entails do we ever achieve – however tenuously – the creative unions and correspondences, the communications and intercourses, which at fortuitous moments arrest us in a lifetime of otherwise vain pursuits. One age might label his attitude antirationalistic, another might call it fideistic skepticism, a third might simply point to the New Testament (see, e.g., 1 Cor. 13), and a fourth might retreat further, perhaps to Job: 'For we are but of yesterday, and know nothing, because our days upon earth are a shadow' (8: 9). In the last fifteen years, this Socratic (Nietzschean) assault on authority and certainty has become the privileged discourse of 'feminist' thinking. While one must admire the political (and, I hope, moral) astuteness that seizes so defensible a high ground as its own, it seems rather dubious that the label will long stick to the stance, if only because the individual human mind seems unable to rest in uncertainties and drives always to empower itself – to speak in phallocentric terms even while condemning them, indeed, in order to condemn them. Sterne seems able to point us toward another language, but our difficulty in ever learning to speak it is suggested by our inability to escape Walter's 'logic': Were a young boy to be named Judas, he would be forever ruined. When we can argue ourselves out of an 'obstinacie in opinion' such as that, a new discourse will have begun.

NOTES

1. Ruth Perry, 'Words for Sex: The Verbal-Sexual Continuum in *Tristram Shandy*', *Studies in the Novel* 20 (1988): 29.

2. Charron wrote in French, *De la sagesse*, translated as *Of Wisdome* by Samson Lennard in ?1612. Sterne definitely quotes from the work at the very end of *Tristram Shandy*, as first pointed out in Françoise Pellan, 'Laurence Sterne's Indebtedness to Charron', MLR 67 (1972): 752–5. The editors of the *Notes* to *Tristram Shandy* (3 of the Florida Edition, ed. Melvyn New, with Richard A. Davies and W. G. Day [Gainesville, FLA: University Presses of Florida, 1984]), point as well to Charron's possible influence in the opening pages (3: 39–40). Charron is basically a compiler and organizer of Montaigne's thoughts; *Of Wisdome* is a rich compendium of the ideas of Renaissance Christian skepticism, one vital strand of which is woven into the quotations offered. It is as well, I suspect, a more important book for Sterne than we have yet fully realized.

3. Laurence Sterne, *The Sermons of Mr Yorick* (London, 1760), 2: 213–14; hereafter cited in text.

4. Matthew Poole, *Annotations upon the Holy Bible* (London, 1688), s.v. Job 2: 9–10.

5. Here, for example, is William Warburton's commentary in *The Divine Legation of Moses*, 6: 2: 'Let us take her, as she is presented to us, on the common footing. She acts a short part indeed, but a very spirited one. [Quotes Job 2: 9.] Tender and pious! He might see, by this prelude of his Spouse, what he was to expect from his Friends. The Devil indeed assaulted Job, but he seems to have got possession of his Wife.

Happiness was so little to be expected with such a Woman, that one almost wonders, that the sacred Writer, when he aims to give us the highest idea of Job's succeeding felicity, did not tell us, in express words, that he lived to bury his Wife.' Several pages later he calls her Satan's agent (*The Works* [London, 1788; rpt. ed., Georg Olms, 1978], 3: 277, 279). For an account of the complex relationship between Warburton and Sterne, see Melvyn New, 'Sterne, Warburton, and the Burden of Exuberant Wit', ECS 15 (1982): 245–74.

6. In addition to the passage from Warburton quoted in n. 5, see, e.g., John Mayer, *A Commentary upon the Holy Writings of Job, David, and Solomon* . . . (London, 1653), s.v. Job 2: 9: 'It may seem strang[e], that when all his Children perished, that his Wife was preserved still alive. . . . the most common received opinion was, that Satan spared her, that by her he might be yet further tempted to curse God. . . . And this seemeth most probable.' Sterne's distance from this sort of thinking is well worth complimenting.

7. See Everett Zimmerman, '*Tristram Shandy* and Narrative Representation', *Eighteenth Century: Theory and Interpretation* 28 (1987): 131–3.

8. Quoted from *The Life and Opinions of Tristram Shandy, Gentleman*, ed. Melvyn New and Joan New (Gainesville, FLA: University Presses of Florida, 1978), 1: 2; hereafter cited in text.

9. James A. Work shaped a generation's attitude toward Mrs Shandy with his comments in his introduction to his popular textbook edition of *Tristram*: 'My mother indeed, though she appears rarely, says little, and has "no character at all", is one of the most delightful of Sterne's creations. . . . she is chiefly notable for her inability – or lack of desire – to say anything for herself. And in her placid, vegetal existence, which is itself a bathetic commentary on the practical value of his [Mr Shandy's] fine theorizing, she . . . acts as a foil to my father' ([New York: Odyssey Press, 1940], lvi–lvii). Work was perhaps thinking to praise Mrs Shandy, but 'placid' and 'vegetal' are not useful words for that purpose.

   A useful corrective to this view is an essay by Leigh A. Ehlers, 'Mrs Shandy's "Lint and Basilicon": The Importance of Women in *Tristram Shandy*', SAR 46 (1981): 61–75. See also the interesting comments on Mrs Shandy in James Swearingen, *Reflexivity in 'Tristram Shandy': An Essay in Phenomenological Criticism* (New Haven, CT: Yale University Press, 1977), 221–6. Perry appreciates Ehlers's essay but dismisses it as a 'humanistic interpretation' (Perry, 'Words for Sex', 30); she does not mention Swearingen.

   A spirited and convincing defense of Mrs Shandy is in Helen Ostovich, 'Reader as Hobby-horse in *Tristram Shandy*', PQ 68 (1989): 325–42. I served as a referee for this essay and when rereading it in print became aware of its influence on my present comments, although I had not retained a copy.

10. Cf. Ian Watt's comment on the scene in the introduction to his edition: 'if Pavlov's dog could have talked, it would, under similar circumstances, no doubt have echoed Mrs Shandy's words' ([Boston, MA: Houghton Mifflin, 1965], xiii). The remark seems

to me unfair, as does Watt's equation of Mr Shandy's 'complete intellectual and emotional impasse with his wife' with Sterne's own difficulties with Mrs Sterne (xii). What interests me most particularly, in fact, is that Sterne seems to associate Walter Shandy with Elizabeth Sterne's failings, his own position with that of Mrs Shandy; see below, n. 14.

11. See New, *Notes*, 3: 51–2, n. to 8.1–3. My own favorite hint is that given in an exchange between husband and wife in one of their beds of justice:

> But indeed he is growing a very tall lad,—rejoined my father.
> ——He is very tall for his age, indeed,—said my mother.——
> ——I can not (making two syllables of it) imagine, quoth my father, who the duce he takes after.——
> I cannot conceive, for my life,—said my mother.———
> Humph!——said my father. (VI. xviii: 526–7).

Mrs Shandy's triumph seems to me splendidly obvious.

12. New, *Notes*, 3: 44, n. to 2.19 ff. For a full discussion, see Louis A. Landa, 'The Shandean Homunculus: The Background of Sterne's "Little Gentleman"', in *Restoration and Eighteenth-Century Literature: Essays in Honor of A. D. McKillop* (Chicago, IL: University of Chicago Press, 1963), 49–68.

13. New, *Notes*, 3: 378, n. to 466.1 ff. Of particular interest to us here is the debate between Filmer and Locke perhaps being alluded to in Trim's recitation of his catechism. Filmer had based his argument in favor of patriarchy in part on the fifth commandment's injunction to honor one's father; Locke chided him in *Two Treatises of Government* with the reminder that the text reads, Honor thy father *and* mother.

14. See Arthur H. Cash, *Laurence Sterne: The Early and Middle Years* (London: Methuen, 1975), 78–86 and *passim*. Cash records the evidence of Elizabeth Montagu, the famous bluestocking who was Mrs Sterne's cousin: 'She was always taking frump at somebody & forever in quarrels & frabbles.' And again: 'Mrs Sterne is a Woman of great integrity & has many virtues, but they stand like quills upon the fretfull porcupine, ready to go forth in sharp arrows on ye least supposed offense; . . . the only way to avoid a quarrel with her is to keep a due distance' (84). How very much more like *Walter* than *Elizabeth* Shandy does she sound!

15. In New, 'Sterne, Warburton'.

16. See New, *Notes*, 3: 442, n. to 572.6, for the possible sexual overtones of 'planting cabbages'.

17. The most readily available edition of the 'Journal to Eliza' is that by Ian Jack (with *A Sentimental Journey*), for the Oxford English Novels series (London: Oxford University Press, 1968), and I have quoted it in my text. However, Lewis Perry Curtis's reprinting of the 'Journal' in *Letters* (Oxford: Oxford University Press, 1935) should also be consulted. The full details of the relationship are sensitively dealt with by Arthur Cash in chapter 7 of *Laurence Sterne: The Later Years* (London: Methuen, 1986),

268–304. An earlier portion of the journal that Sterne actually sent to Eliza has been lost; and none of her writings to him has survived.

18. Apparently, Eliza called Sterne Bramin and he responded, typically enough, with a feminized version, Bramine.

19. Cash, *Later Years*, 288–91 and *passim*.

20. I can agree with Eve Kosofsky Sedgwick's analysis of sentimentalism ('this warm space of pathos and the personal') as a 'complicated male strategy for . . . empower- ment', though I believe the description is far more apropos of the 'Journal to Eliza' than of *A Sentimental Journey*, which she analyzes without much regard for Sterne's humor, irony, or self-correcting, self-reflective language; see *Between Men: English Literature and Male Homosocial Desire* (New York: Columbia University Press, 1985), 67–82. Sedgwick seems to believe that, if she does not proceed in a 'churlish, literal-minded' manner, the work proves too seductive; that it is Sterne's good sense that seduces her is an idea she does not readily entertain. Interestingly, she does not seem to have read the 'Journal' or anything else by or about Sterne, which may be the reason her reading of the *Journey* strikes me as so thesis-dominated, so self-assured, and so possessive of the text. In short, her criticism is 'imperialism with a baby face', as she rather accurately labels sentimentalism; a phallocentric discourse, in Perry's vocabulary.

21. Cf. Cash, *Later Years*, 302: 'Eliza had done as Sterne had urged: she had written unstintingly about her illness – "rhumatism", "fever", "fits", "Delirium". He copied some of her description for Anne James [Curtis, *Letters*, 388]. Certainly he felt much sympathy. But he had not found in her letters what he longed to see, a declaration of her love for him.' Cash convincingly demonstrates that only three of the last five entries were written immediately after July 27; of the remaining two, the one dated August 4 was probably written at the end of September and then predated; and the final entry, November 1, is Sterne's closure to the 'Journal'. It laments: '– And now Eliza! Let me talk to thee – But What can I say, What can I write' (188).

22. See Cash, *Later Years*, 284, n. 68.

23. Laurence Sterne, *A Sentimental Journey*, ed. Gardner D. Stout (Berkeley, CA: University of California Press, 1967), 237; hereafter cited in text.

24. Some attempt was made to identify the Marquesina with a real person, one Marchesa Fagnani, but, as Cash notes, 'the identification is doubtful' (*Later Years*, 235); see also Stout's discussion of the episode (*Journey*, 343–4). Any encounter in the pages of Sterne with a woman whose name is indicated by an *F* followed by three asterisks ought to raise a healthy suspicion.

25. In this chapter, as in 'The Translation', the emphasis is everywhere on the balanced, mirroring, dancelike actions of the couple; e.g. 'She begg'd I would try a single pair, which seemed to be the least – She held it open – my hand slipp'd into it at once – It will not do, said I, shaking my head a little – No, said she, doing the same thing'; and again: 'The beautiful Grisset look'd sometimes at the gloves, then side-ways to the window, then at the gloves – and then at me. I was not disposed to break silence

– I follow'd her example: so I look'd at the gloves, then to the window, then at the gloves, and then at her – and so on alternately' (168). As we shall see, the same alternation is created in the description of the meeting with Maria.

26. A fine recent essay making this point is Donald R. Wehrs, 'Sterne, Cervantes, Montaigne: Fideistic Skepticism and the Rhetoric of Desire', *CLS* 25 (1988): 127–51. Wehrs anticipates the conclusion of my own reading when he writes: 'Like Lacan, [Sterne] views desire as inherently unfulfillable; it projects a narrative course that is necessarily open-ended. However, Sterne suggests that the narrative of desire need not simply substitute, digressively, one metaphoric deferral of fulfillment for another. . . . Instead, his work is "digressive, and it is progressive too – and at the same time" [*TS*, 81] because the narrative of desire leads to a skeptical suspense that opens the way for a faith through which the partiality of every earthly fulfillment becomes tolerable' (141). And again: 'Sterne discerns the trace of divine benevolence behind the perpetual suspension of certainty and the open-ended narratives of desire such suspensions establish' (131). Wehrs's essay appeared simultaneously with my essay, 'Proust's Influence on Sterne: Remembrance of Things to Come', *MLN* 103 (1988): 1032–55, which coincides with his on many points.

27. See Stout, *Journey*, 205–6.

28. Cf. Joseph Chadwick, 'Infinite Jest: Interpretation in Sterne's *A Sentimental Journey*', *ECS* 12 (1978–79): 194: 'Yorick's rhetoric here mixes sentimental with sexual admiration. . . . we cannot define Yorick's interest in Maria as purely sentimental or purely sexual.' See also Arnold E. Davidson and Cathy N. Davidson, 'Yorick contra Hobbes: Comic Synthesis in Sterne's *A Sentimental Journey*', *Centennial Review* 21 (1977): 282–93, esp. the discussion of Maria, 288–90.

29. Cf. 'Journal to Eliza', 184, where Sterne talks of reposing 'all his Cares' and melting 'them *along with hers* in her sympathetic bosom'. The transfer of the nurturing function from Eliza in the 'Journal' to Yorick in the *Journey* is noteworthy.

30. This present reading of *A Sentimental Journey* is derived from my essay, 'Proust's Influence on Sterne'. To that essay I added a 'Post Postscript' in defense of my Christian troping, applicable, I suspect, for this essay as well. That I introduce a Christian vocabulary, just at that point where I should be introducing the radical new language that eschews phallocentrism, will surely puzzle and disappoint. That is, however, the lesson of the exercise, for the reading I am trying to achieve in both essays is one that does not drive forward to inevitable conclusions; does not read Sterne within our own institutional biases (we cannot escape ideology, but we might make some small efforts to discomfort monolithic academic bandwagons); and, in short, a reading that does not make Sterne 'one of us'. To my mind, any truly new mode of discourse (i.e. one not phallocentric) would have to free us all from 'presumption and obstinacy in opinion', leaving us happily and gratefully in 'doubt and suspense' – a *gracious* state of inquiry, if not a state of Grace. The disruptive appearance of this Christian vocabulary strives to do just that.

31. Cf. Charron, *Of Wisdome*, 62: 'there is no desire more naturall than to know the truth: we assay all the meanes we can to attaine unto it, but in the end all our endeavours come short; for truth is not an ordinary booty, or thing that will suffer it selfe to be gotten and handled, much lesse to be possessed by any humane Spirit. It lodgeth within the bosome of God. . . . Man knoweth not, understandeth not any thing aright, in purity and in truth as he ought.' Cf. Wehrs, 'Sterne, Cervantes, Montaigne', 131–2: 'From a Christian perspective, the desire for certitude is potentially heretical, an attempt to assume the attributes of God by abrogating a divinely ordained disjunction between this life, where we see only through a glass darkly, and the life to come, where we shall see face to face.'

32. Cf. Davidson and Davidson, 'Yorick contra Hobbes', 290: 'Sterne . . . knows that such sexual-religious rapture [as experienced with Maria] must be temporary and transient. Not surprisingly, Yorick's new meeting with a woman . . . devolves into an unconditional refutation of the hyperbolic sentiments elicited during his encounter with the mad Maria.' I would suggest, instead, that, rather than refutation, we have ratification of both the truth and the fugacity of moments of Grace.

PART THREE

Sterne and the Body

T ristram Shandy begins and ends with bodies (human and bovine) copulating, and is concerned throughout with bodies, laughing, crying, chasing each other round tables, giving birth, burning, touching, coughing, in pain, dying, wounded, healing, to an extent and in a degree of detail unusual outside anything but a medical text at this time, and almost unique in 'literary' texts after Swift. This did not pass without censorious notice among Sterne's contemporaries, and has become an object of especial critical attention in the twentieth century, beginning perhaps with Sigurd Burckhardt's focus on Sterne's obsession with the physical body, his insistence that we 'read Sterne far more . . . corporeally than has commonly been done', in his early 1960s article 'Tristram Shandy's Law of Gravity' (ELH 28 (1961): 70–88). Important subsequent contributions, reflecting our increasing recent concern with visions and representations of the body, include Louis Landa's study of 'The Shandean Homunculus' (in *Restoration and Eighteenth-Century Literature: Essays in Honour of Alan Dugald McKillop*, ed. Carroll Camden (Chicago, IL: University of Chicago Press, 1963), pp. 44–68); Valerie Grosvenor Myer's 'Tristram and the Animal Spirits' (in her collection *Laurence Sterne: Riddles and Mysteries*, 1984, pp. 99–112); Roy Porter's 'Against the Spleen' (in *Riddles and Mysteries*, pp. 84–98), and Judith Hawley's 'The Anatomy of Tristram Shandy' (1993). Mrs Shandy's pregnancy, Tristram's conception and birth, and Toby's wounded groin are among the most prominent themes for discussion. Donna Landry and Gerald Maclean's 'Of Forceps, Patents, and Paternity' (1989–90) takes a more than usually theorized approach to Tristram's birth in relation to seventeenth- and eighteenth-century obstetrics and midwifery, adopting new historicist and ultimately materialist feminist methods.

These essays are all marked by a combination of extensive investigation of eighteenth-century ideas about the body, with a strenuous critical
regard to the ways in which such ideas motivate and inform Sterne's
writing, as are the two chosen essays in this section. Knowing how the
inner thoughts and feelings of men and women might themselves be
known was always an eighteenth-century concern. The satirist Alexander
Pope suggested that the 'ruling passion' was the key. Sterne speculates
that, if only Momus's glass – a notional pane of transparent crystal –
could have been fixed in the human breast, the observer need only have
'taken a chair softly . . . and look'd in'. Sadly, however, our minds 'shine
not through the body, but are wrapt up here in a dark covering of uncrystalized flesh and blood'. (Hence, Sterne has to resort to his own, or Swift's,
version of the ruling passion, the 'hobby horse'.) That uncrystallized flesh
always obstructs our sight, and the implications and results of those
obstructions in Sterne's novel are the theme of the first of the two eloquent essays here, by Juliet McMaster. The body always gets in the
way. Consciousness of physicality – for characters, such as Tristram or
Phutatorius, and for readers – is always unavoidable. The mind and body
are as intimately connected as a jerkin and its lining. To provide an
account of the 'history of what passes in Phutatorius's mind' is also, as
McMaster points out, to provide a narrative of 'the history of what passes
in his body too'. The rhetoric of the novel constantly reminds us of the
presence of the body: 'there seems to be scarcely a word or an image that
can be sustained at a purely intellectual level: everything tends eventually towards a bodily and sexual inference.' Yet Sterne's rhetoric is not
merely (for the eighteenth century, those worst of things) verbal wit
or prurience, but an account of anatomy and bodily function, and of
the operations of the mind, which has its foundations in seventeenth-
and eighteenth-century thinking, in Burton, Locke and contemporary
medicine, anatomy, pathology and obstetrics.

My second chosen piece is a brief section on Sterne from an essay
by Carol Houlihan Flynn (whose study of the eighteenth-century body
takes a wider compass in her *The Body in Swift and Defoe* (Cambridge:
Cambridge University Press, 1990)). Flynn's main concern, similarly, is
'the dilemma of the spirit being contained by matter that will inevitably
betray'. Here however there is a rather different emphasis. Flynn finds
that 'eighteenth-century novels', and in this essay particularly the novels
of Smollett and Sterne, are 'scrambled, jogging, rocking narratives that
resist interiority while refusing to end'. There are many possible sources
for this generic characteristic, including the pilgrimage, the picaresque
and the romance quest, but Flynn here adumbrates the principle of motion
in the eighteenth-century novel as antidote to that much discussed

eighteenth-century (and twenty-first century) condition, the spleen. In eighteenth-century treatises on the spleen as disease, by such authors as Cheyne, Fuller, Smyth and Ramazini, she finds exercise regularly endorsed as a cure: 'to move the animal spirits, to open up the great sensorium, one must move the body itself'. The important principle is motion, not necessarily exercise; for the eighteenth-century lady or gentleman, the servant could do the hard work. Motion imparted by the agency of another, of a 'body-servant', will be effective against the spleen, without the unfortunate physical side effects of the sweat of one's own brow. Such motion may be imparted by the purposeless (but erotic) oscil-lations of a swing, much recommended by the physicians (and painted by Fragonard), by the trotting of a hobbyhorse, or by the rocking of a coach, just one manifestation in *A Sentimental Journey* of Yorick's 'violent propensity for motion' in fleeing death. Writing itself is motion; more than that, for Smollett and for Sterne, consumptives both, writing is not merely motion but exercise, squirts and jerks not only of ink but also (Flynn suggests) of blood. Their narrative strategies 'are designed to frustrate the logical end of their discourse, fictional closure that repres-ents physical death'. Flynn's extraordinary and compellingly written essay reveals whole new dimensions to the poetics, the erotics and the patho-logies of Sterne's text.

CHAPTER FIVE

'"Uncrystalized Flesh and Blood": The Body in *Tristram Shandy*'*

JULIET MCMASTER

Our minds shine not through the body, we hear in *Tristram Shandy*, 'but are wrapt up here in a dark covering of uncrystalized flesh and blood' (I, 23, 75).[1] It is one of the more melancholy statements in this enduringly sad and immortally funny book. In the debate among eighteenth-century novelists on the relation of the body to character, Sterne differs from his contemporaries, who tend to show a fortunate consonance between the two. We hear of Sophia Western, for instance, after an elaborate description of her appearance, 'Such was the outside of Sophia; nor was this beautiful frame disgraced by an inhabitant unworthy of it. Her mind was every way equal to her person' (IV. II: 155–6).[2] And at the climax of Fielding's novel, Jones leads her to a mirror in order to show her the physical and moral beauty that is to be the 'pledge' of his fidelity: 'Behold it there, in that lovely figure, in that face, that shape, those eyes, that mind which shines through those eyes' (XVIII. XII: 865–6). For Fielding, the mind does shine through the body. Smollett and Richardson, too, routinely provide detailed physiognomical descriptions of their personnel, and appearance is always relevant in a judgement of their characters. The outward and visible aspect of Sir Charles Grandison perfectly matches his inward and spiritual grace,[3] and this harmony has much to do with the fact that the novel in which he appears is a comedy, with a fortunate outcome. Lovelace, on the other hand, has a graceful exterior which belies his moral corruption, and it

---

* Reprinted from *Eighteenth-Century Fiction*, 2 (1990), 197–214

is partly this vitiation of nature's true language of physiognomy which makes *Clarissa* a tragedy. A character's bodily appearance for Richardson is in any case relevant and expressive; and therefore describing it is a useful and much exploited means of characterization.

But since the body in *Tristram Shandy* is viewed as a dark covering of uncrystalized flesh rather than as a lucid medium, we get little in the way of vivid physical description of faces, figures, and so forth. Apart from the Hogarthian figure of Dr Slop,[4] the characters are seldom visually realized. Sterne and Tristram go another way to work, and decide to do the business of characterization through defining their characters' hobby-horses instead (I. XXIII: 77).

This does not mean, however, that the body is unimportant. Far from it. 'Humour, after all,' says Virginia Woolf, 'is closely bound up with a sense of the body.'[5] *Tristram Shandy* certainly has both humour and a sense of the body, and in the highest degree. The book begins *ab ovo*, and with the homunculus; and Tristram reminds us that the homunculus 'consists, as we do, of skin, hair, fat, flesh, veins, arteries, ligaments, nerves, cartilages, bones, marrow, brains, glands, genitals, humours, and articulations' (I. II: 5). Already in the second chapter the emphasis is anatomical. And by the time we get to Ernulphus's curse, we encounter a zestful attempt at exhaustiveness on physiological matters that looks forward to Monique Wittig's liturgies in *The Lesbian Body*:

'May he be cursed inwardly and outwardly. – May he be cursed in the hair of his head. – May he be cursed in his brains, and in his vertex,' (that is a sad curse, quoth my father) 'in his temples, in his forehead, in his ears, in his eyebrows, in his cheeks, in his jaw-bones, in his nostrils, in his foreteeth and grinders, in his lips, in his throat, in his shoulders, in his wrists, in his arms, in his hands, in his fingers.

May he be damn'd in his mouth, in his breast, . . . and in his groin,' (God in heaven forbid, quoth my uncle *Toby*) – 'in his thighs, in his genitals,' (my father shook his head) 'and in his hips, and in his knees, his legs, and feet, and toe-nails' (III. XI: 177)

As the inserted commentary suggests, the different characters are identified by their allegiance to particular parts of the body: Walter Shandy is loyal to the brain and mental operations, and disapproves of the genitals; Uncle Toby responds to the groin (which has equally had a share in developing his character). Trim might well have his own particular sensibilities about knees, Mrs Shandy about ears, Tristram about noses, Dr Slop about fingers and thumbs. The passage not only captures the body and its parts, from the hair of the head to the very toenails, but hooks in the novel's characters along the way.

Mind and body – with the indissoluble links between them, and their simultaneously tragic and comic discontinuity – are surely the major overarching subject of *Tristram Shandy*. The body is not taken for granted, as it may be for pages or chapters together in some fiction. It is

Mind and body . . . are surely the major overarching subject of *Tristram Shandy*

insistently *there*, even if only as an embarrassing 'sort of battered kettle at the heel' (in Yeats's phrase), for all the characters, and in our conception of them. Even though they are not visually realized for us through their physical appearance, we are constantly reminded that they exist in the body, that it determines their responses and limits or enables their actions. They think about it, they have theories about it, they are embarrassed or elated by it, they express themselves through it by their gestures and facial expressions, they live in a constant relation with it, at peace or at war. And their bodies impinge on other bodies. Tristram tells us that the conjunction of the bodies of his parents is to affect their son Tristram permanently, and determine the 'formation and temperature of his body, perhaps his genius and the very cast of his mind' (I. I: 4).

In the preface to *Joseph Andrews* Fielding produced his famous poetics of comedy, as Aristotle had produced the *Poetics* of tragedy. The Ridiculous, he tells us, arises from the exposure of affectation, which strikes the reader with the comic emotions of 'surprise and pleasure' (to balance Aristotle's pity and terror), and thereby purges away 'spleen, melancholy, and ill affections'. *Tristram Shandy* is likewise written 'against the spleen'[6] – and, characteristically, Tristram supplies full medical terminology for the operation of the catharsis of laughter: 'in order, by a more frequent and a more convulsive elevation and depression of the diaphragm, and the succussations of the intercostal and abdominal muscles in laughter, to drive the *gall* and other *bitter juices* from the gall bladder, liver and sweet-bread of his majesty's subjects, with all the other inimicitious passions which belong to them, down into their duodenums' (IV. XXII: 301–2). But Sterne, unlike Fielding, is not interested in the exposure of affectation. If he had written his own poetics of comedy, I suspect, he would have focused on the discontinuity of mind and body as the most fertile source of laughter.

Take the hot chestnut episode, for instance. The idea of a hot chestnut in someone's breeches is amusing, of course, in itself, and apt to prompt a guffaw, like other jokes that overthrow sexual dignity. But this is only the beginning of Sterne's joke. His most characteristic humour lies in his elaboration of the situation. What is crucial to the comedy is that Phutatorius does not know about the fall of the hot chestnut: he is aware of the physical sensation, but not of its cause:

The genial warmth which the chesnut imparted, was not undelectable for the first twenty or five and twenty seconds, – and did no more than gently solicit *Phutatorius's* attention towards the part: – But the heat gradually increasing, and in a few seconds more getting beyond the point of all sober pleasure, and then advancing with all speed into the regions of pain, – the soul of *Phutatorius*, together with all his ideas, his thoughts, his attention, his imagination, judgment, resolution, deliberation, ratiocination, memory, fancy, with ten batallions of animal spirits, all tumultuously crouded down, through different defiles and circuits, to the place in danger, leaving all his upper regions, as you may imagine, as empty as my purse.

With the best intelligence which all these messengers could bring him back, *Phutatorius* was not able to dive into the secret of what was going forwards below, nor could he make any kind of conjecture, what the devil was the matter with it. (IV. xxvii: 321)

Such a passage affords us – as Locke's *Essay* and *Tristram Shandy* do – 'a history . . . of what passes in a man's own mind' (II. ii: 85); and the military manoeuvres of all the forces of Phutatorius's brain – his ratiocination, fancy, and the battalions of his animal spirits – have their keen narrative interest. But the history of what passes in his mind is the history of what passes in his body too, for the faculties of the mind are not confined, it seems, to the cerebral cavity, but may desert their posts. At this moment this particular army is in disarray, its personnel scattered and stumbling over one another like all the king's horses and all the king's men in *Alice*, its messengers scurrying to the wrong places, with the wrong information. The history is prolonged, so that we may savour the few seconds while Phutatorius's senses tell him of the burning heat in his crotch, while his brain cannot divine 'what the devil was the matter with it'. Phutatorius decides in his extremity to bear the pain like a stoic: the mind will vanquish the body. But a third force, his imagination, enters the battle, suggesting the idea that the pain is produced by the bite of some detested reptile. . . . Flesh and blood can bear no more, and they overthrow the command of the mind.

Once Phutatorius has sprung to his feet, exploded with his memorable expletive 'Zounds!' and flung out the chestnut, that particular phase of the joke is over. But Sterne has surrounded the incident with further examples of the comic discontinuity of physical sensation and mental ratiocination. The other clerics at the visitation dinner *hear* Phutatorius's exclamation and *see* him spring to his feet, and like Phutatorius himself they at once set their minds to interpreting these physical manifestations. And again we follow a series of little histories of what passes in each man's mind. Each has a finely developed theory of the cause of their colleague's exclamation, and all assume that his 'mind was intent upon the subject of debate'; yet the

the mind is vanquished by the body; and from the victory arises laughter

debate is 'never once in any one domicile of *Phutatorius's* brain – but the true cause of his exclamation lay at least a yard below' (IV. xxvii: 319). As so often in *Tristram Shandy*, the mind is vanquished by the body; and from the victory arises laughter.

Meanwhile, further history is in the making, the history of what passes in yet another mind, the reader's. The first-time reader, who encounters that potent 'ZOUNDS!——' on the page, knows the cause of it no more than the other characters, or Phutatorius himself; and must follow the mistaken hypotheses of Yorick and company, digest the narrator's aphorism, 'How finely we argue upon mistaken facts!' and pick his or her own path towards interpretation among Tristram's delicate circumlocutions. Somewhere along the route the reader is apt to collapse into a state of helpless laughter. *Tristram Shandy* engages the body as well as the mind of its readers, too.[7]

Walter Shandy has much ado to keep his mind and his body on the same track with one another. There is a moment at which Toby has exasperated him by interrupting an explanation of obstetrical technique that deeply interests him. The needful gesture to restore the discourse to the direction Walter prefers is to lift his wig and wipe the sweat from his head with his handkerchief. Walter is a rhetorician: he cares about appropriate gestures, and wants to perform them well. But he has made the mistake of lifting his wig with the same hand that is needed to pull his handkerchief from his pocket. As he has to reach across his own body, awkwardly groping in the deep right pocket with his left hand, his ideas pile up and bump into one another for want of timely articulation. Sterne dwells on this tableau for several chapters, while Walter's face becomes suffused, Toby demonstrates his charity and his gentle responses, and Tristram can philosophize that 'the circumstances with which every thing in this world is begirt, give every thing in this world its size and shape' (III. ii: 158). We are invited to contemplate the comic picture of Walter in his unlovely pose, while the flow of ideas that he is concerned to maintain is halted and dispersed. It is at this point that Tristram introduces another memorable aphorism:

A man's body and his mind, with the utmost reverence to both I speak it, are exactly like a jerkin, and a jerkin's lining; – rumple the one – you rumple the other. (III. IV: 160)

Mind and body are intimately interconnected, but likewise discontinuous; and from the connection and discontinuity arise the intricacies of the human condition.

Sterne, through Tristram, is always seeking the right metaphor for the relation of mind and body, one that will convey not simple equivalence, but the discontinuities and contiguities of flesh and spirit. Jacket and lining, man and clothing (V. VII: 361), rider and hobby-horse: he wants to suggest the intimate rub and relation, while still preserving the separate identities and antitheses. The shining mind and the dark covering of 'uncrystallized flesh' suggest the loneliness and isolation of the one without the other. The mind has its heady intellectual independence, its untrammelled autonomy; and yet it must operate through flesh: it is trapped, or realized (depending on your point of view at the time) through incarnation. *Tristram Shandy* is a comic prose epic version of Donne's 'The Ecstasy,' and follows a similar progress from the detached intellect to the body:

> But O alas, so long, so far
>   Our bodies why do we forbear?
> They are ours, though they are not we. We are
>   The intelligences, they the sphere.

In so far as *Tristram Shandy* is about the relation of mind to body, the animal spirits, which (according to the quaint and outmoded system that Walter believes in) mediate between the two, almost gain the status of characters in their own right.[8] In *The Anatomy of Melancholy* Burton refers to them as 'the instrument of the soul';[9] Tillyard picturesquely characterizes them as 'the executive agents of the brain'.[10] The animal spirits are introduced in the first chapters as the intended escorts of the homunculus, who were 'scattered and dispersed' by Mrs Shandy's unseasonable question at the moment of Tristram's begetting; and at that phase of the book they are beings subordinate in status only to Tristram himself and his parents:

You have all, I dare say, heard of the animal spirits. . . . Well, you may take my word, that nine parts in ten of a man's sense or his nonsense, his successes and miscarriages in this world depend upon their motions and activity, and the different tracks and trains you put them into, so that when they are once set a-going, whether right or wrong, 'tis not a halfpenny matter, – away they go cluttering like hey-go-mad; and by treading the same steps over and over again, they presently make a road of it, as plain and as smooth as a garden-walk, which, when they are once used to, the Devil himself sometimes shall not be able to drive them off it. (l. i: 4–5)

The passage is a parody, surely, of the description in *Paradise Lost* of the beaten track that Satan establishes between hell and earth:

> Sin and Death amain
> Following his track, such was the will of Heav'n,
> Pav'd after him a broad and beat'n way
> Over the dark Abyss. . . .
>   . . . by which the Spirits perverse
> With easie intercourse pass to and fro
> To tempt or punish mortals. (lines 1024–32)

Tristram is setting up his own comic microcosm, in which the animal spirits make their own road for easy travel between mind and body, sometimes even displacing the Devil himself. The adjective 'animal' serves his purposes well, since it originally derives from *anima*, the soul, but has taken its own evolutionary path towards the beast in us. Tristram's microcosm is a version of his father's: Walter Shandy has strong principles against the movement of the rural population towards London, for according to Walter's world view the movement of the executive agents of the brain should be outward to govern the body; the contrary motion would suggest that the body governs the brain. 'He would run it down into a perfect allegory, by maintaining it was identically the same in the body national as in the body natural, where blood and spirits were driven up into the head faster than they could find their ways down; – a stoppage of circulation must ensue, which was death in both cases' (I. XVIII: 46).

Much has been made of the influence of Locke's *Essay Concerning Human Understanding* as an influence on *Tristram Shandy*; and Sterne himself gives authority for the influence by his respectful reference to the *Essay* as a history of what passes in a man's mind (II. II: 85).[11] But a more congenial model for his novel was *The Anatomy of Melancholy*. The affinities between Sterne's work and Burton's go beyond their shared status as Menippean satires,[12] and beyond the many shameless borrowings, to a kinship in narrative tone, authorial world view, subject matter, and even structure. Tristram, like Burton's persona 'Democritus Junior', is a laughing philosopher, but one humiliatingly prone to the advances of age, mutability, and death. Born in the enlightened eighteenth century, Tristram nevertheless harks back, like his father, to the world picture of the seventeenth century and earlier, as collected from musty authors over twenty centuries, and chaotically rehashed by an Oxford scholar-pedant who gets all his experience and all his excitement from reading. Walter Shandy, as one of Sterne's eighteenth-century critics noted, has 'all the stains and mouldiness of the last century about him'.[13] The four humours, and the vision of the universe they belong to, were outdated by the eighteenth century, and physicians and scientists were busy constructing a new system; but for Walter and Tristram Shandy the balance of the humours in the body still determines temperament: Toby's character is 'of a peaceful, placid nature', because there is 'no jarring element in it, – all was mix'd up so kindly within him' (II. XII: 113); whereas Walter is feisty and aggressive, because of his choler, and 'subacid humour' (II. XII: 113). Mind and body are bound up together. It comes naturally to Tristram to say 'Now, I (being very thin) think differently' (VII. XIII: 493). Tristram's book, like Burton's, is more than a history of what passes in a man's mind: it is an Anatomy, a history of what passes in his body too, because the two cannot be separated. 'The soul and body are joint-sharers in every thing they get: A man cannot dress, but his ideas get cloath'd at the same time' (IX. XIV: 616). Both books are about physio-logy and psychology, and at the same time. Both are the Life *and* the Opinions of their narrators.

One could elaborate the analogy. For instance, Burton's grand climax is his Third Partition on Love-Melancholy, while the declared goal of Tristram's narrative, the 'choicest morsel' he advertises, is the account of Toby's amours. Both authors provide a treatment of love that purports to be comprehensive and exhaustive, 'one of the most compleat systems, both of the elementary and practical part of love and love-making, that ever was addressed to the world' (VI. XXXVI: 466). These two final sections contain much of the same lore about the kinds, causes, examples, and cures of love, with vivid subsections on such matters as the power of the eye in creating love, and the uses of camphor and other refrigerants in allaying lust. (Walter secretly has a pair of Toby's breeches lined with camphorated cerecloth, a recipe gleaned from Burton, which '*membrum flaccidum reddit*'! [VI. XXXVI: 468]). Burton produces an astonishing array of examples of love melancholy, drawn indiscriminately from history, myth, and literature; and Tristram likewise collects for his last book a whole set of sexual relationships, including not only Toby and the widow Wadman and the 'beds of justice' of Walter and Mrs Shandy, but also the amours of Trim and Bridget, Trim and the Beguine, Tom and the sausage-maker's widow, Tristram and Jenny, Obadiah and the maid, and the Shandy bull and cow. Love and sexuality turn out in both books to be the subjects best fitted for dramatizing the intricate interrelation of mind and body.

Locke's *Essay Concerning Human Understanding*, the history of what passes in a man's mind, and Burton's *Anatomy of Melancholy*, which deals largely with what passes in his body, can in fact be seen as dual sources for *Tristram Shandy*, the textbooks on the two great territories and the relation between them that Sterne undertakes to explore. They are the jerkin, and the jerkin's lining – with the utmost reverence to both I speak it.

It is characteristic of Tristram that he has a highly physical conception of mental operations. He explains the relation of wit and judgement by likening them to the knobs on the back of a chair. Toby received his modesty, a moral attribute, from a blow from a stone. Walter makes an opinion his own as a man takes possession of an apple, by mixing up the sweat of his brow and the exudations of his brain with the object, so that it becomes mingled with himself, and therefore his own property (III. xxxiv: 223). Minds are envisaged as physical spaces, with ideas bumping around in them. Susannah's memory is a 'leaky vessel', spilling precious syllables (IV. xiv: 287). Dr Slop's mind seems to be a sea navigated by thoughts which are not always well under way:

But here, you must distinguish – the thought floated only in Dr. Slop's mind, without sail or ballast to it, as a simple proposition; millions of which, as your worship knows, are every day swimming quietly in the middle of the thin juice of a man's understanding, without being carried backwards or forwards, till some little gusts of passion or interest drive them to one side. (III. ix: 167)

'REASON is, half of it, SENSE,' argues Tristram. And he shows himself adept at translating mental processes into terms that can be physically apprehended. It is of a piece with the Shandy mentality that Walter has decided that the soul must have its local habitation in the body. He fixes on the cerebellum as the place, for the empirical reason that his son Bobby, who as the first-born 'made way for the capacity of his younger brothers' by taking the brunt of the pressure during birth on his own cerebellum, turned out to be 'a lad of wonderful slow parts' (II. xix: 151, 153). For all Walter's prowess as a speculative philosopher, his theories have their severe epistemological limitations. He likes to have empirical evidence for his theories, but a single instance will do for proof. So his son's slow parts serve to prove the location of the soul in the cerebellum; his Aunt Dinah's indiscretion with the coachman is the indispensable basis for his theory of names and his conviction of the raging concupiscence of the whole female species; and his grandmother's inflated jointure is the foundation of his grand theory of noses.

The mind responds, of course, to the body's crises. One aspect of the relation between them that reaches the surface of Tristram's narrative is the influence of health and disease on character and on literary composition. Here Tristram writes while seasick, with a developed articu-lateness about what is passing in his own brain:

what a brain! – upside down! – hey dey! the cells are broke loose one into another, and the blood, and the lymph, and the nervous juices, with the fix'd and volatile salts, are all jumbled into one mass – good g – ! every thing turns round in it like a thousand whirlpools – I'd give a shilling to know if I shan't write the clearer for it. (VII. ii: 481)

Tristram and his father monitor their own health and maladies with the self-consciousness of hypochondriacs. The vision of character compre-hends not only the vision of bodies and minds in good working order, but of bodies subject to all the thousand natural shocks that flesh is heir to. Toby with his unhealed wound, poring over his books, is exhorted to fly knowledge as from a serpent: 'Alas! 'twill exasperate thy symptoms – check thy perspirations, – evaporate thy spirits, – waste thy animal strength, – dry up thy radical moisture, – bring thee into a costive habit of body, impair thy health, – and hasten all the infirmities of thy old age' (II. iii: 90). Walter Shandy has his developed theory of 'the whole secret of health' as 'depending on the due contention for mastery betwixt the radical heat and radical moisture' (V. xxxiii: 394). The book is steeped in medical lore:[14] not just the old-fashioned Burtonian adumbration of the operation of the humours, but up-to-date theories on genetics,[15] obstetrics,[16] pathology, and diet. A fictional doctor, Dr Slop, is a pro-minent character, and ready at the drop of a hat to expatiate on the mysteries of his trade. His historical original, Dr Richard Burton, with his book on obstetrics, is often invoked. Another obstetrician, the famous Sir Richard Manningham, is knowledgeably referred to, and another doctor, Richard Mead, appears as the suggestively named Dr Kunastrokius (I. vii: 13). Dr John Smith's theory on the benefits of an alcohol-free diet and a regimen of drinking water receives satirical attention.[17] Various diseases – Tristram's 'vile cough', the scullion's dropsy, the flux fever in the trenches – and various treatments and specifics – blood-letting, the cataplasm, the lint and basilicon that Mrs Shandy calls for after the accident with the window-sash[18] – all have their importance in the narrative, and keep before us the body as a fragile entity, vulnerable, like the mind that inhabits it, to attack, accident, and disease.

The law that pertains among all these anatomically and medically conceived bodies is what Sigurd Burckhardt has described as the law of gravity. 'A messy fatality attends the falling bodies of the novel, the things that stupidly plummet: they always land on the genitals. Rocks, sash windows, chestnuts do far more damage than bullets'.[19] In the same way, and with the same comic force, the faculties of the body are subject

to a gravitational pull downwards. Soul, mind, and brain have aspirations towards upward mobility, but are doomed to bathos. 'Imagination,
judgement, resolution, deliberation, ratiocination' all tumultuously crowd
down; and while the Walters, Tristrams, and Phutatoriuses of the Shandy
world would take off, if they could, on heady flights above the cerebellum,
their actual course usually takes them 'at least a yard below'. The journey
taken by Phutatorius's various mental faculties is in this respect typical.
Language has the same tendency. Tristram can swear until he is blue
in the face that by 'nose' he means nothing but 'the external organ of
smelling' (III. xxxiii: 221), but the more he protests the more he suggests
something at least a yard below. And so with all the multiple and continuous double entendres in the novel; there seems to be scarcely a word
or an image that can be sustained at a purely intellectual level: everything
tends eventually towards a bodily and sexual inference. Likewise every
bodily excrescence – fingers, thumbs, whiskers, noses, ears – as well as
sausages, cannons, and so on, refers eventually to the penis; and every
bodily orifice, indeed every crevice, pond, ditch, pocket, placket, slit, refers
eventually to the pudenda. Literally every 'thing' does. The soul subsides
to the mind, the mind to the body, the body to its lowest 'end'.

The very characters, as identified by their names, grow out of a syn-
ecdoche, the low part standing for the whole. 'Toby' is slang for the
buttocks,[20] and the name calls attention to Uncle Toby's function as the
down-to-earth and practical Shandy brother, the body to Walter's brain.[21]
'Tristram', the 'child of . . . interruption', recalls the *triste* of Aristotle's
quoted dictum, *'omne animal post coitum est triste'* (V. xxxvi: 397).[22]
'Jenny' is the name for the female of the species, especially of donkeys
or (as Tristram prefers to call them) asses. That is, Tristram's 'dear, dear
Jenny' is the female ass.

And hereby hangs a tail. One of the most vivid incidents in St
Jerome's life of St Hilarion shows the sainted ascetic apostrophizing his
body, which has been troubling him during puberty with some lascivi-
ous visions. ' "You ass," he said to his body, "I'll see that you don't kick
against the goad; I'll fill you not with barley, but with chaff; I shall wear
you out with hunger and thirst." '[23] Hilarion's conceit of the lustful body
as ass reaches *Tristram Shandy* (via *The Anatomy of Melancholy*) through
Walter. He deliberately irritates Toby by 'the perverse use my father was
always making of an expression of *Hilarion* the hermit; who, in speaking
of his abstinence, his watchings, flagellations, and other instrumental
parts of his religion – would say – tho' with more facetiousness than
became an hermit – That they were the means he used, to make his *ass*
(meaning his body) leave off kicking' (VIII. xxxi: 583–4). Walter asks
the smitten Toby, 'How goes it with your ASSE?' To which Toby, who is

thinking of the blister on his nethermost part, serenely replies 'My A[rs]e . . . is much better' (VIII. XXXI: 583–5). This explanation of the ass as the body (particularly the lowest end of it) comes late in the novel; but it accounts for the prominence of all those horses, hobby-horses, asses, mules, donkeys, jackasses, and jennys that cavort their quadruped way through *Tristram Shandy*:[24] Yorick's Rosinante, Tristram's mule that he rides through France when he is in flight from death, and Don Diego's mule, which he addresses alternately with his beloved Julia, in Slawkenbergius's Tale. The Abbess of Andoüillets neatly reverses the story of St Hilarion by exhorting her mules to '*bou-ger*' and '*fou-ter*', words which she has heard 'will force any horse, or ass, or mule, to go up a hill' (VII. XXIV: 508). Tristram holds a conversation with an ass in an entrance-way in Lyons: 'with an ass,' he claims, 'I can commune forever' (VII. XXXII: 523). Sterne's characters, that is to say, are in constant communion with the flesh. Tristram implores his reader not to confuse *his* hobby-horse with Walter's ass (VIII. XXXI: 584), but the request is about as disingenuous as the claim that a nose means a nose and nothing else. The relation of the rider to his hobby-horse, carefully explained, is yet another metaphor for the mind's relation to the body; and both sink inevitably towards the unmentionable:

A man and his HOBBY-HORSE, tho' I cannot say that they act and re-act exactly after the same manner in which the soul and body do upon each another: Yet doubtless there is a communication between them of some kind . . . by means of the heated parts of the rider, which come immediately into contact with the back of the HOBBY-HORSE. – By long journies and much friction, it so happens that the body of the rider is at length fill'd as full of HOBBY-HORSICAL matter as it can hold. (I. XXIV: 77)

All these developed relations between characters and animals are intended to remind us again of the varied relations between mind and body. The ass and its variants are cherished, scourged, goaded, bitted, secreted, and paraded. Mind and body, like Walter's ideas and his conduct, are at 'perpetual handicuffs'. Tristram, like the animal spirits, is constantly travelling between them, 'cluttering like hey-go-mad . . . treading the same steps over and over again'. The focus of his interest is that hiatus and connection between the rider's seat and the horse's back, where all the friction is happening. And Tristram's own hobby-horse, 'the sporting little filly-folly which carries you out for the present hour' (VIII. XXXI: 584), with its 'just balance betwixt wisdom and folly' (IX. XII: 614), is *Tristram Shandy* itself, the lasting and visible 'Life' and 'Opinions', words in process of taking on physical being as marks in oil and lamp-black on paper sheets folded and collected in signatures.

An area of the body in which Sterne specializes – the reader will not be surprised to hear – is the genitals. No other novelist had paid such close attention to the biological differences between male and female bodies, or incorporated so outrageously incidents that pertain to the intimate bodily functions of conjugal sexuality, generation, gestation, and childbirth. As a novel by one man, purporting to be the autobiography of another, who writes mainly about still other men – his father, his uncle, and his uncle's manservant – *Tristram Shandy* deals largely with male anxieties, usually sexual ones. But Sterne is alert, too, to the women's side of the picture, and has written a novel more sensitive to women's issues than many of its predominantly male critics have suggested.[25]

Walter Shandy is presented, and judged, as an example not only of the intellect gone berserk, the *philosophus gloriosus* who according to Frye is the proper subject of Menippean satire,[26] but of the mad misogynist. He blames women for most of the evil in the world; and his typical endeavour in his elaborated theories is to marginalize women, and if possible to make them redundant. As Louis Landa has shown,[27] Walter espouses the male side in the scientific debate on the origin of individual life: he believes that the 'bud' of life that becomes the foetus is located in the homunculus of the *semen Marium*, rather than in the mother's egg (which according to this theory provides only a convenient and disposable 'nidus' for the homunculus). He takes delight in the speculation '*That the mother is not of kin to her child*' (IV. XXIX: 328), and argues '*she is not the principal agent*' (V. XXXI: 391) in procreation. Because of his theory that pressure on the cerebellum during labour is dangerous to the intellect of his son, he tries to persuade his wife to undergo delivery by Caesarean – an operation always fatal in the eighteenth century:[28] he is willing to have his wife cracked open like a nutshell for the safer delivery of his son. He bitterly resents the visible bonding of women on the great occasion of childbirth: 'From the very moment the mistress of the house is brought to bed,' he complains, 'every female in it, from my lady's gentlewoman down to the cinder-wench, becomes an inch taller for it; and give themselves more airs upon that single inch, than all their other inches put together' (II. XII: 284).

But Sterne allows us glimpses also of the woman's angle. Against Walter's espousal of the homunculus theory he balances the ovist's view – for Tristram is proud of tracing his history *ab ovo*! Mrs Shandy turns 'pale as ashes' at Walter's proposing a Caesarean, and will have no part of it. She resists his 'man of science', Dr Slop, who as a Roman Catholic would be ready in a crisis to save the child's life at the expense of the mother's (presumably by Caesarean). She is fighting for control of her body, and, limited as her resources are, she manages to bring it about 'that both sides sung *Te Deum*' (I. XVIII: 48). She is a survivor.

It is no news that Walter is a misogynist. But the source of his misogyny is curious, and intricately developed. He is moved less by dislike of women than by envy. Sex disgusts and humiliates him, partly because he is not very good at it, but also because it 'couples and equals wise men with fools' (IX. XXXIII: 645). As a wise man himself (he thinks), he longs to do the whole job of procreation by himself. His model for love is *rational* [love] . . . without mother – where *Venus* had nothing to do' (VIII. XXXIII: 587). Figuratively at least, he can accomplish his fantasy of male conception: When his wife is gestating Tristram, Walter gets on with a pregnancy of his own:

It is the nature of an hypothesis, once a man has conceived it, that it assimilates every thing to itself as proper nourishment; and, from the first moment of your begetting it, it generally grows stronger by every thing you see, hear, read, or understand. This is of great use.

When my father was gone with this about a month . . . (II. XIX: 151)

This is the offspring that Walter most favours, one that is conceived and gestated, as well as begotten, by the male

This is the offspring that Walter most favours, one that is conceived and gestated, as well as begotten, by the male. This foetus/hypothesis comes to term at the same time as his wife's pregnancy, and Sterne sustains the metaphor up to the unfortunate delivery, which parallels Tristram's: Walter is in process of delivering his hypothesis to Toby when 'a devil of a rap at the door . . . crushed the head of as notable and curious a dissertation as ever was engendered in the womb of speculation' (II. VII: 102–3). The arrival of Dr Slop crushes the head of Walter's hypothetical foetus as it crushes the nose of his wife's biological one.

A mate that Walter prefers to Mrs Shandy is the auxiliary verb: with Mrs Shandy he succeeds, with difficulty, in producing only two offspring; but with the auxiliary verb he can 'make every idea engender millions' (V. XLII: 405). By 'conjugating' words instead of women, he announces triumphantly, 'every word, *Yorick*, by this means, you see, is converted into a thesis or an hypothesis; – every thesis and hypothesis have an offspring of propositions' (VI. II: 409). In language he can achieve what he really wants to do: engendering millions without the trouble of a wife.

Walter Shandy is not the only male who envisages childbirth as a masculine affair. Tristram frequently uses a generative metaphor for the creative process; and even Yorick says of a sermon, 'I was delivered of it at the wrong end of me – it came from my head instead of my heart' (IV. XXVI: 317). And indeed their various hobby-horses function for all the men as masturbation, a substitute for lovemaking ('the body of the rider is at length fill'd as full of HOBBY-HORSICAL matter as it can hold'), and ultimately for women. Toby posts down to his model warfare on the bowling green like a lover to his 'belov'd mistress' (II. v: 98): for him fortification is an acceptable substitute for fornication.[29]

The recurring motif of the male longing to take over female biological functions and so to dispense with the women is of course part of Sterne's comedy: one of the latent jokes of the novel is that for all the anxiety about sexual potency that is endemic among the males, for all their fantasies about bigger, better, and more indestructible sexual equipment, they seem really to want to have less and less to do with it.

Sex in the head, that tantalizing entity that D. H. Lawrence so disapproved of, will do as well as sex in the body, for Walter. And it is Sterne's favourite and recurring joke, one further intricacy of the mind–body relation that he is constantly exploring. We have seen that the rider/hobby-horse relation is an analogy for the mind/body one. And just as Walter as male is committed to a mad enterprise to do without women, so Walter as mind, committed to cerebral activity, is also madly trying to dispense with the body. For Walter both woman and body are the 'ass', a beast deserving mainly of kicking, but grudgingly accepted as useful when you cannot get along without it.

Dennis W. Allen, who has written on 'Sexuality/Textuality in *Tristram Shandy*', refers in passing to 'the overall misogyny of the novel'.[30] But though Sterne gives ample coverage to Walter's misogyny, he by no means endorses it.[31] He is not anti-woman, any more than he is anti-body. On the contrary, he not only laughs at Walter and satirizes him, but he inflicts on him the punishment that fits the crime: the Shandys are a dying race.

The body, though it does not directly figure forth the mind, is a concern consumingly and continuously interesting to the narrator and the characters of *Tristram Shandy*. To Walter, it is exasperating and humiliating, an encumbrance he would rather be without; and he exists in a state of war with his own and other people's. Toby, on the contrary, is at peace with his body: he is so little self-conscious about it that he thinks the widow Wadman is talking about geography and not anatomy when she asks him where he received his wound; and his face and limbs settle themselves into attitudes naturally and eloquently expressive. For Tristram and Sterne, the very disjunction of mind and body furnishes a vision of life, and a source of pain and laughter. The body is variously viewed by the characters as a microcosm for the state, a castle of health, an object of learning, and a field for theories and speculation. It exists, that is, in the mind as well as in the flesh. Consciousness of physicality is omnipresent in the novel, which figures forth in Tristram the narrator a mind that is constantly occupied with itself as incarnation.

NOTES

1. *The Life and Opinions of Tristram Shandy, Gentleman*, ed. James Aiken Work (New York: Odyssey Press, 1940). References are by volume, chapter, and page number of this edition.
2. *The History of Tom Jones*, ed. R. P. C. Mutter (Harmondsworth: Penguin Books, 1966). References are by book, chapter, and page number of this edition.
3. See my '*Sir Charles Grandison*: Richardson on Body and Character', *Eighteenth-Century Fiction* 1 (1989): 83–102.
4. This description stands out as the only instance of such precise visual delineation in the novel, and in deliberate compliment to Hogarth, who provided an illustration in which Dr Slop is prominent (II. xvii: 121): 'Imagine to yourself a little, squat, uncourtly figure of a Doctor *Slop*, of about four feet and a half perpendicular height, with a breadth of back, and a sesquipedality of belly, which might have done honour to a serjeant in the horse-guards. . . . Such were the outlines of Dr *Slop's* figure, which, – if you have read *Hogarth's* analysis of beauty, and if you have not, I wish you would; – you must know, may as certainly be caracatur'd, and convey'd to the mind by three strokes as three hundred' (II. ix: 104–5). Sterne's other characters are *not* caricatures, and require by contrast both 'great out-lines' and 'familiar strokes and faint designations' (I. xxii: 72–3).
5. Virginia Woolf, 'On Not Knowing Greek', in *The Common Reader* [first series] (London: Hogarth Press, 1925), p. 56.
6. See Roy Porter, 'Against the Spleen', in *Laurence Sterne: Riddles and Mysteries*, ed. Valerie Grosvenor Myer (London: Vision Press, 1984), pp. 84–98.
7. See Gabriel Josipovici's study of *Tristram Shandy* in *Writing and the Body* (Princeton, NJ: Princeton University Press, 1982), pp. 32–3.
8. See Valerie Grosvenor Myer, 'Tristram and the Animal Spirits', in Myer, cited above.
9. Robert Burton, *The Anatomy of Melancholy*, ed. Floyd Dell and Paul Jordan-Smith (New York: Tudor Publishing, 1951), I, 1, 2, 2, p. 129.
10. E. M. W. Tillyard, *The Elizabethan World Picture* (London: Chatto & Windus, 1943), p. 64.
11. But see W. G. Day, '*Tristram Shandy*: Locke may not be the Key', in Myer, pp. 75–83. Day lists the critics who have pursued the Sterne–Locke connection (including Fluchère, Traugott, and others), but demonstrates that Sterne's references to, and paraphrases from, Locke's *Essay* are far from respectful.
12. See Northrop Frye, *Anatomy of Criticism* (Princeton, NJ: Princeton University Press, 1957), p. 309.

13. John Ferriar, *Illustrations of Sterne &c.* (London: Cadell & Davies, 1798), p. 57. Ferriar documents at length Sterne's ample borrowings from Burton; see pp. 56–95.

14. 'Medicine . . . provided [Sterne] with the language, the medium, through which he sought to understand his own, and the human, condition.' Roy Porter, p. 94.

15. See what is to my mind the most fascinating single paper on *Tristram Shandy*, Louis A. Landa's 'The Shandean Homunculus: The Background of Sterne's "Little Gentleman" ', in *Restoration and Eighteenth-Century Literature: Essays in Honour of Alan Dugald McKillop*, ed. Carroll Camden (Chicago, IL: University of Chicago Press, 1963), pp. 44–68.

16. See Arthur H. Cash, 'The Birth of Tristram Shandy: Sterne and Dr Burton', *Studies in the Eighteenth Century*, ed. R. F. Brissenden (Toronto: University of Toronto Press, 1968), pp. 133–54.

17. In chap. v of vol. VIII, which contains the apostrophe 'O ye water-drinkers!' I suspect Sterne is alluding to John Smith's *The Curiosities of Common Water, or the Advantages thereof, in Preventing and Curing Many Distempers* (Dublin, 1725).

18. See Leigh A. Ehlers, 'Mrs Shandy's "Lint and Basilicon": The Importance of Women in *Tristram Shandy*', *South Atlantic Review* 46 (January, 1981): 61–75.

19. Sigurd Burckhardt, '*Tristram Shandy*'s Law of Gravity', *Journal of English Literary History* 28 (1961): 72.

20. See Eric Partridge's *Dictionary of Slang and Unconventional Usage*. Ian Watt, among others, has pointed out that ' "Toby" had long been established as a euphemism for the posterior'. Introduction to the Riverside edition of *Tristram Shandy* (Cambridge, MA: Houghton Mifflin, 1965), p. xxiii.

21. See Frank Brady: 'Toby, who did not philosophize but felt, represents the feelings and the body.' '*Tristram Shandy*: Sexuality, Morality, and Sensibility', *Eighteenth-Century Studies* 4 (Fall, 1970): 42.

22. Robert Alter, '*Tristram Shandy* and the Game of Love', *American Scholar* 37 (1968): 322.

23. *Early Christian Biographies*, ed. Roy J. Deferrari (Washington, DC: Catholic University of America Press, 1952), pp. 248–9.

24. See Fritz Gysin, *Model as Motif in Tristram Shandy* (Bern: Verlag, 1983), pp. 77ff.

25. I have developed this argument elsewhere, in 'Walter Shandy, Sterne, and Gender: A Feminist Foray', *English Studies in Canada* 15 (December, 1989): 441–58.

26. Frye, p. 309.

27. Landa, cited above.

28. See Cash, p. 141.

29. See A. R. Towers, 'Sterne's Cock and Bull Story', *English Literary History* 24 (1957): 22.

30. Dennis W. Allen, in *Studies in English Literature* 25 (1985): 661.

31. For the importance of women in *Tristram Shandy*, see Ruth Marie Faurot, 'Mrs Shandy Observed', *Studies in English Literature* 10 (1970): 579–89; and Leigh A. Ehlers, cited above.

CHAPTER SIX

'Running Out of Matter: The Body Exercised in Eighteenth-Century Fiction'*

CAROL HOULIHAN FLYNN

'Fabricating at great rate' his *Sentimental Journey*, Sterne guarantees a correspondent that the work 'shall make you cry as much as ever it made me laugh – or I'll give up the Business of sentimental writing – & write to the body.'[1] He reveals in this boast the edgy, nervous relationship he has to a method of writing that ironizes the tears he wrings from his subject, the body he is always displacing in language. To write 'to the body' is to approach it directly and follow its course into death. Its progress is sure, Sterne makes clear as he quantifies the blood he coughs up while tracing the source of his discontent. Engaging in 'hectic watchings' (I: 104) (the term is a tubercular one), born into a 'scurvy world' (I: 8), Sterne turns body into a text that must be interrupted to keep it from ending, for the straight plot line of gravity can only lead into closure most fatal.

> **Sterne turns body into a text that must be interrupted to keep it from ending, for the straight plot line of gravity can only lead into closure most fatal**

The act of writing itself creates physical communion with problematic flesh. Preparing to describe Walter Shandy's grief over Tristram's

* Extracted from G. S. Rousseau and Roy Porter (eds), *The Languages of Psyche: Mind and Body in Enlightenment Thought* (Berkeley, CA: University of California Press, 1990), pp. 147–85

crushed nose, the writer enters this part of his story 'in the most pensive and melancholy frame of mind, that ever sympathetic breast was touched with', his 'nerves relax' and he feels 'an abatement of the quickness of [his] pulse'. His cautious composure, so different from 'that careless alacrity with it, which every day of my life prompts me to say and write a thousand things I should not', seems to be associated with the serious-ness of his subject. More typical are

the rash jerks, and harebrain'd squirts thou art wont, *Tristram*, to transact it with in other humours, – dropping thy pen, – spurting thy ink about thy table and thy books, – as if thy pen and thy ink, thy books and thy furniture cost thee nothing.

(I: 254)

Is the ink Sterne's blood, costing indeed something, sign of his transub-stantiated text? Or merely ink? Flesh and blood, paper and words com-mingle violently as Sterne throws fair sheets of text into the fire and, for relief, 'snatch[es] off [his] wig' to throw it perpendicularly upward, defying the gravity he writes against (I: 350).

Writing against the spleen to extend, in the process, his own life, Sterne, through exertion, comes up against the very problem he is trying to solve, for in exercising his vital animal spirits, he is also, in his rash transactions, spurting his ink, his energy, his life's blood about the room. 'In writing,' Ramazini noted, 'the whole Brain with its Nerves and Fibres are highly tense, and a Privation of their due Tone succeeds.'[2] Writing, like study, is, after all, bloody work. Witness the trials of Uncle Toby, displacing his wound through hard study guaranteed to feed the flames of melancholia as he pursues the intricate mazes of the labyrinth promis-ing 'this bewitching phantom, KNOWLEDGE . . . O my uncle! fly—fly—fly from it as from a serpent. – Is it fit, good-natur'd man! thou should'st sit up with the wound upon thy groin whole nights baking thy blood with hectic watchings?' (I: 103–4).[3] And how can Toby fly from the knowledge threatening to consume him, a knowledge, not of javelins and bridges and sentry boxes, but the deeper knowledge of 'whole nights baking thy blood with hectic watchings' after death? In the text, the answer is clear. Toby must mount his hobbyhorse and ride away from the wound itself.

A hobbyhorse. Not an overlooked vehicle to be sure, but one, I think, more directly connected to Sterne's narrative strategies and one closer to Cheyne's chamber horse than to 'hobbies' emptied of the physicality they promise. Sterne employs his hobby to move, lurch, jerk, and jog the matter of his text across a page that is alarmingly substantial, and he does so to exercise spirits that are too active for a badly decomposing 'real' body.

Sterne's own mythologized equestrian escapades suggest a violent propensity for movement, just what, after all, the doctors prescribe.

Writing from Montpellier, he complains that the 'Thiness of the pyrenean Air brought on continual breaches of Vessels in my Lungs, & with them all the Tribe of evils insident to a pulmonary Consumption – there seem'd nothing left but gentle change of place & air.' 'Gentle', however, is a word that becomes altered by the movement itself and, once Sterne puts himself into motion, 'having traversed the South of France so often that I ran a risk of being taken up for a Spy, I . . . jogg'd myself out of all other dangers.'[4] Wildly excursing with a mad wife who thinks she is the Queen of Bohemia, demoniacally racing across Crazy Castle sands,[5] he violates therapeutic prescriptions for moderate exercise just as thoroughly as his morbidly energetic race against death flouts Nicholas Robinson's sound admonition to his consumptive patients. 'All the dejecting Passions should be banish'd,' Robinson advises, 'and Objects only admitted that may create gay, merry and chearful Scenes. . . . I should think it highly detrimental, too much to play with the gloomy Prospects of Death, unless manifest Symptoms appear of his approaching Dissolution.'[6] It would be, I imagine, difficult not to gag on such banal bromides. Sterne shows no signs of swallowing the discourse of cheerful moderation. His gaiety will crack at its edges as he perversely calls up 'gloomy Prospects of Death' (37–8), two of them, impenetrable black monuments to Yorick's mortality, only to flout them, to exorcise their spirit through a brisk, cracked energetic course of exercise.

*

Resurrecting 'poor Yorick' at will, Sterne jerks his invincible – because already dead – character across fictive landscapes that strain beneath the weight of curveting, frisking hooves. Sentimental travelers 'Crack, crack—crack, crack—crack, crack', across France (II: 599), and on domestic ground are prone to take 'a good rattling gallop', to risk routinely life and limb in order to arouse the appropriate spirit:

Now ride at this rate with what good intention and resolution you may, – 'tis a million to one you'll do some one a mischief, if not yourself – He's flung – he's off – he's lost his seat – he's down – he'll break his neck – see! (I: 356)

Motion, not ripeness, is all. Ripeness must, in fact, be interrupted, for to ripen is to rot. Growth becomes in nature death – unless the natural channels are diverted. Tristram knows that, as he compulsively displaces his origins, pushing them always beyond his own comprehension, short-circuiting in the process his logical narrative end.

To escape the real problems of body, the quarts and gallons of blood that Tristram decides not to measure, Sterne sets up several diversionary strategies. To escape being 'killed' by kind questions addressed to the nature and location of his wound, My Uncle Toby displaces his corporeal state through military maneuvers. Trim, his surrogate, in love and war, one of those accommodating 'body servants' so necessary to exercise the vital spirits, makes it possible for Toby to swing between states of benevolence and bloody gore as he races his hobbyhorse from the Bowling Green to Dunkirk and back again without getting anywhere at all. Walter, less tactile, depends upon auxiliary verbs to move the soul, that great sensorium of verbal connections:

Now the use of the *Auxiliaries* is, at once to set the soul a going by herself upon the materials as they are brought her; and by the versability of this great engine, round which they are twisted, to open new tracks of enquiry, and make every idea engender millions. (I: 485)

Aided by the auxiliary yet active parts of speech not unlike accommodating servants willing to administer brisk rubbings of the flesh-brush for their mistress's own good, Walter sets the great white bear dancing across the page to not quite end another book:

A WHITE BEAR! Very well. Have I ever seen one? Might I ever have seen one? Am I ever to see one? Ought I ever to have seen one? Or can I ever see one?

Would I had seen a white bear – (for how can I imagine it?) If I should see a white bear, what should I say? If I should never see a white bear, what then?

If I never have, can, must or shall see a white bear alive; have I ever seen the skin of one? Did I ever see one painted? – described? Have I ever dreamed of one?

Did my father, mother, uncle, aunt, brothers or sisters, ever see a white bear? What would they give? How would they behave? How would a white bear have behaved? Is he wild? Tame? Terrible? Rough? Smooth?

—Is the white bear worth seeing?—

—Is there no sin in it?

Is it better than a BLACK ONE? (I: 487)

Walter's final question exposes the absurd limits to his own system, promising endless discourse, newly opened tracks of inquiry that would 'make every idea engender millions' of words going absolutely nowhere, ending up in tautological exercises that, nonetheless, 'set the soul a going by herself' and keep, in the process, the wheel of life running 'long and chearfully round' (I: 401).

Tristram compulsively pursues motion for its own sake. 'So much of motion, is so much of life, and so much of joy . . . that to stand still, or get on but slowly, is death and the devil,' he claims, rejecting Bishop Hall's desire for heavenly rest. *'Make them like unto a wheel'* becomes not a 'bitter sarcasm' made against the restless spirit of fallen man, but a benediction allowing, however mechanically, transcendence. 'I love the Pythagoreans . . . for their . . . *"getting out of the body, in order to think well"*. No man thinks right whilst he is in it' (II: 592–3).

Tristram travels by coach, by hobbyhorse, and by sentimental chance, depending, when particularly weary, upon sturdy surrogates to move his dangerously hardening soul. To get out of the body, Sterne depends upon moving his and his reader's soul mechanically, but also pathetically, by allowing a sentimental escape from the hard realities of life. Auxiliary agents of feeling, body servants as indispensable as Trim, will become in *Sentimental Journey* necessary for the sentimental commerce Yorick conducts.[7] Just as the White Bear carried into and out of Walter's discourse calls attention to the arbitrary, fragmentary nature of any discourse, so the isolated, often inconclusive sentimental tales filling both novels emphasize their transitory, yet necessary, quality. Tristram, in fact, highly recommends the pitiful Maria piping her sorrows as a good sentimental side trip to Yorick, the sentimental traveler in search of emotional and motional diversion. Maria's madness and pathos is just the thing to exercise the spirits and rouse the soul.[8] Feelings, the property of patients genteel enough to suffer from the spleen, are expensive to sustain and will continue to depend, sentimentally, largely upon the sufferings of other, hardier souls valued for their compliance and visibility.

All these side trips, all this openness to the pleasing sensation of disruption, prohibits narrative coherency. That is, in fact, the point. Tristram 'so complicate[s] and involve[s] the digressive and progressive movements, one wheel, within another, that the whole machine, in general, has been kept a-going; – and what's more, it shall be kept a-going these forty years, if it pleases the fountains of health to bless me so long with life and good spirits' (I: 82). In the hectic spirit, he sets out to move through time and space Dr Slop, Obadiah, Uncle Toby, Corporal Trim, Yorick, Walter, and himself – and on occasion, that inveterate lover of coach travel, Aunt Dinah, players all in his 'dance . . . song . . . or . . . concerto between the acts' of birth and death.

Compulsively calling attention to the seams and struts of his narrative, Sterne makes clear with cloying irritation the effort it takes *not* to be splenetic. If I were to choose a kingdom, Tristram muses, let it be filled with 'hearty laughing subjects'. The Rabelaisian dream of a 'body politick as body natural' as body laughing is poignantly undermined by his salute to the reader he takes leave of 'till this time twelve-month, when (unless this vile cough kills me in the meant time) I'll have another pluck at your beards' (I: 402). Not only does his own body natural intrude upon his vision of 'subjects' with the 'grace to be as WISE as they were MERRY', but his assertion of authority reveals even more the unlikely nature of his fictional structure. His hearty subjects must laugh, humorists subject to a regimen of joy that strains against its imperative. Crack, crack—crack, crack—crack, crack – watch the 'characters' prance and paw as they course across a narrative designed to get them nowhere. The less nimble need to be occasionally carted off the stage, for movement, not direction, is all. 'Getting for-wards in two different journies together, and with the same dash of the pen', playing parlor tricks with time and space as he walks across the marketplace of Auxerre with my father and my uncle Toby just as he enters Lyons with a 'post-chaise broke into a thousand pieces ... moreover this moment' rhapsodizing on the banks of the Garonne (II: 621–2), Sterne

> **Crack, crack—crack, crack—crack, crack – watch the 'characters' prance and paw as they course across a narrative designed to get them nowhere**

exhausts the reader with his frantic attempts at capering in the Shandy manner.

By denying his vehicle, his text, stability, by 'breaking it up into a thousand pieces', Sterne collapses it finally in a 'COCK and a BULL'. Strategies of interruption and digression energize – hectically – a dis-course that can even mobilize 'auxilary verbs' to 'open new tracks of enquiry, and make every idea engender millions'. But in the case of the wonderful dancing bear, such multiplication is essentially nongenerative. The bear moves through the text, but doesn't get anywhere – he doesn't even make sense. New tracks of inquiry lead to dead ends that require yet another detour. Thus Tristram multiplies his own activity textually: 'I have three hundred and sixty-four days more life to write just now, than when I first set out; so that instead of advancing, as a common writer, in my work with what I have been doing at it – on the contrary, I am just thrown so many volumes back' (I: 341). Advancing, and then 'thrown back', the writer swings back and forth between birth and death, between those 'acts' that threaten closure. The swinger escapes time, escapes death, as long as he can sustain movement ultimately as sterile as Walter's recalcitrant bull. For there is, within the text itself, a resistance to the cracks and jerks and jogs and pokes that creates a hectic, masturbatory exhaustion of the 'animal spirits' Sterne tries to resuscitate. The irritability that Sterne wants to transform into 'good humor' reveals the strains of sublimation.

NOTES

1. *A Sentimental Journey*, ed. Gardner Stout (Berkeley and Los Angeles, CA: University of California Press, 1967), 19–20.
2. B. Ramazini, *A Treatise on the Disease of Tradesmen* (London, 1740), 401.
3. Quotations are from *The Life and Opinions of Tristram Shandy*, ed. Melvyn New and Joan New (Gainesville, FLA: University Presses of Florida, 1978–84).
4. *The Letters of Laurence Sterne*, ed. Lewis Perry Curtis (Oxford: Oxford University Press, 1965), 205.
5. In *Scrapeana* (York, 1792), John Croft reports that Elizabeth Sterne imagined herself the Queen of Bohemia. To amuse her, 'and induce her to take the air', 'Tristram, her husband . . . proposed coursing, in the way practised in Bohemia; for that purpose he procured bladders, and filled them with beans, and tied them to the wheels of a single horse chair. When he drove madam into a stubble field, with the motion of the carriage and the bladders, rattle bladder, rattle; it alarmed the hares, and the greyhounds were ready to take them' (22, as cited in David Thomson, *Wild Excursions: The Life and Fiction of Laurence Sterne* [New York: McGraw-Hill, 1972], 123). Arthur Cash finds this to be 'one of the least trustworthy stories about Sterne' (*Laurence Sterne: The Early and Middle Years* [London: Methuen, 1975], 286), but something in it rings true. Wilbur Cross states that of all the pastimes that 'took Sterne out of doors, none pleased him quite so much' as 'racing chariots along the sandy beach' near Crazy Castle ' "with one wheel in the sea" ' (*The Life and Times of Laurence Sterne* [New Haven, CT: Yale University Press, 1925], I: 121).
6. Nicholas Robinson, *A New Method of Treating Consumptions* (London, 1727), pt. 2, 48.
7. In his 'Preface' written in the Desobligeant, Yorick decides that 'the balance of senti-mental commerce is always against the expatriated adventurer: he must buy what he has little occasion for at their own price – his conversation will seldom be taken in exchange for theirs without a large discount – and this, by the by, eternally driving him into the hands of more equitable brokers for such conversation as he can find, it requires no great spirit of divination to guess at his party' (*Sentimental Journey*, 78–79).
8. The pitiful condition of Le Fever also serves to rouse Toby from his sickbed. Most of the sentimental incidents in both *TS* and *SJ* seem designed to elicit a short, strong response that will invigorate its feeling spectator.

PART FOUR

Sources, Imitation, Plagiarism

S terne stole. Or, to put it another way, Sterne's novels, more particularly *Tristram Shandy*, are webs of allusion to, and borrowing from,
the writings of others. Or, to put it a third way, *Tristram Shandy*,
particularly in its parodic and mimetic tendencies, is recognizably a text
which implicates itself in a European tradition of learned wit, whose key
authors include Rabelais, Montaigne, Robert Burton and Swift, a text
which sometimes acknowledges its debts and sometimes (in a manoeuvre
which is itself a marker of that tradition) does not.

How, then, should one put it? Are we to regard Sterne as a thief, or
can we theorize and historicize his position in richer, and less morally
negative, ways? The late eighteenth-century writer John Ferriar was the
first to carry out detailed scholarship on Sterne's borrowings. As H. J.
Jackson points out in the opening lines of the first of the two essays
printed in this section, Ferriar's original impulse was charitable: 'I wish to
illustrate, not to degrade him'. Five years later, however, Ferriar may be
found accusing Sterne of the moral fault, or criminal act, of 'plagiarism'.
Plagiarism, along with forgery, has become a vital issue in the study of
literature of the second half of the eighteenth century, and theory has
recently begun to develop a more developed and less morally unper-
plexed view of the literary sleight of hand that underlies the work of,
notably, Macpherson, Chatterton and the Shakespearean forger William
Henry Ireland; important recent studies include Paul Baines's *The House*

of Forgery in Eighteenth-Century Britain (Aldershot: Ashgate, 1999) and Nick Groom's 'Forgery and Plagiarism' (in *Companion to Literature from Milton to Blake*, ed. David Womersley (Oxford: Blackwell, 2000), pp. 94–113). Sterne does not quite belong to the category of forger; he is more a borrower than a feigner, despite his willingness to create such knowingly bogus texts as Slawkenbergius's Tale. An important and central trend in modern Sterne criticism, established in Douglas Jefferson's seminal '*Tristram Shandy* and the Tradition of Learned Wit' (1951), has delineated Sterne's relation to a centuries-old history of mainly humanist learned satire characterized by quotation, allusion, parody, all kinds of playful recombination. A familiar instance of an aspect of this, gleefully repeated in modern criticism, is Sterne's remark at the beginning of Volume V of *Tristram Shandy*: 'Are we for ever to be twisting, and untwisting the same rope? for ever in the same track – for ever at the same pace?' – a complaint against the endless re-cycling of knowledge and writing, which is itself (silently) borrowed from Burton's *Anatomy of Melancholy*. Swift had played a game according to the same sorts of parodic rules when he sturdily asserted his own independence and originality in his 'Verses on the Death of Dr Swift':

> To steal a hint was never known,
> But what he writ was all his own.
>
> (lines 317–18)

But this assertion is also borrowed, in this case from John Denham's 'On Mr Abraham Cowley' (lines 29–30).

Neither in Swift nor in Sterne is this game merely plagiarism; for both, to steal from other authors adjurations against literary stealing is part of a self-conscious ironic textual strategy, an act of quiet but mischievous complicity with those from whom they steal. In Jackson's article we find a serious attempt to uncover the fellow satirist's acknowledgment that Sterne makes to Burton – '*non ego, sed Democritus dixit*', it is not I, but Democritus who has spoken – and to explore the creative uses Sterne makes of his 'thefts'. Jackson's overriding point is about the satiric and comic applications of Burtonian allusion, 'the comic discrepancy between the original and the acquired significance of Burton's words'. Sterne like Burton speaks in 'another's person, an assumed habit and name'. Burton's persona, Democritus Junior, becomes Yorick or Tristram.

Burton's sentiments and ideas are transformed and re-cast, distorted and recontextualized, in ways which expose Tristram's scholarly unreliability or Walter's pedantry, and provide the reader with the repeated and often disarming surprise of comic recognition.

Jackson's essay is a critical and ground-breaking investigation of Sterne's relation to, and manipulations of, a particular source. Jonathan Lamb, in an essay which is a significant preparation for one of the most important books on Sterne of recent years, *Sterne's Fiction and the Double Principle* (1989), deals with a wider range of Sterne's numerous originals (Montaigne, Cervantes, Burton, Locke, Rabelais, Longinus, Pope, Hogarth, Shakespeare, Obadiah Walker and Sterne himself), and postulates theoretical explanations for Sterne's methods in the mimetic aesthetic theory of Sterne's own time. Sterne's use of such textual predecessors is not only a humanist's taste for and exploitation of a learned and satiric tradition (though that, too, is a theoretically and ideologically sophisticated position), but a complex and self-defining intertextuality, which may be characterized neither as mere theft nor as mere novelty. All consciousness and all knowledge, as Locke (and indeed Aristotle) taught, is imitation; without imitation, knowledge is impossible and thinking has no materials to work on. 'A true imitator' (in Lamb's words) 'does much more than simply spatchcock other texts into his own, or dutifully give a foreign idea an "agreeable turn": other men's thoughts are not a supplement to his own but the very means by which his own thought takes place.' *Tristram Shandy* is (like Burton's *Anatomy of Melancholy*) not merely a *cento*, a paste-book of others' passages, a magpie's collection of inert though brightly coloured stones, but a synthesizing and transformative re-working of the ideas, and significances, of many different textual sources. Allusion, echo, quotation are not theft but the rhetorical and figurative processes by which Sterne created his own paradoxically original work.

CHAPTER SEVEN

'Sterne, Burton, and Ferriar: Allusions to the *Anatomy of Melancholy* in Volumes V to IX of *Tristram Shandy*'*

H. J. JACKSON

The Manchester physician John Ferriar is ultimately responsible for the common belief that Sterne plagiarized from Burton's *Anatomy of Melancholy* in *Tristram Shandy*.[1] When he first published the results of his research into the sources of Sterne's writings in 1793, Ferriar refused to describe Sterne as a plagiarist, saying, 'I wish to illustrate, not to degrade him.'[2] But by the time his essay was reprinted in an enlarged form and reached a wider audience as the *Illustrations of Sterne* in 1798, he had changed his mind. For reasons which will be explored in the final section of this paper, his manner towards Sterne became more severe, and he referred to his 'plagiarism' from a number of writers, particularly Robert Burton. As an attentive reader of *Tristram Shandy*, Ferriar was able to suggest three reasons for such literary larceny: he said first of all that Sterne had meant to ridicule the 'gravity' of out-of-date writers like Burton; secondly, that he had conceived of Walter Shandy (*ab ovo*) as a character of Burtonian erudition and eccentricity; and finally, that he had borrowed learned quotations from the *Anatomy* in order to impress the reader and make 'a great figure as a curious reader'.[3] Ferriar's research was remarkably thorough and his conclusions were plausible, but for almost two centuries they have deterred readers and critics of *Tristram Shandy* from making any concentrated attempt to reassess Sterne's 'debt' to Burton. A number of substantial borrowings from the *Anatomy*, however, went unnoticed by Ferriar and later critics; their discovery may now be taken as an occasion for reopening the question of the relationship between Sterne and Burton.

* Reprinted from *Philological Quarterly* 54 (1975): 457–70

It has been clear for some time that Sterne had a copy of the *Anatomy* before him as he wrote certain sections of *Tristram Shandy*, beginning with the opening of Volume V. It has not been as obvious that he expected at least some of his readers to work with *Tristram Shandy* in the same way, comparing parts of its text with Burton's; but a reconsideration of the evidence shows that he must have done so. Sterne deliberately seeded the later volumes of *Tristram Shandy* with quotations taken (not without acknowledgement) from Burton's work, and he appears to have meant them to function as allusions, adding an ironic dimension to the novel. For the author himself, for perhaps a handful of 'curious readers' of his time, and for the Prince Posterity who might possess an annotated edition of *Tristram Shandy*,[4] the allusions to the *Anatomy* are big with jest. They are 'digressive, and . . . progressive too' (p. 73): on the one hand, they advance the action of the novel; and on the other, they invite a good reader, one who does not have the vulgar habit of 'reading straight forwards' (p. 56), to stop to consider the relationship between two texts which share the same words. They affect the active reader as a kind of verbal *trompe l'oeil*, for they force him to perceive two fundamentally different patterns at once. The conjunction of the two is invariably surprising and generally comic, although the butt of the joke is not always the same.

It may be possible to explain the intention and effect of the allusions to Burton in *Tristram Shandy*, but Sterne's silence about this aspect of his work remains mysterious. He must have been aware that few of his contemporaries knew the *Anatomy* well enough to identify the allusions without more authorial guidance than he gave. For almost all readers of Sterne's day, the borrowed phrases and sentences were indistinguishable from the original materials in the text of the novel; and for them, Ferriar's revelations could lead to only one conclusion, that Sterne was guilty of 'the most scandalous fraud and plagiarism which has yet been detected in the annals of our republic of letters', as a reviewer wrote.[5] In spite of this predictable response to the exposure of his debts, Sterne was evidently content to keep the complex allusiveness of his book as a private joke for as long as he lived,

> **Sterne was evidently content to keep the complex allusiveness of his book as a private joke for as long as he lived, making it one more game in which the Jester triumphed over most of his Jestees**

making it one more game in which the Jester triumphed over most of his Jestees.[6]

I

The most significant omission from Ferriar's catalogue of borrowings from the *Anatomy* was the clue to Burton's identity which was given on the title pages of Volumes V and VI, published in December, 1761. Sterne originally gave those volumes only two epigraphs:

> *Dixero si quid fortè jocosius, hoc mihi juris*
> *Cum venia dabis.—*

HOR.

> *—Si quis calumnietur levius esse quam decet theologum,*
> *aut mordacius quam deceat Christianum—non Ego, sed*
> *Democritus dixit.—*

ERASMUS (p. 339)

The crucial phrase, *'non Ego, sed Democritus dixit'*, does not appear with the rest of the second quotation in Erasmus's preface to the *Encomium Moriae*. It is, however, the clue which should send the reader to the *Anatomy of Melancholy* to find the following passage, in which Burton quoted the lines from Horace and Erasmus but substituted his own famous pseudonym, 'Democritus Junior', for Erasmus's Folly.

> If I have overshot myself in this which hath been hitherto said, or that it is, which I am sure some will object, too phantastical, 'too light and comical for a divine, too satirical for one of my profession', I will presume to answer, with Erasmus in like case, 'Tis not I, but Democritus, *Democritus dixit*: you must consider what it is to speak in one's own or another's person, an assumed habit and name – a difference betwixt him that affects or acts a prince's, a philosopher's, a magistrate's, a fool's part, and him that is so indeed – and what a liberty those old satirists have had; it is a cento collected from others; not I, but they that say it.

> *Dixero si quid forte jocosius, hoc mihi juris*
> *Cum veniâ dabis.*[7]

Burton's footnotes, printed in the margins of Sterne's seventeenth-century edition of the *Anatomy*,[8] provided attributions and the Latin text for the quotation from Erasmus.

The *Anatomy* was identified as the source of these epigraphs by Wilbur Cross in 1909, but without comment.[9] Treated as a direct allusion rather than as a covert theft, the epigraphs are extremely interesting. Once the allusion has been recognized, Sterne's 'Democritus', the source of some 'light and comical' passages in *Tristram Shandy*, can be confidently identified: he is neither Democritus of Abdera, nor Thomas More whom Erasmus called 'Democritus Junior', but the Democritus Junior whose name appeared on the title page of the *Anatomy of Melancholy*. On the very first page of Volume V of *Tristram Shandy*, then, Sterne covered his debts to Burton with one general acknowledgement, *'non Ego, sed Democritus dixit'*. The epigraphs illustrate the common tendency of Sterne's quotations from the *Anatomy*, for while they are in isolation appropriate for *Tristram Shandy*, they become much more significant when they are seen to refer to Burton's work. Their original context, with its statement of satiric intent, its discussion of the value of a persona, and its description of the *Anatomy* itself as 'a cento collected from others', is a useful commentary upon *Tristram Shandy*. By the allusion to Burton, Sterne gave notice that he too had constructed a patchwork, a cento based in part at least upon the most celebrated cento in English; and it must have seemed to him both just and ironic that a novel 'wrote . . . against the spleen' (p. 301) should have drawn upon an anatomy of melancholy.

Sterne's turning to the *Anatomy* has usually been supposed to have been the result of flagging inventiveness; but even as slight an example as this pair of epigraphs may serve to suggest how creatively Sterne used passages from Burton. The first writer of fiction to see comic potential in Burton's very serious moral and medical work, he audaciously applied these quotations to his own quite different book; he then thinly disguised the allusion by inverting the order in which the quotations appeared (and inversion was to be a favorite technique in dealing with borrowed materials), but left enough of the sense of the original to alert an active reader to the trick he was playing. In choosing to incorporate quotations from another author's work in his own, Sterne can hardly be accused of sparing his energies. On the contrary, like Mr Shandy with the *Tristra-paedia*, he spun the supposedly plagiarized sections of *Tristram Shandy* 'out of his own brain, – or reeled and cross-twisted what all other spinners and spinsters had spun before him, [so] that 'twas pretty near the same torture to him' (pp. 372–3). Why he should have exercised his ingenuity simultaneously in concealing and betraying his source – quoting directly from the *Anatomy*, for example, when paraphrase might have gone un-detected – is incomprehensible except as a device by which he thought that both the novel and the reader should have something to gain.

II

The greatest concentration of materials borrowed from the *Anatomy* occurs, as Ferriar demonstrated, in the first three chapters of Volume V of *Tristram Shandy*; and the first passage there which Ferriar 'illustrated' was the following:

Shall we for ever make new books, as apothecaries make new mixtures, by pouring only out of one vessel into another?

Are we for ever to be twisting, and untwisting the same rope? for ever in the same track – for ever at the same pace? (p. 343)

The analogies of the apothecaries' mixtures and the rope came from Burton:

As apothecaries we make new mixtures every day, pour out of one vessel into another; and as those old Romans robbed all the cities of the world to set out their bad-sited Rome, we skim off the cream of other men's wits, pick the choice flowers of their tilled gardens to set out our own sterile plots. . . . [W]e weave the same web still, twist the same rope again and again. . . . (I: 23, 24)

Ferriar observed that it was 'very singular' that in such an 'evident copy' Sterne 'should take occasion to abuse plagiarists'.[10] He seems to have missed both the possibility of a calculated irony in Sterne's having 'plagiarized' a denunciation of plagiarists, and the significance of the original context of the borrowed phrases. In the *Anatomy*, Burton made a distinction between real and apparent plagiarism as part of a defense of his policy of quotation. By the allusion to Burton's work, Sterne showed that he anticipated criticism for his own practices. He followed the allusion with a covert apology:

Shall we be destined to the days of eternity, on holy-days, as well as working-days, to be showing the *relicks of learning*, as monks do the relicks of their saints – without working one – one single miracle with them? (p. 343)

It is interesting to note that Ferriar quoted this exculpatory sentence in the 1793 version of his essay, with a generous comment, 'Here we must acquit Sterne: he has certainly done wonders, wherever he has imitated or borrowed.'[11] However, he left both the quotation and his comment out of the 1798 *Illustrations*.

In these introductory sentences, Sterne implied that his use of materials from Burton's neglected *Anatomy of Melancholy* was not to be a tedious display of 'the *relicks of learning*' but a kind of resurrection. He went on, by a logical progression which is still obscure to readers unaware of the source or implications of his borrowings, to give two demonstrations of the kind of 'miracle' he had in mind. He began by recalling the magnificent opening paragraphs of the *Anatomy* (I: 130) in a long sentence of his own:

Who made MAN, with powers which dart him from earth to heaven in a moment – that great, that most excellent, and most noble creature of the world – the *miracle* of nature, as Zoroaster in his book περὶ φύσεως called him – the SHEKINAH of the divine presence, as Chrysostom – the *image* of God, as Moses – the *ray* of divinity, as Plato – the *marvel* of marvels, as Aristotle – to go sneaking on at this pitiful – pimping – pettifogging rate? (p. 343)

Ferriar echoed the question in his only comment on this passage, 'Who would suspect this heroic strain to be a plagiarism? yet such it is undoubtedly. . . .'[12] He said nothing about the connected and cumulative effect of the series of 'plagiarisms' which he had recorded in a single chapter; and again he failed to recognize the incongruity of the allusion. Sterne did not quote Burton verbatim: to a few phrases from the *Anatomy* he added illustrations and decorations of his own, successfully transforming a lament for the fall of man into an attack upon imitators. In the attitude of a popular author, he wrote, 'I wish from my soul, that every imitator in *Great Britain, France,* and *Ireland,* had the farcy for his pains' (p. 343); at the same time, of course, he was acting as an imitator himself.

The second and last 'miracle' in Chapter 1 was performed in the composition of the 'Lady Baussiere' episode in the Fragment upon Whiskers. Ferriar quoted the parallel passages from *Tristram Shandy* (p. 346) and the *Anatomy* (III: 34–40) in the *Illustrations*,[13] with only a rather puzzled reference to 'this curious copy'.[14] The texts involved are too long to be given here, but something may be said of the way in which the Lady Baussiere episode fits into the emerging pattern of allusions to the *Anatomy* in Volume V of Sterne's novel. Sterne worked his literary miracle by selecting a small part of Burton's dramatization of the lack of charity in the world, and turning it into a comic representation of absent-mindedness. Taking Burton's refrain, 'Ride on', he created a dramatic incident with a lady, a palfrey, a page and a terrace at the end of the ride. He laid the way for direct quotation in the second half of his set piece by imitation in the first: the passing of the host, and the old man holding a box 'begirt with iron' (p. 346) were his additions to the scene. Furthermore, he inverted the order of the original, ending where Burton had begun, with the 'decayed kinsman' (III: 35). The whole episode shows how creatively Sterne could deal with 'the *relicks of learning'.* He did not take passages from the *Anatomy* indiscriminately or quote them unaltered. He chose his materials carefully, and treated Burton's prose as though it were a mosaic which he could break up and reassemble in patterns of his own. He did not offer Burton's ideas at face value either, but tended to use them with an irony which could be appreciated only if the original was known. The denunciation of imitators by an imitator; the paradoxical similitude of the fall of man and the decline of an author; and the travesty of Burton's words on charity in Sterne's tale of double-entendre – all contribute to the calculated incongruities of Volume V.

Sterne's quotations from the *Anatomy* became bolder and more conspicuous through the first three chapters of Volume V, and reached a climax in the most celebrated 'plagiarism' of all, Walter Shandy's oration on the death of his son Bobby (pp. 350–6). As Ferriar showed,[15] the oration was taken piecemeal from a 'consolation against the death of friends' in Burton's work (II: 176–85).[16] Ferriar interrupted his citation of parallel passages only to draw attention to the outrageousness of Sterne's plagiarism, saying, for example, 'Sterne should have considered how much he owed to poor old Burton',[17] or, in a later case of Walter Shandy's using Burton's words, 'Sterne has picked out a few quotations from Burton's Essay on Love-Melancholy, which afford nothing very remarkable, except Sterne's boldness in quoting quotations'.[18] But in his desire to prove Sterne's indebtedness to Burton, Ferriar consistently overlooked the implications of the passages chosen and underestimated the way in which Sterne recast Burton's prose to blend with a completely new background. In the case of Mr Shandy's oration, there is less than usual to be gained by referring to the context of the consolation in Burton's *Anatomy*, but the changes made in Burton's collection of commonplaces about death deserves some attention. Intending to incorporate words and phrases from the *Anatomy of Melancholy* in a comic context, as he had done before, Sterne prepared a situation appropriate to them, built up to them by imitation and paraphrase, and then presented Burton's words as fragments in a dramatic pattern. After the narrator's elaborate introduction, Walter Shandy's harangue is undercut by stage directions, interruptions, and hilarious misunderstandings.

The *Anatomy* has been known since Ferriar's time as a source of learned quotations for Walter Shandy.[19] More recently, critical attention has turned towards Tristram, and it has been seen as appropriate that he, too, should be furnished with learning taken at second hand from Burton.[20] What has been overlooked, however, is the modification in Sterne's use of the *Anatomy* which was dictated by the difference between father and son. Walter Shandy's book-learning, however ludicrous, is real, and he usually quotes his authorities correctly. Tristram, on the other hand, is shown repeatedly bungling attempts to display his knowledge, and the collapse of his pretensions contributes to the comedy of the novel.[21] In introducing his father's oration on death, for example, he offers a long list of possible sources for a set of commonplaces about grief

> **Tristram . . . is shown repeatedly bungling attempts to display his knowledge, and the collapse of his pretensions contributes to the comedy of the novel**

(pp. 350–1), although the attribution was confidently made in the *Anatomy* (II: 179–80). His discussion of 'what love is' (pp. 466–8), though based on Burton as are his father's analyses of love, is confused and inconclusive. He passes on a group of serious case histories from the *Anatomy* (I: 171) as a 'tawdry' story 'of a nun who fancied herself a shell-fish, and of a monk damn'd for eating a muscle' (pp. 479–80). He mis-quotes and mistakes the author of one Latin sentence plucked from Burton,[22] and unnecessarily attributes another to 'I know not who'.[23] Similar to these mistakes are some of the ludicrous errors – ludicrous, at least, to a learned audience – which have hitherto been ascribed to Sterne himself. Tristram's citing *'Aristotle's Master-Piece'* for Aristotle's *Book of Problems* (p. 102 and n.), and his hasty description of della Casa's *'nasty Romance of the Galateo'* (p. 618 and n.) are only two of many such mistaken references in the narrative. In the larger context of the novel, Tristram's blunders may be seen as part of the pervasive satire against pedantry and as further signs of his overwhelming incompetence as narrator. What must be emphasized, however, is that many of his errors can be discovered only by direct reference to the text of the *Anatomy of Melancholy*, for Sterne deliberately distorted quotations and citations from the *Anatomy* in order to represent Tristram as a pedantic but unstable scholar.

> **Tristram's blunders may be seen . . . as further signs of his overwhelming incompetence as narrator**

III

After the first three chapters of Volume V, Sterne may appear to have abandoned – or repented of – the practice of quoting from the *Anatomy of Melancholy*, but in fact he continued to adapt passages from Burton. Ferriar recorded several later examples of the materials from the *Anatomy* which appear as a recurrent motif in Volumes V to IX of Sterne's work,[24] but a number of others have not been noticed before. Perhaps the most charming of these is one which occurs in Volume VI, in Uncle Toby's 'apologetical oration' on the subject of war – a speech which corresponds to his brother's discourse on death. Sterne's use of the *Anatomy* here seems particularly mischievous, for Toby cannot be supposed to be a 'curious reader', and quoting from the *Anatomy* is therefore quite inappropriate for him. His speech is implicitly contrasted with his brother's oration as a piece of spontaneous oratory.

– 'Tis one thing, brother *Shandy*, for a soldier to hazard his own life – to leap first down into the trench, where he is sure to be cut in pieces: – 'Tis one thing, from public spirit and a thirst of glory, to enter the breach the first man, – to stand in the foremost rank, and march bravely on with drums and trumpets, and colours flying about his ears: – 'Tis one thing, I say, brother *Shandy*, to do this – and 'tis another thing to reflect on the miseries of war; – to view the desolations of whole countries, and consider the intolerable fatigues and hardships which the soldier himself, the instrument who works them, is forced (for six-pence a day, if he can get it) to undergo. (p. 461)

This paragraph, down to the homely parenthesis of 'six-pence a day, if he can get it', was taken from an outright attack upon war in Burton's *Anatomy*; but Sterne inverted the moral bias as well as the sequence of ideas when he transposed the passage into *Tristram Shandy*, as a glance at the original will show.

By means of which it comes to pass that daily so many voluntaries offer themselves, leaving their sweet wives, children, friends, for sixpence (if they can get it) a day, prostitute their lives and limbs, desire to enter upon breaches, lie sentinel, perdu, give the first onset, stand in the fore-front of the battle, marching bravely on, with a cheerful noise of drums and trumpets, such vigour and alacrity, so many banners streaming in the air, glittering armours, motions of plumes, woods of pikes and swords, variety of colours, cost and magnificence, as if they went in triumph. . . . (I: 60)

Earlier in his attack, Burton had paraphrased Erasmus's words on the unnaturalness of war:

. . . what plague, what fury brought so devilish, so brutish a thing as war first into men's minds? Who made so soft and peaceable a creature, born to love, mercy, meekness, so to rave, rage like beasts, and run on to their own destruction? (I: 57)

This idea also found its way into Toby's oration:

Need I be told, dear *Yorick*, as I was by you, in *Le Fever*'s funeral sermon, *That so soft and gentle a creature, born to love, to mercy, and kindness, as man is, was not shaped for this?* (p. 462)

If nothing but the theme of Yorick's sermon had been lifted from the *Anatomy*, a reader who recognized the allusion might take it simply as a sign Yorick, like Walter and Tristram Shandy, was a reader of old books; but since an important part of Toby's speech was drawn from the same source, he must look for some more comprehensive explanation of Sterne's borrowings. One further example will confirm this need.

Burton's words were distributed among minor characters as well as being given to the principals in the later volumes of *Tristram Shandy*, and in almost every case they were set in a context radically different from the *Anatomy*. In Toby's oration, materials from Burton were used to support a position which Burton himself opposed. For another episode which has not previously been identified as Burtonian, Sterne cast borrowed phrases as a dialogue, inverting Burton's conclusion by leaving it to an essentially unsympathetic character. The sentence from the *Anatomy* upon which the dialogue was based is, 'Consider the excellency of virgins; *Virgo coelum meruit*, marriage replenisheth the earth, but virginity Paradise . . .' (III: 224). It is introduced in *Tristram Shandy* when Walter Shandy's audience rebels against his hostile description of 'natural' love – the description itself being drawn from another part of the *Anatomy*.

—I think the procreation of children as beneficial to the world, said *Yorick*, as the finding out the longitude—

—To be sure, said my mother, *love* keeps peace in the world—

—In the *house*—my dear, I own—

—It replenishes the earth; said my mother—

But it keeps heaven empty—my dear; replied my father.

—'Tis Virginity, cried *Slop*, triumphantly, which fills paradise.

Well push'd nun! quoth my father. (p. 588)

The dialogue is delightful for the way in which it represents the opposing attitudes which the reader has come to expect in Yorick, Slop, and Mr and Mrs Shandy; and the passage from the *Anatomy* lent itself particularly well to what we know of the life and opinions of each character involved in the debate. But a comparison of the two texts shows that ideas which existed in harmony in Burton's system are used as signs of discord in the Shandy parlour. In this brief exchange, as in most instances of Burton's words being adapted for particular characters in the novel, the reader is made aware of the shortcomings of the Shandys. Burton's consolation upon death is moving, but Walter Shandy's is absurd; Burton's learning is impressive, but Tristram's is feeble and misapplied; Burton's moral system is consistent and compelling, but Toby's, however generous in impulse, is patently illogical. At times both parties – both 'patterns' in the verbal illusion which Sterne created by repeated reference to the *Anatomy* – become objects of mockery. Sterne evidently found Burton 'Laugh-at-able',[25] like Walter Shandy, for his grave pedantry; when Walter, believing 'that there is no passion so serious, as lust' (p. 592), writes a letter of advice to Toby, he naturally draws upon the antiquated medical data of the *Anatomy of Melancholy*. But whether the joke is turned against Burton, against the Shandys, or against the defenseless reader himself, the common effect of allusions to the *Anatomy* is surprise. Sterne's readers do not expect to find quotations from Burton in *Tristram Shandy*, and when they do, they are surprised. When they investigate the significance of the quotations, they should be further surprised and delighted by the comic discrepancy discovered between the original and the acquired significance of Burton's words.

IV

It is perhaps the strangest part of Sterne's complicated joke that it went undetected, or at least unpublicized,[26] for almost thirty years, and that when the borrowings were recognized, the jest was not. John Ferriar read his essay, 'Comments on Sterne', to the Literary and Philosophical Society of Manchester on 21 January 1791; it was published in the fourth volume of the Society's *Memoirs* in 1793, and was then reprinted in a revised form as *Illustrations of Sterne* in 1798. In the *Illustrations*, for the first time, Ferriar accepted and employed the word 'plagiarism': 'Who would suspect this heroic strain to be a plagiarism? yet such it is undoubtedly. . . .'[27]

A number of reasons may be suggested to account for this influential change of tone. In the first place, Ferriar's evidence was incomplete. Although it is possible that further borrowings from the *Anatomy* will be discovered in *Tristram Shandy*, since Sterne disguised quotations with considerable ingenuity, it is clear that some of the most significant ones were missing from Ferriar's catalogue. The epigraphs to Volumes V and VI provide the only oblique reference to Burton's name, and if the *Anatomy* is not identified as the source of passages like the 'apologetical oration' on war and the debate on marriage, Sterne's extensive and conspicuous use of learned materials makes it easier to classify him simply as a plagiarist.

Secondly, it is worth pointing out that reviewers welcomed the opportunity of renewing attacks upon Sterne. When Ferriar's 'Comments' was published, they responded with a call for a direct denunciation of Sterne's crime against Burton.[28] Pressure of this kind may have influenced Ferriar as he revised his essay for republication.

A third reason for Ferriar's accepting the verdict of plagiarism probably outweighs the other two: that is, the change in the status of the *Anatomy of Melancholy* between 1761 and 1798. When Sterne wrote Volume V of *Tristram Shandy*, Burton's work had not been reprinted for almost a century and was generally neglected; but before the end of the century there was a revival of interest in the *Anatomy*, with special attention given to its history as a mine for plagiarists.

Anthony Wood's *Athenae Oxonienses* (1691) first publicized the rumor that 'Gentlemen . . . put to a push for invention' frequently turned to Burton for assistance.[29] Wood's account of Burton and the *Anatomy* was used as the basis of a number of articles on Burton in the biographical dictionaries of the late eighteenth century, although not all included the legend of plagiarism.[30] Scholarly readers would have found passing references to the *Anatomy* in increasing numbers towards the end of the century – in Percy's *Reliques of Ancient English Poetry* (1765),[31] in Thomas Warton's *History of English Poetry* (1774–81),[32] and in five editions of Shakespeare's plays published between 1773 and 1793.[33] A wider audience could read of Johnson's interest in the *Anatomy* in the biographies by Hawkins[34] and Boswell,[35] and in Mrs Thrale's edition of his letters.[36]

Apart from these general notices and recommendations, writers of the later eighteenth century stimulated interest in Burton's work by drawing attention to the tradition of plagiarism associated with it and by adding several distinguished names to the list of writers supposed to be in Burton's debt. Letters written by Thomas Herring, Archbishop of Canterbury, were published in 1777 after the author's death. In one of them, Herring mentioned the *Anatomy* favorably, recommended Anthony Wood's account of Burton, and offered an observation of his own. He said that 'the wits of queen Anne's reign, and the beginning of George I's, were not a little beholden to him [Burton]'.[37] Many later references to Burton quoted Herring's tribute: in 1782, for example, the publisher and antiquarian John Nichols included it in two of his own books, the *Biographical and Literary Anecdotes of William Bowyer* and the *History of Hinckley*.[38] The legend of plagiarism grew in the 1780s. In 1785, Thomas Warton's edition of Milton's minor poems appeared to demonstrate that *L'Allegro* and *Il Penseroso* had been inspired by the *Anatomy*;[39] in 1786, John Nichols drew attention to a story taken from Burton in the *Tatler*;[40] and in 1788, Mrs Thrale published a letter of her own in the *Letters to and from the late Samuel Johnson*, in which she enthusiastically endorsed the theory of widespread plagiarism from the *Anatomy* and named Milton, Savage, Swift (meaning the *Tatler*), and Shakespeare as some of Burton's debtors.[41] By 1790, it was a well-known fact that the *Anatomy* was vulnerable to plagiarists; and during the 1790s, Sterne was all too easily absorbed into the tradition. Ferriar himself described the *Anatomy* as 'a source of surreptitious learning to many others besides our author'.[42]

Ferriar called Sterne a plagiarist, and although 'plagiarism' is an inaccurate description of Sterne's practices in the later volumes of *Tristram Shandy*, it is a word still commonly used. The revelations of the *Illustrations* had an unfortunate effect upon Sterne's reputation; but at the same time, with an irony which Sterne might have enjoyed, they were very good for Burton's. It took the scandal of Sterne's supposed plagiarism to bring copies of the *Anatomy* into circulation, for Ferriar's book was the immediate cause of a new edition of the *Anatomy* which appeared in 1800[43] – the first in over a hundred and twenty years, and the first of many nineteenth-century reprintings. In an indirect way, Ferriar was instrumental in bringing about the conditions right for the reading of *Tristram Shandy*, since he was responsible for putting copies of Burton's *Anatomy* into every well-equipped library.

NOTES

1. Ferriar's discussion of Sterne and Burton was first published as an essay entitled 'Comments on Sterne' in the *Memoirs of the Literary and Philosophical Society of Manchester*, 4 (1793), 45–86; it was then included in *Illustrations of Sterne: with Other Essays and Verses* (London, 1798), pp. 56–92, 98–9. There are accounts of the relationship between Sterne's and Burton's works in a number of modern studies of Sterne. The most important of these are Wilbur L. Cross, *The Life and Times of Laurence Sterne* (New York: Macmillan, 1909), pp. 139–40, 260 (and Cross's statements about Sterne and Burton were not changed in the 1925 and 1929 editions of his work); Henri Fluchère, *Laurence Sterne, de l'homme à l'oeuvre* (Paris: Gallimard, 1961), pp. 372–8; and J. M. Stedmond, 'Sterne as Plagiarist', *English Studies* 41 (1960): 308–12. Stedmond's article also appears in a revised form as an appendix to his book, *The Comic Art of Laurence Sterne* (University of Toronto Press, 1967), pp. 165–71.
2. Ferriar, *Memoirs*, p. 47.
3. These three points are made in the *Illustrations* on pp. 55–6, 56–7 and 88–90, and 83–4 respectively.
4. One is reminded of Tristram's project, announced in the first volume of his memoirs, of providing maps and appendices at the end of the twentieth volume 'by way of commentary, scholium, illustration, and key to such passages, incidents, or inuendos as shall be thought to be either of private interpretation, or of dark and doubtful meaning after my life and opinions shall have been read over (now don't forget the meaning of the word) by all the world. . . .' *The Life and Opinions of Tristram Shandy, Gentleman*, ed. James Aiken Work (New York: Odyssey Press, 1940), p. 36. Future references to this edition will be given in parentheses after each quotation.
5. *European Magazine*, 24 (1793), 269.
6. 'The *Mortgager* and *Mortgagee* differ the one from the other, not more in length of purse, than the *Jester* and *Jestee* do, in that of memory' (p. 27).
7. Robert Burton, *The Anatomy of Melancholy*, ed. Holbrook Jackson (London: Dent, 1932; rpt. 1968), I: 121. Future references to this edition will be given in parentheses after each quotation, with volume numbers preceding page numbers.
8. Sterne appears to have owned a copy of the 1652 sixth edition of the *Anatomy*. The bookseller's catalogue which included Sterne's library and one other library – and

which listed only the 1652 edition – has been reproduced under the rather misleading title, *A Facsimile Reproduction of a Unique Catalogue of Laurence Sterne's Library* (New York: James Tregaskis & Son, and Edgar H. Wells, 1930).

9. *Life and Times*, p. 264.

10. *Illustrations*, p. 66.

11. Ferriar, *Memoirs*, p. 60.

12. *Illustrations*, p. 68.

13. *Illustrations*, pp. 69–71.

14. *Illustrations*, p. 71.

15. *Illustrations*, pp. 71–80.

16. One pair of parallel sentences could be added to Ferriar's catalogue of materials borrowed for the third chapter of Volume V. Part of Sterne's – or rather, Tristram's – description of Walter Shandy at a time of crisis was imitated from Burton. In *Tristram Shandy*, the passage reads, 'he neither wept it away, as the *Hebrews* and *Romans* – or slept it off, as the *Laplanders* – or hang'd it, as the *English*, or drowned it, as the *Germans* . . .' (p. 351). Burton says, 'The Italians most part sleep away care and grief . . . ; Danes, Dutchmen, Polanders, and Bohemians drink it down; our countrymen go to plays' (ɪɪ: 185).

17. *Illustrations*, p. 73.

18. *Illustrations*, p. 83.

19. Ferriar discussed Sterne's use of Burton's learning in the *Illustrations*; Stedmond describes Sterne as 'eager for erudition' in his article, 'Sterne as Plagiarist', p. 312; and Fluchère analyzes ways in which data from the *Anatomy* are assimilated into *Tristram Shandy* in *Laurence Sterne*, p. 372.

20. Stedmond, 'Sterne as Plagiarist', pp. 310–11: 'Mr Shandy must sprinkle his discourses with learned references to authorities, and Tristram, as his father's son, must also display some touches of quaint erudition. Sterne could scarcely find a better symposium than the *Anatomy* to supply such strokes.'

21. Another aspect of this characterization of father and son is discussed by A. R. Towers in 'Sterne's Cock and Bull Story', ɛʟʜ 24 (1957): 12–29. In displays of learning, as well as in the sexual comedy of *Tristram Shandy* which is the subject of Towers's article, Walter Shandy may be said to embody the 'comedy of frustration' and Tristram the 'comedy of impotence'.

22. '*Quanto id diligentius in liberis procreandis cavendum*, sayeth Cardan' (p. 463). Cf. *Anatomy*, ɪ: 215: '. . . *quanto id diligentius in procreandis liberis observandum!* . . .'

23. '*Rhodope Thracia tam inevitabili fascino instructa, tam exacte oculis intuens attraxit, ut si in illam quis incidisset, fieri non posset, quin caperetur. –* I know not who' (pp. 576n–7n). Cf. *Anatomy*, ɪɪɪ: 90 n.2.

24. The only obvious debt to the *Anatomy* in Volume IX is the epigraph on its title page (p. 595); but it seems to me possible that the famous phrase, 'a cock and a bull' (p. 647), at the very end of the novel may, among its many implications, include a slight allusion to *Anatomy*, ɪɪ: 82, 'talk of a cock and bull over a pot'.

25. Laurence Sterne, *Letters*, ed. Lewis P. Curtis (Oxford: Clarendon Press, 1935), p. 74.

26. John 'Shandy' Henderson, an actor who died in 1785, should perhaps be given credit for the first advertisement of Sterne's debt to Burton. According to a reviewer for the *European Magazine* who wrote after Ferriar's paper had been read in Manchester but before it was published, Henderson had 'perused with great attention, just before his death, a book formerly much celebrated, though now seldom looked into, entitled, "Burton's Anatomy of Melancholy", and from thence extracted various parallel passages, which Mr Sterne had availed himself of in the course of his entertaining works' (*European Magazine* 21 [March, 1792]: 167–8).

27. *Illustrations*, p. 68.

28. See the quotation from the *European Magazine*, p. 50 above.

29. Wood, I: 535.

30. A paraphrase of Wood's account which first appeared in the *New and General Biographical Dictionary* of 1761 was adopted in the enlarged second edition of the *Encyclopaedia Britannica* in 1778, and in Stephen Jones's *New Biographical Dictionary* in 1794. James Granger's popular *Biographical History of England* (1769–74) gave a more critical description of the *Anatomy* which was later echoed in the revised *Biographia Britannica* (1784) and in Boswell's 'Hypochondriack' papers.

31. Thomas Percy, *Reliques of Ancient English Poetry* (London, 1765), I: 221–2.

32. Thomas Warton, *The History of English Poetry* (London, 1774–81), I: 62n; I: 432n; III: 295–6; III: 425n; III: 434n; III: 471; III: 483.

33. In the 1793 Johnson-Steevens edition of Shakespeare's plays, which brought together notes from the editions of 1773, 1778, and 1785, as well as from Malone's 1790 edition, references to the *Anatomy* occur as follows: III: 26n; III: 417n; V: 6n; VIII: 16n; VIII: 95n; VIII: 344n; XI: 16n; XI: 382n; XII: 504n; XIV: 437n; XV: 532–3n.

34. Sir John Hawkins, *Life of Samuel Johnson*, 2nd ed. (London, 1787), pp. 39–40.

35. James Boswell, *Life of Johnson*, ed. George Birkbeck Hill, rev. L. F. Powell (Oxford: Clarendon Press, 1934–50), esp. II: 121; II: 240; III: 415.

36. Hester Lynch Thrale Piozzi (ed.), *Letters to and from the late Samuel Johnson, Ll.D.* (London, 1788), I: 202; I: 310; II: 247–8.

37. Thomas Herring, *Letters . . . to William Duncombe, 1728–1757* (London, 1777), p. 150.

38. John Nichols, *Biographical and Literary Anecdotes of William Bowyer* (London, 1782), pp. 569, 570–1; *The History and Antiquities of Hinckley* (London, 1782), pp. 132–4.

39. Thomas Warton (ed.), *Poems upon Several Occasions, English, Italian, and Latin, with Translations, by John Milton* (London, 1785), pp. 93–4.

40. John Nichols (ed.), *The Tatler* (London, 1786), I: 13–14.

41. Thrale, *Letters*, II: 247–8.

42. *Illustrations*, p. 58.

43. A statement to this effect is made in the publisher's advertisement to *The Anatomy of Melancholy* (London: Vernor and Hood, 1800), I: xiii.

CHAPTER EIGHT

'Sterne's System of Imitation'*

JONATHAN LAMB

I continued to reason how much further one could proceed with this
reflection and multiplication of what is imitated: that is to say, whether one
could not only duplicate, but triplicate and quadruplicate it, and
go as far as one liked, finally, as it were one imitator imitating
another imitator, and so on and so on . . . (Alessandro Piccolomini)

Ever since John Ferriar compiled a regular institute of Sterne's borrowings the novelist's reputation has been divided between praise for his
spontaneity and originality on the one hand, and an awed respect for
the extent and subtlety of his thefts on the other. Sterne makes no bones
about exhibiting these two sides of his literary character and seems to see
no need to reconcile them: he is both the man who cautiously burned more
wit than he published and the 'inconsiderate Soul . . . who never yet knew
what it was to speak or write one premeditated word';[1] the man who in
Tristram Shandy cleverly plagiarizes Robert Burton's attack on plagiarism
and the one who, in the same novel,

> **praise for his spontaneity and originality . . . awed respect for the extent and subtlety of his thefts**

* Reprinted from *Modern Language Review*, 76 (1981), 794–810

declares that he begins 'with writing the first sentence – and trusting to Almighty God for the second'.[2] Like Tristram Shandy, Sterne seems to alternate between discretion and carelessness, between government of and by the pen, expressed as the difference between writing fasting and writing full (p. 436). These days it is usual to concentrate on his originality, his contempt for rules, his debunking of 'conventions', his readiness to experiment with the novel-form, in short his modernism. By contrast, those critics who have studied the texts and methods he used to supplement his originality have tended to conclude that he had an old-fashioned taste for literature and wit and that what is odd about him is what is out of date.[3] In this essay I want to strike a balance between these two views by considering Sterne's way of writing as fairly typical of his time and by showing that his most spontaneous and irregular production, *The Journal to Eliza*, obeys the same laws as his more finished work.[4]

Although in his politics Sterne was a Whig, and invented in 'uncle Toby' a hero who has little in common with the Tory satirists on the subject of the War of the Spanish Succession, in his writing he parodies the chiliastic visions of true-blue Moderns with as much vigour as Swift. Those who really believe that the arts and sciences are advancing towards their acme of perfection or who believe that wit and judgement will create between them an ultimate 'effusion of light' (*TS*, pp. 64, 198) are mocked with paradoxes and with the facts of their own unredeemed nature. Sterne's view, like Fielding's, is that life is not going to change very much and that any attempt to transcend its imperfections and ambiguities, like Walter Shandy's systems or the Man of the Hill's delight in the nectar of infinity, is ridiculous. The 'world' of *Tristram Shandy* is an Augustan one where 'incorporated minds', in Johnson's phrase, try to find some tolerable room on the isthmus of a middle state, a place where trifles have their importance and where 'small heroes' try to cope with destinies they never forged. That there is no amelioration of the human condition other than the light in which we choose to regard its discomforts and puzzles is the theme of most of Sterne's jokes. In the dedication he writes to a fellow sufferer, Sterne offers laughter as a fence against infirmities, not as a cure of them. In many respects 'Shandeism' is like the practical scepticism of *Rasselas, Tom Jones*, and *Humphry Clinker* in its determination to expect from life only what life will afford.

With an outlook similar to his Tory contemporaries it is not surprising that Sterne should share many of their literary tenets. He is not burlesquing Pope's rule:

A perfect Judge will *read* each work of Wit
With the same Spirit that its Author *writ*

when he asks 'madam' to tame her curiosity or when he invites the reader to imagine, and even write, his or own part of the narrative. In allowing the reader a dialectical share of the written product he is asking for that sagacity which Fielding frequently demands from his reader (especially in his tender scenes), comprising sufficient experience, humanity, and sympathy to make the *poco meno* as detailed and believable as the *poco più*. Sterne is as opposed as Swift to that passive curiosity (so close to prurience in his opinion and Fielding's) which makes a beast of the 'lazy grunting Reader'.[5] Ideally author and reader occupy a common ground on which what is already known fruitfully intersects with what is written and read: 'What oft was thought but ne'er so well exprest'. Sterne's version of this precept is given in a letter to an American admirer where he says that the reader's ideas are 'call'd forth by what he reads, and the vibrations within, so entirely correspond with those excited, 'tis like reading *himself* and not the *book*' (*Letters*, p. 411). It is a case of finding Pope's 'something' which 'gives us back the Image of our Mind'.

In neo-Classical literary theory the author experiences an analogous intersection between his own ideas and a text, whether it is the Book of Human Nature which Fielding transcribes in writing *Tom Jones* and which Johnson told Boswell diligently to read, or whether it is an actual text modelled on that great original. In the end the best literature and the Book of Human Nature are the same: Scaliger finds Virgil and Nature to be identical, while Virgil finds in Homer the same identity between what is and what is written. Classical literature forms a kind of institute of all human experience, hence Swift's horror at Bentley's officious attempts to lessen its authority and his mockery of the Moderns' assumption that contemporary experience will add to the stock. The dunce-narrator of *A Tale of a Tub* faces an embarrassing shortage of 'new Matter' when he writes his book because he has not understood, in the words of the *Spectator*,

that Wit and fine Writing doth not consist so much in advancing things that are new, as in giving things that are known an agreeable Turn. It is impossible for us who live in the later Ages of the World, to make Observations in Criticism, Morality, or in any Art or Science, which have not been touched upon by others. We have little else left us, but to represent the Common Sense of Mankind in more strong, more beautiful, or more uncommon Lights. (No. 253)

Joseph Warton, a critic skilled in tracing the genealogies of stories and ideas, concludes with Voltaire that 'All is imitation . . . Boiardo has imitated Pulci, Ariosto has imitated Boiardo. The geniuses, apparently most original, borrow from each other'.[6] For his own part Sterne gestures freely at his models, noting the critical distances between himself, Swift, and Rabelais and drawing attention to what is 'cervantic' in his sense of humour, not forgetting at the same time to emphasize 'the air and originality' of his book (*Letters*, pp. 76–7). The nature of the originality and the imitation will become clearer by looking at *Tristram Shandy* and some of the books that have contributed to it.

Walter Shandy's career illustrates the problems a man of erudition faces when he has an ambition to be original. Although it is his axiom that 'an ounce of a man's own wit, was worth a tun of other peoples' and his belief that a man may pick up an opinion 'as a man in a state of nature picks up an apple' (*TS*, pp. 147, 221) and show as inalienable a right to it, it is nevertheless the case that all his systems are cobbled together out of other men's books. No matter how exempt from the stream of vulgar ideas or the common road of thinking Walter thinks he is, and no matter how oddly he assembles his theories and applies them, it is evident from Chambers's *Cyclopaedia*, Burton's *Anatomy of Melancholy*, and Obadiah Walker's *Of Education* that his ideas once dwelt in other heads. He makes this point himself when he praises Ernulphus's anathema as a digest and institute of all possible modes of swearing and defies anyone 'to swear *out* of it' (*TS*, p. 183). Not that Ernulphus is original on this account: he merely provides the meeting point between all prior and all subsequent knowledge of oath-making (as Slawken-bergius does in the field of noses) to show that there is nothing new under the sun and that all is imitation. Walter's 'singular and ingenious' hypothesis is no more than a theory of imitation that his son, with some minor provisos, espouses too. Even Tristram's most original inventions, the digressive-progressive system of writing and the life-writing paradox, are not as original as he claims they are: Longinus praises Thucydides's management of digressions so that 'at length after a long Ramble, he very pertinently but unexpectedly returns to his Subject, and raises the Surprize and Admiration of all';[7] and Montaigne and Cervantes discuss the puzzles that arise when a life is being lived as well as written, not to mention Walter's frustrations with the *Tristrapaedia*.[8] Parodically Tristram concedes the point when, amidst his father's energetic quotation of his grief for Bobby's death, he traces the course of Eleazer's sentiment from the Ganges to Yorkshire and comically refines upon Sir William Temple's theory of the geography of imitation.[9] And when he declares that he intercepts 'many a thought which heaven intended for another man' (*TS*, p. 540) he outlines a potential community of ideas which is achieved whenever his interceptions are made, as they often are, at the level of libraries rather than the middle air.

At its most utilitarian Sterne's borrowing on his hero's behalf is merely a way of finding convenient sources of recondite information with which to ornament a theme like love, education, or death. So Burton's partition on Love-Melancholy is used heavily during the Amours, just as Walker is used extensively for the *Tristrapaedia*. As an act of vanity borrowing can be the means to claiming prestigious friends: Rabelais, Montaigne, Cervantes, Locke, Shakespeare. But whatever Sterne's first motives are in borrowing, he often develops secondary ones which make the discovery of a theft his triumph and not the detective's or which give an added allusive strength to a professed imitation. Consistent with his intention not to exert a false authority over the reader's imagination Tristram advises us to 'Read, read, read, read, my unlearned reader! read' (*TS*, p. 226); and it is only by reading that we will appreciate his plagiarism of Burton's attack on plagiarism, or be aware of the careful distinctions being drawn between sense and nonsense in Walter's definition of a good tutor, or find the sequel to his interrupted definition of 'analogy' (*TS*, pp. 414–15).[10] Likewise it is by reading that we can piece together the clues about his intentions or opinions that Sterne is dropping for our benefit. Slop's arrival is keyed to a couple of allusions to *The Dunciad* ('majesty of mud' and 'obstetric hand') that, combined with the simile of Hamlet's ghost, suggest a Smedley-cum-Douglas-cum-apparition emerging dirtily from below with just the sort of exaggerated theatricality that marks the dunces' performances in Pope's satire. Sterne has also wrapped this sequence in three allusions to Hogarth's *Analysis of Beauty* (*TS*, pp. 100, 105, 122) which refer to the line of beauty and to the greater or less amount of detail needed in the composition of a figure, 'the insensible more or less'; and they form a pictorial bridge between Slop's sesquipedality of belly and the natural grace of Trim's sermon-reading.[11] More than that they were consciously intended by Sterne 'mutually [to] illustrate [Hogarth's] System & mine', a system of careful alternation between tact and circumstantiality that he had already called 'the happiness of the Cervantic humour' (*Letters*, pp. 99, 77) and which Pope had praised as 'the *true Sublime* of *Don Quixote* . . . the perfection of the Mock-Epick'.[12] Clearly Sterne was using and thinking of his Cervantic-Hogarthian system in two different but related ways, as a satirical weapon of deflation and as a humorous tool of enlargement. The one is signalled by his allusion to *The Dunciad*, where exaggeration is reductively mock-epic, and the other by his allusions to Hogarth, where exaggeration serves to highlight and cherish the comedy of average human behaviour. That the sermon Trim reads is Sterne's own, printed at York in 1750, and that Slop's overthrow is a version of the one Montaigne describes in his essay 'Use makes Perfectness' serves to show that Sterne's faculty for allusive imitation is almost boundless.

Sometimes a borrowing is made in order to mock the author borrowed from. Sterne's respect for Locke did not exclude witty revenge being taken on the philosopher for his attacks on figurative language, and this is done mostly at the expense of Locke's occasional metaphors. When he calls the name of complex ideas 'as it were the knot that ties them fast together' and stresses the importance of that knot in keeping the parts of the idea united, he allows Sterne the opportunity of making the name the very opposite of a neat bond.[13] Although Obadiah's knots are 'good, honest, devilish, right, hard knots, made *bona fide*' (*TS*, p. 168) they are untied into all sorts of puns: 'knots' of speed, 'knot' as noose, 'knot' as life's obstacle, marriage 'knot', and even the umbilical 'knot' which Slop will have to tie when he has undone the other ones. Depending on names rather than on the natural associations of the mind is shown to be a risky business. Contrariwise Locke's idea of a dictionary, where the meaning of 'words standing for things' might be fixed by 'little draughts and prints made of them' (III: 11, 25), is borrowed by Tristram as a metaphor for facial expressions: 'There are some trains of certain ideas which leave prints of themselves about our eyes and eye-brows . . . we see, spell, and put them together without a dictionary' (*TS*, pp. 346–7).

The associative habit of mind that Sterne defends from Locke's nominalism is closely related to the borrowing habit. A true imitator does much more than simply spatchcock other texts into his own, or dutifully give a foreign idea an 'agreeable turn': other men's thoughts are not a supplement to his own but the very means by which his own thought takes place. His commonplace-book and his memory are to all intents and purposes identical and every passing idea in his head, which will inevitably have a literary reference if not a literary origin, instantly assembles associated literary ideas around it. This is what Walter is doing in his

other men's thoughts are not a supplement to his own but the very means by which his own thought takes place

oration on death, taming his grief by fettering it in the sentiments of ancient and neoteric stoics between which his mind moves with an almost natural associative agility. Just as fluidly Tristram's mind can shift from one borrowed sentiment to another as if they were decreeing the development of his thought and the pressure of his feelings. A sentiment from Montaigne leads naturally into one from Rabelais, and a quotation from Rabelais leads to an oath fetched not from Ernulphus but from *Don Quixote*.[14] The process is like Trim's knowledge of the fifth commandment, which is reached by going through the previous four: Tristram finds what he believes and feels very often by travelling through texts, *reading* himself in them and writing down the result. It is a sort of travelling commonly found in the eighteenth-century and early nineteenth-century comic novel: Parson Adams, Charlotte Lennox's Arabella, Catherine Morland, and Edward Waverley all try to find a path through life by books; yet the burlesque or pedantic elements of this imitative heroism are greatly outweighed by the freshness and vigour of minds that are formed by literary experiences or sharpened by literary expectation. This is a paradox that Sterne is well aware of and his favourite sources, as well as his characters, reveal his deep interest in the phenomenon of bookish naivety which accompanies true sincerity, and imitation which manifests an original integrity.

Montaigne and Burton are the two contemplative models, as it were, and Don Quixote the active one. Between them they represent the two sides of imitation: responding to literature as pure experience on the one hand, and converting experience into literary analogue on the other. All three confront the business of imitation in the spirit of classical criticism. When he decides to imitate the mad antics of Beltenebros, Quixote justifies his decision according to the rule of imitation that is observed in painting and 'in all other arts and sciences that serve for the ornament of well-regulated commonwealths'. Choosing to season his imitation with one or two of Orlando's frenzied actions, he carefully determines on those 'most essential and worthy imitation' (I: 181–2). Montaigne and Burton both make the point that borrowing is no theft provided the imitation measures up to the source (as Quixote's certainly does): Burton calls it 'assimilating what he has swallowed', and Montaigne says it would be indigestion to do otherwise.[15] They stress how different the borrowed thing becomes in its new setting, 'theirs . . . and yet mine', says Burton, and Montaigne: 'a Work that shall be absolutely his own'; while Quixote declares the singular perfection of his imitation consists in running 'mad without a cause, without the least constraint or necessity' (*DQ*, I: 183). Their originality lies in the manner of doing it, 'the composition and method', and Montaigne warns his reader to regard not 'the Matter I write, but my Method in writing. . . . For I make others say for me, what, either for want of Language, or want of Sense, I cannot myself well express' (*Essays*, II: 115). What seems to be a considered and highly self-conscious procedure of imitation is transformed into an extraordinarily intimate exhibition by means of the method of assimilation. 'I expose myself entire', Montaigne confesses, and Burton says, 'I have laid myself open (I know it) in this treatise, turned mine inside outward' (*Essays*, II: 72; *AM*, I: 27). In his Beltenebrising Quixote reveals parts so private, 'such rarities, that Sancho even made haste to turn his horse's head, that he might no longer see them' (*DQ*, I: 194).

Of the three methods of imitation Burton's shows most vividly how an odd individual can inhabit a book world and use its contents to reveal himself. His experience does not extend beyond the shelves of his college's well-stocked library, all his travelling is done by map, but because his theme is melancholy, a *disorder* afflicting the whole world as well as himself, he can never find an appropriate or standard response to the information of books. Although texts are exclusively his source for estimations of reality they offer him neither order nor a coherent body of symptoms. So Burton is constantly expatiating, 'ranging in and out', his moods constantly shifting between despair and optimism, anger and helpless laughter, all stimulated by the books he is endlessly traversing. His sentences have a loose subordinate structure designed for the instant incorporation of diverse material and they present a constant temptation to elaborate ideas and heighten moods: the word 'sermon' (*AM*, I: 35), or the simple proposition 'I am contented with my fortunes' (II: 188), tend to spawn examples, synonyms, modifications, and quotations in such profusion that Burton often leaps the gap and begins to impersonate his subject. The proposition 'He loves her, she hates him' is gone into so thoroughly that Burton is transformed into the forlorn 'he': 'I give her all attendance, all observance, I pray and entreat' (III: 231). When he cannot stop his words or the feeling they are intensifying he commits what he calls 'overshooting', as in 'Democritus Junior to the Reader' where he becomes Democritus in earnest in spite of the reader. He moves towards his emotional declaration by quotation and allusion (Erasmus, Horace, Martial, Terence) then suddenly realizing what he has done he retreats in the same manner, by way of Tasso, Tacitus, Bacon, saying finally 'in Medea's words I will crave pardon' (I: 122–3). Literature is the means both to promoting and excusing his decision to write satire, it is the vehicle for feelings of temerity and shame that Burton partly experiences and partly performs. It contributes to the larger performance in which he writes about melancholy in a melancholy manner, exhibiting in his treatise all the contradictions and irregularities that belong to the disease. Burton's real melancholy is both excited and controlled by books and his imitations of them, just as Quixote's imitation of Beltenebros is both the effect and the representation of madness. In both cases the otherwise unframeable contexture of a peculiar self finds an addition to its experience and a method of self-expression by an act of imitation.

In his essay 'Upon Some Verses of Virgil' Montaigne addresses himself to the subject of eroticism in life and literature, old as he is, in order to discover the true principle of excitement. He does not find it in Martial's over-naked verse, but in Lucretius and Virgil, whose 'words of flesh and bone' are the result of seeing 'farther and more clearly into things' and finding in them a 'Sense [which] illuminates and produces the Words' (*Essays*, III: 120–1). Discretion and obliquity are the keys to good love-poetry, an artful modesty of language in which 'words signifie more than they express'. This is what makes Virgil's Venus more beauti-fully alive than the original, and it is the same obliquity which makes the practice as well as the literature of love truly exciting. This is 'naturalized art', bringing actions and words as close to their objects as possible, and it is Montaigne's too: his 'Torrent of Babble' is exactly his, and yet not his; his 'apish imitating Quality' (III: 124) has ensured that what seems carelessness is really the obliquity and discretion he has learned from the poets and from Plutarch. He has warmed his old blood with their words of flesh and bone, and used his own to 'represent my self to the Life'. They are the words that make the book consubstantial with its author, known in him and he in it; and the representation of himself in such a book discovers experiences he would never have had, as giving ear to whimsies 'because I am to Record them' and studying books not to make his book but because 'I had made it' (II: 509–10).

When Sterne invests Tristram with his knowledge of Montaigne's *Essays*, the *Anatomy of Melancholy*, and *Don Quixote* he gives him room to experiment with all aspects of imitation: the discovery of life in literature, literature in life; the conversion of what is read into what is acted, the translation of what is lived into what is read. The Shandy family are chiefly concerned to convert literature into action, like Quixote: Toby's bowling green is analogous to the infant Tristram in so far as they are both used to realize texts upon (the *Flanders Gazette* and the fruits of Walter's study). Disasters occur when the text is removed (the Treaty of Utrecht), or when the realization goes wrong and ceases to conform to the model, or when something happens for which there is no textual authority (the circumcision until it is redeemed by the advent of a book). But when things go wrong literature comes unconsciously into the minds of those who think they are bereft of it. In his Apologetical Oration Toby quotes consciously from Yorick's sermon a sentiment borrowed from Burton, having already unconsciously borrowed from the same source himself (*TS*, pp. 461–2; *AM*, I: 57, 60). When Walter lifts himself off the bed to exclaim against his ill luck and to offer himself some consolation, he starts quoting the beginning of Yorick's sermon 'Trust in God' (*TS*, p. 277).[16] Similarly when he apologizes to Toby for having been rude about his hobbyhorse he insensibly uses Cassius's words to Brutus: 'Forgive, I pray thee, this rash humour which my mother gave me' (*TS*, p. 115),[17] prompting Tristram to make the comparison explicit in the next chapter but one. When Trim makes his speech on death equipped with no deeper reading than his muster-roll, he nevertheless manages to quote from the same essay of Montaigne's that Walter is using (TS, p. 365).[18] It is as if the mind, faced with painful or unexpected circumstances, naturally forms a sentiment out of them and makes an accidental discovery of life's literary qualities; or at least it is as if Tristram wishes us to think so. Certainly in his own case he is moved, rather than simply inclined, to find an authority for his feelings when they reach a higher pitch by overshooting in Burton's or Cid Hamet Benengeli's words.

Whether a character is being natural or studied, an imitation and therefore something of a performance takes place: texts control the emotions, as in Walter's discourse on death, and release them, as in Trim's. Either way imitation guarantees a mode of expression for sentiments that otherwise might have

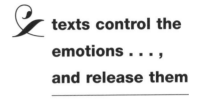

texts control the emotions . . . , and release them

none, so that in the heat of anger or the coolness of consideration oaths are made (as Montaigne says his are) by imitation and according to Ernulphian necessity. The imitative component in hobbyhorses is what makes them such apt instruments for character-drawing because it exhibits what the character wishes to present of himself (the 'personate actor' in Burton's phrase (AM, I: 15)) and it also is the means of turning his inside outward. Nature as art and art as nature meet at the point of imitation: Quixote promises himself real pain in his impersonation of Beltenebros ('the blows which I must give myself on the head, ought to be real, substantial, sound ones, without any trick, or mental reservation' (DQ, I: 187)), while the real pain Walter feels at the attacks on his son's virility forces him to turn at once to books for solace and utterance.

Tristram organizes his narrative according to a system of double imitation; that is, he borrows both the structure and the matter of his situations, sometimes from different sources. Walter's letter of instructions to Toby, for instance, is based on Quixote's to Sancho but consists of advice out of Burton. Toby's oration is *like* Quixote's defences of arms against learning but is also pieced out with the *Anatomy of Melancholy*, in the same way that Walter's quotation of Yorick forms a scene that recalls Quixote's complaint after he has been trampled by the bulls (DQ, II: 383). The arrangement can be even more complex, as during the reading of Ernulphus when Tristram makes a Burtonian oath and a Benengelian wager to affirm the Cervantic contrast between Slop's reading and Toby's whistling. This is like Yorick's death, which in its situation is like Quixote's (a beating followed by the loss of illusions and then life), but which is accomplished in Sancho's words and recorded in Shakespeare's. At its most subtle the technique can exactly reproduce the effects of the

147

original: Trim's unconscious imitation of Montaigne imitates Sancho's unconscious imitation of Plutarch (*TS*, p. 365; compare *DQ*, II: 440), and Sancho's speech is imitated again by Tristram when he wants to say something about sleep that is entirely natural and therefore better than 'the dissertations squeez'd out of the heads of the learned' (*TS*, p. 290). It is a clever irony and illustrates, as all these examples do, the inescapability of imitation.

Turning his own life into literature through the medium of literature Tristram unites the methods of Burton and Montaigne. As well as a fund of erudition Burton offers him the warmth and suddenness of imitative practice, and it is his overshootings that he concentrates on. The Lady Baussière rides on to the rhythm of Burton's callous rich man; Tristram pulls himself back from the brink of a vision of carnal bliss with the words Burton uses to extricate himself from nuns' and widows' melancholy;[19] and on his own account Tristram will overshoot himself into a warm contempt for rules (*TS*, p. 281) or into a devil of a chapter where the readers are advised to look to themselves (p. 350). And sometimes the habit of saying too much will suit the form of a Benengelian apostrophe, where Tristram will launch himself towards the object of his feelings, as Burton so often does, by inhabiting his text and speaking in it; and sometimes he will ring the changes on a word like 'cant' or 'nose' as Burton does on 'sermon' or 'mad'. It is in Burton's manner that Tristram makes his most poignant declaration: he is 'sick! sick! sick! sick!' (*TS*, p. 481) as scholars' labours are 'mad, mad, mad' (*AM*, I: 47). Montaigne, on the other hand, does not supply a model of imitative emotion, rather he shows what sorts of unions can take place between the mind and its object after that emotion has been raised. Constantly studying his relation to experience he ends up dreaming that he dreams, liking the 'deadest deaths' and finding a paradoxical completeness in writing a book that is its own subject, consubstantial with its sources and its author, because 'this Form is, in me, turn'd into Substance'.[20] When Tristram is fully aware of his life and book as the same thing his imitations have the 'ambitious subtilty' of Montaigne's associations: attacking plagiarism by plagiarizing Burton's equally plagiarized attack has the reflexive density of his borrowing Montaigne on the subject of borrowing (*TS*, p. 316) or his invocation of Benengeli's invocation (*TS*, p. 628; compare *DQ*, II: 285). His mind is so attuned to the business of imitation that there is no difference between writing and action, and he produces the very thing he is imitating.

That the emotions must be stimulated in the reading, assimilation, and production of literature is, of course, a sentimental axiom widely embraced by Sterne's contemporaries, but only he has investigated its implications for imitation far enough to find an appropriate critical theory. The process begins with his contempt for anything that is written in a straight line, emerging from the head as a cold unmetaphorical, 'sententious parade of wisdom'. Prose which separates itself from its subject, 'tall opake words, one before another, in a right line, betwixt your own and your readers' conception' (*TS*, p. 200), will smother any fire in the person using it and utterly inhibit any vibratory response from the audience. In their sermons Sterne and Yorick have avoided preaching that is designed merely 'to shew the extent of our reading, or the subtleties of our wit – to parade it in the eyes of the vulgar with the beggarly accounts of a little learning, tinsel'd over with a few words which glitter, but convey little light and less warmth' (*TS*, p. 317). Sterne's earliest attempt to discuss the difference between this bad sort of imitation and warmer performances of flesh and bone is in his *Fragment in the Manner of Rabelais* where, in two short chapters, a sympathetic churchman called Longinus Rabelaicus ('one of the greatest Critick's in the western World, and as Rabelaic a Fellow as ever piss'd') is proposing to write a 'Kerukopaedia' or system and institute of sermon-making; meanwhile in the next room Homenas (the dwarfish borrower of *Tristram Shandy*) is making his sermon by transcribing some of Samuel Clarke's choice paragraphs and thoughts 'all of a Row'.[21] Homenas's tears of shame at being discovered in his theft completely refrigerate his borrowed sublimity; on the other hand Longinus Rabelaicus's scheme, for all its pedantic sound, is an art to combine the making and the giving of sermons, 'a Way to do this to some *Tune*', suggesting the harmony of Tristram's fiddler 'whose talents lie in making what he fiddles to be felt, who . . . puts the most hidden springs of my heart into motion' (*TS*, p. 372). At the same time it is a plan to do for sermons what Ernulphus does for oaths, to create a pool of all possible sentiments so that no one can preach out of it.

In his important sermon 'Search the Scriptures' Sterne turns again to the difference between language that is essentially moving and that which is coldly elegant and nice, and once again he mentions Longinus's name. Using translation as a standard he undertakes to defend the scriptural or oriental sublime against critics (and Addison was one) whose delicacy prevents them from seeing its beauties. He begins by making the distinction Yorick makes in *Tristram Shandy* between eloquence which consists in 'an over-curious and artificial arrangement of figures, tinsel'd over with a gaudy embellishment of words, which glitter, but convey little or no light to the understanding' and the language of the heart, in this case the biblical eloquence, which consists 'more in the greatness of the things themselves, than in the words or expressions'.[22] In translation the classical sublime suffers because it lies in the expression, whereas the lofty ideas of the scriptural sublime survive the 'most simple and literal translations . . . and break forth with as much force and vehemence as in the original'. Longinus's praise of the sublime in Genesis is instanced, and he is paid a version of the compliment paid to Longinus Rabelaicus: 'the best critic the eastern world ever produced'. Sterne joins a debate here that had much to contribute towards the development of the English sublime in 'The Age of Sensibility',[23] and it seems likely that some of his illustrations were prompted by reading Longinus in William Smith's translation. Not only does he take some of Longinus's examples of the classical sublime to show how poorly they translate (Neptune shaking the earth and the description of Pallas's horses), he also shares Smith's enthusiasm for the scriptural sublime, particularly the description of the war-horse in *Job*, and no doubt read the discussion of that passage in the *Guardian*, 86, to which Smith alludes (*OS*, p. 171, n. 3). The distinction which the *Guardian* critic, Smith, and Sterne all enforce is of course Longinus's. In the famous seventh section of *On the Sublime* (pp. 14–15) he recommends that poetry and prose be carefully scrutinized to see 'whether it be not only Appearance':

We must divest it of all superficial Pomp and Garnish. If it cannot stand this Trial, without doubt it is only swell'd and puff'd up, and it will be more for our Honour to contemn than to admire it . . . Whatever pierces no deeper than the Ears can never be the true Sublime. That on the contrary is grand and lofty, which the more we consider, the greater Ideas we conceive of it; whose Force we cannot possibly withstand; which immediately sinks deep, and makes such Impressions on the Mind as cannot be easily worn out or effaced.

It is the same distinction Tristram and Yorick use to mock the French, whose sublime consists in mere words ('*more* in the *word*; and *less* in the *thing*')[24] and who believe that 'talking of love, is making it' (*TS*, p. 634). On the other hand, when the expression is a function of a real idea operating on the whole man (Trim's dropping of the hat, Slawkenbergius's 'lambent pupilability of slow, low, dry chat', or uncle Toby's *Lillabulero*), it 'leaves something more inexpressible upon the fancy, than words can either convey – or sometimes get rid of' (*TS*, p. 361). When words are used, they must be endowed with the expressive power of action or gesture and exert sufficient force to ensure a feeling response in the audience. This is the rhetorical and moral basis of Sterne's sermons and novels, for empty expression is not only bad in itself, it is also used to hide imperfections of the heart.

Sterne's use of the translation-test in establishing the superiority of the scriptural sublime points out one of the ways that Longinus contributes to his system of imitation. As a preacher Sterne felt it his duty to be the energetic medium between the force of scriptural language and the hearts of his congregation, so his 'dramatic' sermons are translations of the primitive and sublime ideas of the holy text into expressions that are made as forceful and immediate as possible by concrete language and a variety of rhetorical devices. The sermons are not simply elaborations or explanations of the text but enactments or imitations of the divine original, the fruits of a mind 'naturally elevated by the true Sublime, and so sensibly affected with its lively Strokes, that it swells in Transport and inward Pride, as if what was only heard had been the Product of its own Invention' (os, p. 14). Sterne was proud of his sermons in this way, despite their being filled with a good stock of Latitudinarian texts as well, because they testified to a necessary sympathetic power in him which he could transfer to his parishioners or, to use his own coinage of Longinus, having 'read' his own heart in the Bible text, this audience might then read theirs in his. In his novels Sterne arranges a variety of literal and figurative translations, from Slawkenbergius's last tale to those prints and etchings in the countenance, all of which require that sixth sense of the heart to interpret rightly. In *A Sentimental Journey* he fully develops the metaphor of translation to include all language, whether of the face, the body, the tongue, or an actual text, and this universal language provides the 'volumes' of material that Yorick translates into his two volumes of book. But there is a technique of translation in *Tristram Shandy* that is related directly to the one he developed for his sermons, and that is to take a text not from the Bible but from proverbial wisdom like 'All is not gain that is got into the purse' or 'Nothing in this world is made to last for ever' or 'It is with LOVE as with CUCKOLDOM' (*TS*, pp. 216, 560, 540). No doubt Sterne shared Quixote's opinion that proverbs are a non-systematic fund of truth, 'all so many sentences and maxims drawn from experience, the universal mother of sciences' (*DQ*, I: 138), and he has Tristram dramatize them in the same way that his sermons dramatize a scriptural text. The text for Trim's speech on death ('Are we not here now – and gone in a moment?') is, as Tristram says, 'one of your self-evident truths' (*TS*, p. 362), but when it is re-animated by Trim's rhetorical use of his hat 'nothing could have expressed the sentiment of mortality . . . like it'. Toby's gentleness, rendered in rather ornamental proverbial form by his nephew as having 'scarce a heart to retaliate upon a fly' (*TS*, p. 113), is illustrated in a dramatic realization of the proverb as Toby catches, apostrophizes, and liberates an actual fly.

There is a strong 'Rabelaic' element in these restorations of proverbial truth to the human activity from which it derives. In almost every case the body participates with the tongue to give the borrowed text the force of an original sentiment, as often in *Gargantua and Pantagruel* Panurge will use body language to redeem words and ideas from abstraction. Toby's literal and metaphorical kindness to flies exactly resembles those situations where Panurge enacts the proverb that applies to him by eating his corn while it is green, having a flea in his ear, or sitting between two stools.[25] Whatever truth has been lost from the proverb by timeless repetition is renewed by an active or dramatic imitation which makes words once more conversant about *things*. Indeed this sort of rhetoric, or translation, tends to dissolve the difference between text and example, word and thing, so that Trim, dramatically applying his body to the reading of Yorick's already dramatic sermon, becomes so moved that he cannot distinguish between what is descriptive and what is real. There are Cervantine analogues for this state of affairs, for example Quixote's mistaking the representation of *Gayferos and Melisandra* for the real thing, but Sterne is concerned to stress the value of the sympathy that accomplishes these translations of the active meaning of a text into gesture, speech, and ultimately another text. He is also discovering, with or through Rabelais, a version of the comic sublime that has its origin in scripture. When Panurge prophesies victory over the Dipsodes by breaking a staff over two wineglasses, and when Tristram, in his Rabelaisian Preface, takes Pantagruel's advice about finding wisdom in ordinary things and comes to the crux of his argument by pointing to his cane chair, they are using a primitive figurative language called by Warburton, in his discussion of biblical examples of it, 'the voice of the sign'.[26] It is not a case of supplanting words with gestures but of finding the complemental force of both that makes words, bodies, and things speak. This tendency carries both authors towards a kind of punning (also found in the Bible) that establishes an identity of action and naming: it is constantly to be found in Rabelais's etymologies of names and in his puns on *wine* ('Notez, amis, que de vin divin on devient'; *Cinquième Livre*, Ch. 45) where the deed and its verbal or liturgical signification become one; and Tristram is doing the same thing when he 'drops' remarks and drops *Remarks* (*TS*, p. 529). The same identity is established by Trim's hat which does more than represent the sentiment of mortality: 'It fell dead', and in doing so it returns the self-evidence of the truism to the much more powerful self-evidence of the voice of the sign.[27]

Sterne's choice of the name 'Longinus Rabelaicus' indicates that he was aware of the potential connexion between the two before he thought of writing his first novel: in Smith's edition of Longinus he found the theory of eloquence that deals with things rather than words copiously illustrated, and in Rabelais he found it put into comic practice. But Longinus offers even more. When Tristram overshoots into a warm disregard for rules, and dispenses with the critical cant about chapters in the same phrase his Epistemon uses to cast doubt on the value of a Kerukopaedia ('a story of a roasted horse'), he adds, 'O! but to understand this . . . you must read Longinus' (*TS*, p. 282). In Longinus's treatise we can find a rule for almost every one of Tristram's irregularities, and in this particular case Tristram, who is already imitating the performed warmth of Burton, is claiming a portion of the praise Longinus awards to Demosthenes when he says, 'With him Order seems always disordered, and Disorder carries with it a surprizing Regularity' (*os*, p. 56). Not only does Longinus stress the importance of imitation ('Let this, my Friend, be our Ambition; be this the fix'd and lasting Scope of all our Labours' (*os*, p. 36)), he also discusses in great detail the art of seeming impulsiveness, the 'brave Irregularities' that result from the deployment of rhetorical figures that are 'then most dextrously applied' when they 'cannot be discerned' (*os*, p. 51). The use of sudden silence, circumstantiality, apostrophe, digression, and impersonation exhibits that 'pliant Activity' of minds able to mark and transmit the flux and reflux of emotion so that 'they alter their Thoughts, their Language, and their manner of Expression a thousand times' (*os*, p. 58). The figures of *asyndeton* and *hyperbaton* are the ones Tristram is using when he seems oddest of all: his dashes, exclamations, and especially his 'transposing Words or Thoughts out of their natural and grammatical Order' (*os*, p. 57), which he carries to the point of transposing whole chapters, are his brave irregularities committed with Longinus's authority. These two figures also provide him with an official explanation of what Burton and Montaigne are doing. Montaigne is a past master in the art of giving 'his Audience a kind of Anxiety, as if he had lost his Subject, and forgot what he was about' and then unexpectedly returning to his subject (*os*, p. 60), while Burton is equally skilled at digressing with a warmth that 'carries your Imagination along with him in this Excursion' by elaborating an image and often dramatizing it (*os*, p. 64). What seems to be Tristram's odd originality is an art of performed feeling that has its rules in Longinus and its models in Montaigne's *Essays* and the *Anatomy of Melancholy*, and which contributes to his comic

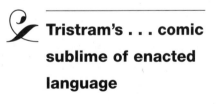

Tristram's . . . comic sublime of enacted language

sublime of enacted language. It is the imitation of naturalized art, one that avoids the extreme of sheer disorder on the one hand and of cold correctness on the other.

Longinus teaches Sterne another lesson, not by precept but by example. Boileau spoke for many eighteenth-century critics when he said of the seventh section of *On the Sublime* that 'this is a very fine Description of the Sublime, and finer still, because it is very Sublime itself' (*os*, p. 115, n. 2). It was a compliment Addison sought to pay Pope's Longinian exercise, the *Essay on Criticism*, and which Warburton re-tuned in his high estimation of the *Essay on Man*;[28] and it is a compliment Sterne deserves too. Tristram's use of hyperbaton is often characterized by the production of the very thing he is talking about: writing about a digression he makes one (*TS*, p. 618) and talking about gaps in his narrative he falls into one (p. 462). These comic sublimities arise from his decision never to separate the words he uses from the objects and feelings they name, so that they dwell *in* more than *about* their point of reference and, as the *Guardian* critic puts it, 'flow from an inward principle' in the thing described. It is the same sublimity that is brought to those imitations of Burton, Montaigne, and Benengeli which contrive to be what they are also about, and they show that the best parts of Sterne's commonplace-book were not filled with well-worn sentiments that might be given an agreeable turn but with examples of irregularity that have the self-evident quality of 'voices of the sign' or words of flesh and bone. These are the texts translated so directly and yet subtly from real experience of things or of other texts that they can be retranslated into *Tristram Shandy* with no loss of force. Tristram's imitations necessarily involve the expression as well as the sentiment because both his originality and his finest plagiarism depend on his seeing no difference between a live idea and its most appropriate form. With all the appearance of spontaneity lines are drawn and things 'come out of themselves' because Tristram is master of the art of turning fortune and his library into nature and of perceiving in the result, with a Longinian eye, that it could not have been otherwise and that others have done it before him.

If *Tristram Shandy* were to be regarded as an institute or system of life-writing practice then it would partly explain why Sterne found that he could not live out of it. When his work burst upon the London literary scene he responded to the acclaim in the character of Tristram and, later, of Yorick. Having invented a character who translates his life into a book by 'reading' his experiences and his texts and then transcribing them into his own, Sterne adopted the foible of Tristram's family by turning the book into his own life and talking Shandean nonsense with the best. Not quite in the sense that Warburton uses the disparaging phrase, Sterne was 'making himself' (*Letters*, p. 96) by imitating his imitations and fashioning a social style out of Tristram's asyndeton and hyperbaton. There can have been no sweeter triumph than his introduction to the Comte de Bissy when he 'found him reading Tristram' (*Letters*, p. 151), an exquisite confusion that he re-translated into 'The Passport. Versailles' in *A Sentimental Journey*. Really there is no contradiction between the imitative sincerity of Tristram, enacted in words on the page, and Sterne's, which 'cut no figure, *but in the doing*' (*Letters*, p. 157): both exhibit 'that careless irregularity of a good and easy heart' (*Letters*, p. 117) that is formed on the principles of naturalized art. Sterne was able to explore Montaigne's paradox, of being known in his book and his book in him, while functioning like Quixote of the second part in being constantly aware of himself as a literary fact and as a real person, *and* in being pestered with false sequels to himself. As a result his next novel illustrates the theme of literature and life meeting in a rather different way from *Tristram Shandy*, where literature is seen as a fund of forms and ideas that life takes to express itself with. Although literature and life bump into one another in Shandean ways in *A Sentimental Journey*, there is a constitutive as well as an expressive function to some of the incorporated texts. A paraphrase of Genesis about hands creates the circumstances of manual intimacy with Mme de L***, which in turn creates a metaphor of travelling by hand that is realized later in 'The Fille de Chambre. Paris', when real hands meet once again over a text (Crebillon's two volumes of *Les Egarmens du Coeur et de l'Esprit*) whose title predicts the consequence of the meeting and whose story contains a scene in which the hero and his beloved exchange sentiments over a book.[29] In these related sequences texts are promoting the action and controlling its outcome as well as expressing the feelings of the participants; they are determining the course of the story by providing the occasions of feelings and the nature of their sequels. No doubt Sterne was trying to render some of the effects of the considerable alterations his first novel had produced in his own life.

While writing this novel Sterne was also writing his *Journal to Eliza*, and he compared the two manuscripts to the two front wheels of his chariot: 'I cannot go on without them' (*Letters*, p. 364). What they have in common, and what distinguishes them quite markedly from *Tristram Shandy*, is a division between the body and the soul, action and sentiment, that is never properly bridged. At the upper level are sentimental feelings, often expressed in scriptural language, which are ethereal and disembodied; while at the lower level physical embarrassments take place that mock the spiritual aspirations. For example Yorick's physical ascent of Mt Taurira is outstripped by the spiritual rarefactions of 'Maria', 'The Supper', and 'The Grace', only to be followed by the plunging bathos of 'The Case of Delicacy'. In the *Journal to Eliza* Yorick is forced to interrupt the poignancies of a heart 'unsupported by aught but its own tenderness' to report that his doctors suspect him of having the pox. There are many more witty attempts to adjust these two levels in *A Sentimental Journey* than in the *Journal*; but what is interesting about the latter is that each level has its own imitative strategy that competes with the other.

When Eliza Draper sailed away to India aboard the *Earl of Chatham* Sterne built a dream-world out of literary artifice. The *Journal* is described as an English translation of a French manuscript containing the correspondence of two people represented 'under the fictitious Names of Yorick & Draper' (*Letters*, p. 322). Very soon it is translated once more into the pages of its companion text, and the future editor of *A Sentimental Journey* is instructed how to write the footnote on 'Eliza'. In every respect this is a literary relationship conducted in pen and ink and vying with other famous literary love affairs such as those of Swift and Stella, Scarron and Maintenon, Waller and Saccharissa (*Letters*, p. 319). All the way from Lord Bathurst's table in London to the ghostly Cordelia's ruins at Byland, Yorick is introducing Eliza's name to literary company and literary archetypes, and she contributes her part by penning letters that exalt the art of writing 'to a science' (*Letters*, p. 320). In this world, where 'there wants only the *Dramatis Personae* for the performance' (*Letters*, p. 364), Yorick identifies himself as 'a Dreamer of Dreams in the Scripture Language' (*Letters*, p. 366) and keys his highest moods to biblical phrases. Spiritual melancholy is linked to *King Lear* and especially to *Hamlet*: 'Alas! poor Yorick!—remember thee! Pale Ghost—remember thee—whilst Memory holds a seat in this distracted World—Remember thee,—Yes, from the Table of her Memory, shall just Eliza wipe away all trivial men—& leave a throne for Yorick' (*Letters*, p. 346). By sentimental magic the jester is turned into the king's ghost and Eliza is turned into Hamlet, and this twice-dead Yorick finds a romantic and equally ghostly confidante in the dead Cordelia. Again and again Yorick refers to himself as a ghost or a spirit, 'an etherial Substance' and a 'gawsy Constitution' that lives scarcely conscious of its existence and that looks forward only to the purest mental pleasures from meeting the object of its love once more. Having retreated to reflection and books, Yorick feeds his mind and discards his body with fictions and performances that have nothing to do with action and which are tricked out in a false sublime drawn from Shakespeare and the Bible. Bathos is supplied from only one source, *Tristram Shandy*. Sterne's own book intrudes to name or characterize disasters that will not be sentimentalized. The symptoms of the pox arriving inopportunely to mock 'Yorick's Spirit' are an embarrassment so comically disastrous that 'Shandy's Nose – his name – his Sash-Window are fools to it' hence it would 'make no bad anecdote in T. Shandy's Life' (*Letters*, pp. 329–30). The same force of Shandean prophecy is at work in the sequel, for the mercury treatment he is prescribed is taken from the authoritative work of Tristram's old enemy Kunastrokius (otherwise Dr Mead) and Yorick is obliged to submit to it 'as my Uncle Tody did, in drinking Water . . . *Merely for quietness sake*' (*Letters*, p. 347). Similarly, when some of his nights are made restless by visions and hot blood that are less than sentimental, he believes they have been forecast by that 'Prophetic Spirit wch dictated the Acc^t of Corp^l Trim's uneasy night when the fair Beguin ran in his head' (*Letters*, p. 326). The book has decreed what Yorick would prefer not to experience, accordingly he turns the prospect of his wife's imminent visit into Shandean business and prose: 'A Book to write—a Wife to receive & make Treaties with—an estate to sell—a Parish to superintend' (*Letters*, p. 376), aptly enough imitating Tristram's chapter of *things*. Mrs Sterne is no widow Wadman but she represents the carnal antithesis to the shadowy Eliza since she is after nothing but cash and is suffering from 'a weakness on her bowels ever since her paralitic Stroke' (*Letters*, p. 363). She will cause Yorick to sigh as many 'Hey ho's' as Toby did after the Treaty of Utrecht, and a Shandean finger points the moral (itself very Shandean) of these trials and discomforts: '☛—Every thing for the best!' (*Letters*, p. 347).

Longinus's metaphor for bad amplification, the multiplication of words that is unaccompanied by sublime meaning, is the separation 'as it were of the Soul from the Body' (*os*, p. 32) and it is as if Yorick has realized it in his *Journal to Eliza*: his upper half is sublimating itself amongst literary fragments and allusions while his lower one is collapsing into Shandean predictions. That there seems to be no point of equilibrium is made comically plain in Sterne's letter to 'Hannah' in which he promises to 'give up the Business of sentimental writing—& write to the Body' if his *Journey* does not make her cry as much as it has made him laugh (*Letters*, p. 401). Curiously Yorick uses the same metaphor as Longinus to describe the reason for writing the *Journal*, Eliza's departure: ''Twas the Separation of Soul & Body—& equal to nothing but what passes on that tremendous Moment' (*Letters*, p. 374). As a metaphor of his dissociated state made out of the literal separation that will take place at his death, it suggests both why the strategy of the sentimental sublime will fail and the reasons he had in using it. It is as if Yorick has planned to antedate his death by dying metaphorically into pure spirit, retaining his consciousness at the expense of everything else and converting all evidence of a real death yet to come into metaphors and tokens of one that has already occurred. His haemorrhages flow from a lover's bleeding heart and stain handkerchiefs which then become earnests of the absolute fidelity for which, as a ghost and a spectre, he waits to be rewarded. With all anchorage in things and bodies deliberately forsaken the sentiment cannot help but attenuate and get lost in professions that have nothing but scraps of Shakespeare to perform with. Shandean bathos arrives with the reminder that there is still some real life left and also a real death yet to die, in fact it re-establishes the comic association of sex and death that is so common in *Tristram Shandy*. When Tristram breaks a blood vessel over Jenny he wryly acknowledges the dangers of going down to the centre as he goes off to get himself treated, whereas Yorick tries to evade them by making gruesome symbolism out of the disaster and turning himself into 'Death alive', as Richard Griffith called him.

The *Journal to Eliza* ends with the contest between Shandean imitations and sentimental ones unresolved, but in two last letters Sterne presents it once more. To Mrs Montagu he declares gallantly that he will laugh at disasters like Cervantes and Scarron and die in a joke. To Mrs James he writes a melancholy valediction acknowledging that his spirits are fled and asking pardon for his Shandean follies; yet at the same time Shandean imitation almost insensibly takes over as he recommends, Le Fever-like, his only child to the protection of an uncle Toby in the shape of Mr James. That is his last imitation and in it he fulfils the promise he made to Hall-Stevenson: 'I shall leave you all at last by translation, and not by fair death' (*Letters*, p. 186).

NOTES

1. See *Letters of Laurence Sterne*, edited by Lewis Perry Curtis (Oxford, 1935), pp. 77, 117 (hereafter *Letters* with page references in text).
2. *Tristram Shandy*, edited by James A. Work (New York, 1940), pp. 342–3, 540 (hereafter *TS* with page references in text).
3. See, for instance, D. W. Jefferson, '*Tristram Shandy* and the Tradition of Learned Wit', *Essays in Criticism* 1 (1951): 225–48.
4. I have found the following articles useful in compiling this one: C. J. Rawson, 'Two Notes on Sterne', *N & Q* 202, NS 4 (1957): 255–6; J. M. Stedmond, 'Genre and *Tristram Shandy*', *PQ* 38 (1959): 37–51, and 'Sterne as a Plagiarist', *ES* 41 (1960): 308–12; Gardner D. Stout, 'Some Borrowings in Sterne from Rabelais and Cervantes', *ELN* 3 (1965): 111–17.
5. *A Tale of a Tub*, edited by A. C. Guthkelch and D. Nichol Smith (Oxford, 1958), p. 203.
6. Joseph Warton, *An Essay on the Genius and Writings of Pope*, 2 vols (London, 1782), II: 54.
7. Dionysius Longinus, *On the Sublime* (London, 1739), p. 60. Reprinted in the translations of Nicholas Boileau-Despréaux and William Smith by Scholars' Facsimiles and Reprints (New York, 1975), hereafter *OS* with page references in text.
8. Of his adding to but not correcting subsequent editions Montaigne says, 'From thence however there will easily happen some transposition of Chronology; my Stories taking place according to their patness, and not always according to their

Age'; and he goes on to draw the famous distinction between 'I now, and I anon': *Essays of Michael Seigneur de Montaigne*, translated by Charles Cotton, 3 vols (London, 1711), III: 247 (hereafter, *Essays*). This seems very akin to Tristram's splitting himself up into two lives: 'I perceive I shall lead a fine life out of it out of this selfsame life of mine', p. 286). When Don Quixote discovers that the first part of his adventures is already written and published he marvels that 'there was such a history extant, while yet the blood of those enemies he had cut off, had scarce done reeking on the blade of his sword', and he asks Samson Carrasco if 'the author promises a second part?' (*Don Quixote*, translated by Peter le Motteux, Everyman edition, 2 vols (London, 1906; reprinted 1972), II: 19–20). This confrontation with his own experience as text begins all the life-literature paradoxes of the second part, culminating in the meeting with Don Alvaro Tarfe, a character from Avellaneda's spurious sequel (page references are to *DQ* hereafter).

9. 'Of Learning', noted by James A. Work, 'The Indebtedness of *Tristram Shandy* to certain English Authors, 1670–1740', unpublished dissertation (University of Harvard, 1934), p. 135.

10. Compare Obadiah Walker, *Of Education* (Oxford, 1673; reprinted Scolar Press, 1970), pp. 46–7, 78–9. The definition is taken from Chambers's entry 'Analogy'.

11. Compare William Hogarth, *Analysis of Beauty* (London, 1753; reprinted Scolar Press, 1971), pp. 62, 66, 135.

12. 'Postscript to the *Odyssey*', *The Twickenham Edition of the Poems of Alexander Pope*, edited by John Butt and others, 11 vols (London, 1939–69), x: 388.

13. *Essay Concerning Human Understanding*, ed. by A. Campbell Fraser, 2 vols (Oxford, 1894), II: 50 (III: 5, 10).

14. *TS*, p. 367. Compare the paragraph with Montaigne's distrust of his judgement: 'Whoever shall call to memory how many, and how many times he has been mistaken in his own Judgment, is he not a great Fool if he does not ever after suspect it' (*Essays*, III: 403); and with Rabelais who maintains things 'even unto the fire *exclusive*' (*Gargantua and Pantagruel*, translated by Sir Thomas Urquhart and Peter le Motteux, Everyman edition, 2 vols (London, 1929; reprinted 1966), I: 138 (Prologue, *Pantagruel*). The quotation of Tickletoby's disaster and the advice to the reader which it introduces (*TS*, p. 266) is confirmed with an oath 'by St Paraleipomenon', formerly a knight with a Shandean hatchment in *Don Quixote*, II: 254: 'Sir Paralipomenon, Knight of the Three Stars'.

15. *Anatomy of Melancholy* (*AM* in subsequent references), Everyman edition, 3 vols (London, 1932; reprinted 1961), I: 25; Montaigne, *Essays*, I: 200.

16. Compare *The Sermons of Mr Yorick*, 2 vols (Oxford, 1927), II: 147.

17. Compare *Julius Caesar*, IV, III: 119: 'When that rash humour which my mother gave me | Makes me forgetful'.

18. Compare 'To Study Philosophy, is to learn to die', *Essays*, I: 89, 90.

19. Compare *TS*, p. 346: *AM*, II: 36; *TS*, p. 495: *AM*, I: 417.

20. See *Essays*, I: 95; III: 125, 317, 397.

21. See Melvyn New, 'Sterne's Rabelaisian Fragment: A Text from the Holograph Manuscript', *PMLA* 87 (1972): 1083–92 (p. 1088).
22. *Sermons*, II: 229–30.
23. See Northrop Frye, 'Towards Defining an Age of Sensibility', *ELH* 23 (1956): 144–52, where he discusses the influence of the translated Bible on the work of Smart, McPherson, and Blake.
24. *A Sentimental Journey*, edited by Gardner D. Stout Jr (Berkeley and Los Angeles, CA, 1967), p. 159.
25. *Gargantua and Pantagruel*, I: 265, 278; II: 355 (*Pantagruel*, Chs 2, 7; *Cinquième Livre*, Ch. 44).
26. See William Warburton, *The Divine Legation of Moses Demonstrated*, 2 vols (London, 1837), II: 34–47. He gives examples from Jeremiah 35 and Ezekiel 31.
27. Northrop Frye's discussion (cited above) of the 'primitive' or 'barbaric' metaphor that establishes identity rather than likeness bears a good deal on this one.
28. *Spectator*, 253; *The Works of Alexander Pope Esq*, edited by W. Warburton, third edition, 9 vols (London, 1753), III: 50–1, note.
29. *The Wanderings of the Heart and Mind or Memoirs of Mr de Meilcour*, translated by Michael Clancy (London, 1751), p. 155. The bashful Meilcour manages to make conversation with Hortensia about the book she is reading, 'the history of an unfortunate lover'.

PART FIVE

Narrative and Form

This concluding section is made up of two essays on two differing but nonetheless intimately related formal aspects of *Tristram Shandy*: Sterne's handling of his narrative (if indeed it is safe to use that word of a novel which seems to problematize narrative so comprehensively), and the apparently idiosyncratic manner in which Sterne uses the resources of typography, page layout and other features and resources of the physical book.

J. Hillis Miller's essay belongs more clearly to the first of these two formalist strands, the narratological, more especially the deconstructionist theorizing of narrative. 'Where shall I begin', asked the White Rabbit. 'Begin at the beginning,' replied the King of Hearts, 'and go on till you come to the end: then stop.' Human beings have a longing for narrative, for stories that follow a right order, trace the line of a credible logic, and arrive at a proper destination: Ulysses' return to Ithaca, the redemption and death of King Lear, the marriage of Elizabeth and Darcy. Such conclusions make a wished-for sense out of the badly designed confusions of our real lives. 'Meaning,' as Miller puts it, 'lies in continuity, in a homogeneous sequence making an unbroken line.' Notoriously, *Tristram Shandy* seems to have very little truck with the human desire for order and sequence. The book begins with an interruption. A little later in the first volume, Sterne explicitly rejects the narrative linearity associated with the rise of what we have come to call the 'novel' when he sends 'Madam' back to read a previous chapter, specifically in order to 'rebuke a vicious taste which has crept into thousands besides herself, – of reading straight forwards . . . in quest of the adventures'.

In the twentieth century many narratologists, from Russian formalists to deconstructors, have queried the mimetic functions of the novel as a genre, laid bare its artifices, denied the determinacy of its narratives, resisted its seductive tendencies to closure. *Tristram Shandy* has been seen as providing particularly potent evidence for this project. For Hillis Miller, as earlier in the twentieth century for Shklovsky, *Tristram Shandy* is the most representative of all novels, serving him for his central exemplum in this deconstructive speculation on the 'narrative middle' (narrative beginnings and endings having already received their theoretical dues). *Tristram* figures, in the freehand lines with which Sterne schematizes the progress and returns of his story, the inevitable discontinuities, disintegrations and indirections of all prose fictional narrative structures. Throughout, *Tristram* is 'a hilarious parody and undoing of the idea of a continuous and complete life story', showing 'that all narrative lines come into existence in defiance of the fact that a narrative can neither begin nor proceed continuously once it has begun, nor ever stop or reach its goal once it has, in defiance of these impossibilities, begun continuing'.

Miller's breathtaking excursus on the figure of the 'line', and the filiations of Sterne's masterpiece with many other lines in western narrative traditions, is no doubt the seminal deconstructive account, and has evoked a number of responses. In an important and powerful essay Robert Markley has clarified the rationales of 'Narrative Middles', and related Miller's approach particularly to American deconstructive theoretics and stylistics. Markley insists that 'the style of deconstruction . . . holds out the exhilarating opportunity of investigating not merely local meanings but the problematic of meaning, the silences, the abyss, of western metaphysics'. That bold claim sets out in its most explicit form a binary opposition between 'theoretical' and text-centred approaches, the dismissive 'merely' occluding centuries of carefully analytic textual reading. Markley finds Miller (like Shklovsky) not much concerned with the text which is his ostensible subject: 'Miller does not try to interpret Sterne's novel but offers instead a "continuation" of *Tristram Shandy*'s "magnificent demonstration" of "the impossibility of distinguishing irrelevance from relevance, digression from the straight and narrow"' ('*Tristram Shandy* and "Narrative Middles"' (1985), pp. 182–3). (This perhaps does not do complete justice to Hillis Miller, in this essay as elsewhere one of the most supple and subtle of Derridean close readers.)

Melvyn New on the other hand, in an essay published in the early 1990s, rejects the modernist (rather, postmodernist) insistence that all literature can be shown to be open and indeterminate, and opposes that tendency in the work on Sterne of Miller, Markley, Flores, Lamb and others. For all its turnings and digressions, *Tristram* as a document, and particularly as a document which constantly appeals to and includes all sorts of other explanatory and encyclopaedic documents, restages 'the instinct, the drive to order and comprehend through our language whatever is not yet our language. The urge not merely to begin but to complete the narrative of ourselves is evident everywhere in *Tristram Shandy*.' *Tristram* is not only a text but also a text in a particular cultural and bibliographic context, a book which belongs to a community of books. Sterne, 'this rural Anglican clergyman', belongs in a specific eighteenth-century cultural location, and is not to be found at home 'in the indeterminate, existential, absurd, phenomenological, solipsistic universe where we nowadays seem to find him'. If Sterne was a sceptic and an intellectual prankster, he valued too the aspiration to knowledge and understanding (these are all characterizations which place him in his own time). As New puts it, 'Sterne keeps us aware . . . that while every attempt to create a world of certainty and truth will fail, the attempt is what ties us to the community of humanity . . . the present emphasis in narrative theory on the epistemology of indeterminacy is a tendency he might have predicted but never have succumbed to' ('Sterne and the Narrative of Determinateness' (1982), pp. 322, 329).

Christopher Fanning, in the second essay in this section, brings Sterne's narrative methods more fully into engagement with the physical characteristics of his book. Beginning with the same issues of narrative coherence, Fanning turns his attention to 'space' in the fictional world, in the technique of fiction, and, especially, in the printed form of Sterne's work. The spatial layout of Sterne's printed page is to a significant (though uncertain) extent a result of his conscious design, visibly and effectively different from that of his 'novel'-writing contemporaries. Fanning sets out to show how textual layout and spacing, the typographical presentation of speech and dialogue, and the use of such features of punctuation as varied lengths of hyphen, enact and perform meaning in Sterne's text, in the sermons and, more especially, in *Tristram Shandy*. Such features of *mise en page* both guide and problematize the reading of *Tristram*; the oral reader cannot adequately express its passages of parallel text, concurrent translation, simultaneous speakers, footnotes, asterisks and freehand lines, black and blank and marbled pages. *Tristram* is 'not just a score for performance' (and indeed Fanning shows this is a score beyond performance), but 'a performance in itself'.

The inescapable physicality of Sterne's book, his uses of typography and meta-typography, have been familiar fields of discussion. Fanning's essay however may be seen as part of a more recent project of examination of the history and forms of the book, of the practices of its production and the potentialities of its features, which has made steady progress among recent students of the Renaissance and seventeenth century, and is now being taken up by students of writings of Sterne's century, particularly following pioneering work by James McLaverty on the printing processes and forms of the poetry of Alexander Pope ('The Mode of Existence of Literary Works of Art: the Case of the *Dunciad Variorum*', *Studies in Bibliography*, 37 (1984), 82–105). Though Sterne's sparse and spaced page indeed does not much resemble the thick and variegated texture of such works of parody scholarship – such 'mock books' – as Swift's *Tale* and Pope's *Dunciad*, his intentional and directed use (or abuse) of the possibilities of print and textuality, more especially of the typographical and paratextual devices of the annotated learned text, surely relate him to this aspect of Scriblerian satire. J. Paul Hunter's extended and detailed investigation of print technology and bookmaking in both Sterne and Pope in his essay 'From Typology to Type: Agents of Change in Eighteenth-Century English Texts' (1994) offers a model for future work on this rich and suggestive historico-cultural issue.

CHAPTER NINE

'Narrative Middles: a Preliminary Outline'*

J. HILLIS MILLER

I f Edward Said has discussed beginnings and Frank Kermode the senses of ending, the coherence of the part in between is no less a problem. The middle may be put, for the moment, under the friendly, but by no means entirely rainproof, umbrella of Soren Kierkegaard. 'My life,' says 'A' in *Either/Or*, 'is absolutely meaningless. When I consider the different periods into which it falls it seems like the word *Schnur* in the dictionary, which means in the first place a string, in the second, a daughter-in-law. The only thing lacking is that the word *Schnur* should mean in the third place a camel, in the fourth, a dust-brush.'[1]

Meaning, whether in a narrative, in a life, or in a word, lies in continuity, in a homogeneous sequence making an unbroken line. The human need for continuity is so strong that a man will find some principle of order in any random sequence. One might note, for example, that a daughter-in-law is indeed a string, almost in the Jamesian sense of 'ficelle'. A daughter-in-law is an indispensable, though somewhat extraneous, means of maintaining the continuity of a lineage from father to son to grandson. No doubt one could, given a little ingenuity, assimilate the camel and the dustbrush to the line of that *Schnur*. Part of the difficulty of the middle, all that series in a narrative between beginning and end, is not the encounter with fragmentation or irrelevance, but the difficulty of establishing some principle by which one could be sure

---

* Reprinted from *Genre*, 11 (1978), 375–87

something is extraneous. How could one be certain a given element is in fact an inassimilable episode ('There should be no episodes in a novel,' said Anthony Trollope[2]), or an 'irrelevant detail'?[3]

Whether one thinks of a novel from the point of view of the writer writing it, or of the reader reading it, or as the mirroring of an objective series of historical events, or as the following of the line of a life, or as the making up 'out of whole cloth' of a coherent story, one is likely to use models of causal chaining or of organic growth to describe the desirable hanging together of a narrative. So powerful is this assumption of linear continuity that it may easily be imputed to some random collocation of contiguous morsels.

Plot, double plot, subplot, narrative strands, graph or curve of the action, chain of events – this compelling image of a story as a line which might be projected, plotted, graphed, or diagrammed as a continuous spatial curve, or as a zigzag, as some form of visible figure, has a long history in Western thought. This history forms an extended line of lines, in genealogical filiation. The 'origins' of this line of lines may be found in the double source of our culture in the Greeks and in the Hebrews. The Psalmist's 'The lines are fallen unto me in pleasant places; yea, I have a goodly heritage' (Psalms 16:6) is often echoed and has become almost a cliché, as when Trollope's Josiah Crawley sardonically reverses it in *The Last Chronicle of Barset*. Greek lines include the twice-bifurcated dialectical line of *The Republic*, and the line image implicit in the Greek word for historical narrative, *diegesis*, with its suggestion that a history or a story is the leading out of a line of events or its tracking down later. To skip over such intervening lines as the spiral track of Dante's *Purgatorio* and the compass lines of Donne, there is a modern sequence, more closely adjacent to the novel proper, threading its way through the development of nineteenth- and twentieth-century literature. This more recent series goes from the Hogarthian lines of beauty and of grace through the splendid parodies of these in Sterne, on to Edmund Burke, then to the aesthetic arabesques of Friedrich Schlegel and the spirals of Goethe, to the citation of Corporal Trim's flourish by Balzac as the epigraph to *La peau de chagrin*, to Baudelaire's thyrsis, to Henry James's figure in the carpet, and to all those lines, genealogical, topographical, and facial, in Thomas Hardy's work. In America there is a splendid branch line which goes from Poe's arabesques to Emerson's 'Circles' ('There are no straight lines in nature'), through the shoreline of Whitman's 'Out of the Cradle Endlessly Rocking', and elsewhere in his poetry, to Stevens's defiance of Emerson and Whitman in 'The Stars at Tallapoosa' ('The lines are straight and swift between the stars. . . . The mind herein attains simplicity'), to Ammons's admirably exuberant 'Lines', where the line proliferates madly in its curvings, re-curvings, and crossings: 'lines exploring, intersecting, paralleling, twisting, / noding: deranging, clustering'.

Sterne and Schlegel will serve here to document a preliminary exploration of what is put on the line by this figure. In both cases the writing or reading of a novel, or the course of a story, or the line of a life, is thought of as the energetic production of a filament. This strand is generated by the balance of antagonistic forces, within and without. This gradually produces a visible figure, open to theory, that is, open to the speculative unifications of some onlooker, some narrator. ('Theory' is from the Greek *theasthai*, to watch, observe. 'Theater' has the same source.) Alternatively, these activities of writing, reading, or living, the making of a life or of history, are thought of as the retracing of such a line already produced. Tracing, the making of a track, or retracing, the following of a track already made – the ambiguity of a first which is already second, of an event which has always already happened, of a pathbreaking which is always also a path-following, is always present in all versions of the narrative line as a production, a performance, a happening. If even the first is already a repetition, it contains always within itself the possibility of further repetitions – citations, parodies, subversions, doublings with a difference, subplots, counterplots to match the main plot.

Behind Sterne's outrageous graphings lie Hogarth's lines of beauty and of grace, referred to several times with approbation early in *Tristram Shandy* and then hilariously parodied in two places. That Hogarthian line, whether in the two-dimensional or almost two-dimensional form of the line of beauty, or in the three-dimensional spiral of the line of grace, was itself copied from antiquity, where it is already a sign, even the sign of a sign. The enigmatic representation of the line of grace, spiral form around a cone, in Hogarth's 'Tailpiece, or the Bathos' (1764) is itself copied from 'fig. 26' of the first plate of the *Analysis of Beauty* (1753). The enigma lies in the two inscriptions or legends explaining the spiral around a cone, one from Tacitus, the other from Maximus Tyrius. The spiral itself stands for the cone around which it is wrapped in asymptotic yearning. The cone in turn, surprisingly, stands for the perfection of the female body, for Venus. I say 'surprisingly' because a cone might at first seem more a male than a female symbol, depending on whether one takes it inside out or outside in, as sword or as sheath. This cone, however, is a 'pyramidal shell', and it tapers not to a point, but to a 'small circumference'. The first inscription, from Tacitus's *History*, Bk. I, ch. 3, reads: 'Simulacrum Deae non effigie humana: continuus orbis latiore initio tenuem in ambitum, metae modo, exsurgens, [s]et ratio in obscuro' ['The image (*simulacrum*) of the goddess does not bear the human shape; it is a rounded mass rising like a cone from a broad base to a small circumference. The meaning of this is doubtful,' trans. Church and Brodribb]. The second inscription, from the *Dissertationes* of Maximus Tyrius, reads: 'Venus a Paphiis colitur, cuius Simulacrum nulli rei magis assimile, quam albae Pyramidi' ['By the Paphians Venus is honored; but you cannot compare her statue to anything else than a white pyramid', trans. Thomas Taylor].[4] The key word in both these inscriptions is *Simulacrum*: image, copy, icon, artificial or phantasmal likeness. The line of beauty in the flesh, seductively graceful curve of breast, waist, hip, and thigh, is represented by a hollow cone. This is then further abstracted as a spiral line moving around that cone toward an effaced central point or axis at the blunted apex, sign of the missing interior. The line will never meet that virtual point, though it will approach closer and closer to it in infinite looping approximations.

This line is then taken by Sterne away from its 'origin', the mysterious attractions of the female body, expressible only as the sign of the sign of an absence in the Hogarthian curve. The Hogarthian line is made by Sterne the image for the spinning out of a story, narrative line or life line. Seduction becomes production, drawing from without generation from within, or the following, after the fact, by some narrator, of that generation. The passages from Sterne are splendidly comic extrapolations of the Hogarthian line of beauty. The first is in chapter forty of volume six:

I am now beginning to get fairly into my work; and by the help of a vegetable diet, with a few of the cold seeds,[5] I make no doubt but I shall be able to go on with my uncle *Toby*'s story, and my own, in a tolerable straight line. Now,

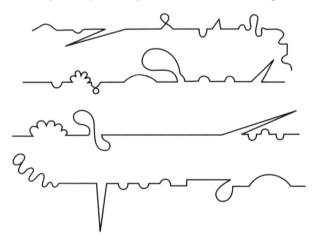

These were the four lines I moved in through my first, second, third, and fourth volumes—In the fifth volume I have been very good,—the precise line I have described in it being this:

By which it appears, that except at the curve, marked A, where I took a trip to *Navarre*,—and the indented curve B, which is the short airing when I was there with the Lady *Baussiere* and her page,—I have not taken the least frisk of a digression, till *John de la Casse*'s devils led me the round you see marked D.— for as for *c c c c c* they are nothing but parentheses, and the common *ins* and *outs* incident to the lives of the greatest ministers of state; and when compared with what men have done,—or with my own transgressions at the letters A B D —they vanish into nothing.

In this last volume I have done better still—for from the end of *Le Fever*'s episode, to the beginning of my uncle *Toby*'s campaigns,—I have scarce stepped a yard out of my way.

If I mend at this rate, it is not impossible—by the good leave of his grace of *Benevento*'s devils—but I may arrive hereafter at the excellency of going on even thus;

---

which is a line drawn as straight as I could draw it, by a writing-master's ruler, (borrowed for that purpose) turning neither to the right hand or to the left.

This *right line*,—the path-way for Christians to walk in! say divines—

—The emblem of moral rectitude! says *Cicero*—

—The *best line*! say cabbage-planters—is the shortest line, says *Archimedes*, which can be drawn from one given point to another.—

I wish your ladyships would lay this matter to heart in your next birthday suits!

—What a journey!

Pray can you tell me,—that is, without anger, before I write my chapter upon straight lines—by what mistake—who told them so—or how it has come to pass, that your men of wit and genius have all along confounded this line, with the line of GRAVITATION?

With admirably subversive wit, yoking heterogeneities violently together, this passage gathers together many of the figures of the narrative line. It gathers them not to twine them into a unified chain or rope, but to play one figure against the others in a running, constantly interrupted series undercutting the possibility of an innocently solemn use of any one of the figures. Though the passage claims allegiance to the continuity of the straight line, its rhythm is abrupt, broken at every moment by Sterne's dashes and by the sudden shift to a new figure or topic. 'What a journey!' The line of a narrative, Sterne assumes, should ideally be the production of a perfectly straight sequence going from beginning through middle to end, retelling with no digressions or episodes Uncle Toby's life and his own. This generation of a narrative line is conflated with the actual drawing of a straight line by rule, according to a norm (*norma*: Latin for ruler). This conflation calls attention to the figurative, conventional quality of the image of the narrative line. At the same time it calls attention to its absurdity. It is a good example of Sterne's splendid gift for destroying a figure by taking it literally, with mock solemnity. He reminds the reader that a narrative is in fact nothing like a straight line drawn with a ruler, or that if it were it would be without interest. The interest of a narrative lies in its digressions, in episodes that might be diagrammed as loops, knots, interruptions, or detours making a visible figure.

> **The paradox of the narrative line lies in the impossibility of distinguishing irrelevance from relevance, digression from the straight and narrow**

What then happens to the concept of digression? The paradox of the narrative line lies in the impossibility of distinguishing irrelevance from relevance, digression from the straight and narrow. *Tristram Shandy* as a whole is the magnificent demonstration of this, for example in the way the passage promising a line henceforth as straight as a ruler can draw it is followed by the totally 'digressive' journey of Book VII. The paradox of the narrative line lies also in the incompatibility between moral rectitude and narrative interest. A wholly 'moral' story would be a straight line without features, altogether boring, like a journey in which nothing happens, while every distinguishing feature of a given story is at the same time a moral transgression. 'And make straight paths for your feet, lest that which is lame be turned out of the way,' said Paul in the Epistle to the Hebrews (12:13).

The same contrast between the featureless straight line and the line curved to become a sign, so carrying meaning and becoming a plot, but at the same time becoming transgressive, deviant, forms and reforms itself in the nine lines superimposed on the seemingly innocent figure of a narrative as a linear series of events: the line of a journey, with its side-trips and airings; the line of a logical argument, broken by digressions;

the grammatical line of words in a piece of writing, which may be interrupted by parentheses, *c c c c c*, and so on; the line of history with the zigzagging ins and outs of ministers of state; the ruled line of 'moral rectitude', broken by lamenesses, wanderings, transgressions leading the feet away from the straight and narrow; the straight line of a row of cabbages in a garden; the geometrical line defined by Archimedes in *On the Sphere and Cylinder*, I, Assumption I: 'Of all lines which have the same extremities the straight line is the least'; the line of gravitation, with a characteristic multiple pun on gravitation as Newtonian attraction, as the vertical descent of bathos or the art of falling, and as the grave solemnity of the horizontal line of moral rectitude, each meaning interfering with the others and 'confounding' them; and finally, to come full circle back to Hogarth and the Venusian line, as the straight line of an ideally economical birth-day suit, where, I take it, there is the surfacing of an erotic pun which has been lurking under the surface throughout the passage. The birth-day suit is, as the notes to one edition say, 'clothes worn at a birthday celebration', but it surely also means nakedness. The figure sets the dullness of a straight line drawn from one point to another on a female body against the Hogarthian curved line of beauty which strays seductively from the straight road, following the contours of breast, waist, and thigh, to lead its beholder hopelessly astray in digressions, transgressions, parenthesis, episodes, and airings, wanderings from the straight path like the episodes in *Tristram Shandy*.

Dazzling set of different linear figures gathered in a loose hank, superimposed, tangled, interfering with one another like multiple incompatible signals graphed simultaneously on an oscilloscope – the passage in *Tristram Shandy* disarticulates the line, pulverizes it, reduces it to fragmentary bits. It does this by showing its arbitrary or figurative quality and by showing the comic inability of this figure to account for or plot the various regions of experience it is supposed to represent. The straighter the line, the more Archimedean it is, the less significance it has as a representation of anything human, the less susceptible it is to being repeated again as a recognizable sign, and the less it invites, unlike the line of beauty, to reproduction. On the other hand, the more information the line carries, the more curved, knotted, hieroglyphic, it is, the less it can any longer be called a line, and the closer it approaches the totally overdetermined state of a tangled ball of broken bits of yarn or of a cloud of dust in Brownian movement, impossible to graph by any line.

An erotic motivation, like that of the birthday suit, though with an opposing affect, generates the other literally represented line on a page of *Tristram Shandy*. Corporal Trim warns Uncle Toby that marriage is confinement, like the inquisition: 'once a poor creature is in, he is in, an' please your honour, for ever'. Celibacy, the single state, the state of unattachment, is, on the contrary, liberty, the liberty of the arabesque:

Nothing, continued the corporal, can be so sad as confinement for life—or so sweet, an' please your honour, as liberty.

    Nothing, Trim—said my uncle Toby, musing—

    Whilst a man is free,—cried the corporal, giving a flourish with his stick thus—

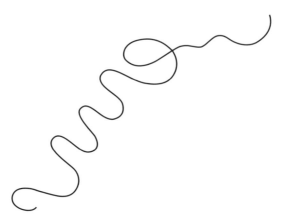

    A thousand of my father's most subtle syllogisms could not have said more for celibacy. (IX: ᴠ)

Tristram Shandy throughout is a hilarious parody and undoing of the idea of a continuous and complete life story. It shows that all narrative lines come into existence in defiance of the fact that a narrative can neither begin nor proceed continuously once it has begun, nor ever stop or reach its goal once it has, in defiance of these impossibilities, begun continuing. As one example of this, Corporal Trim's flourish in its irregularity is a subversive parody of the Hogarthian line of beauty. Trim's flourish is still a line, however. If marriage is imprisonment, the immobilization of the stick, celibacy is freedom, but freedom to move in response to 'gravitational' forces. Freedom is not reaching the goal, that Venusian infinitely distant or absent point, apex of the cone. Corporal Trim's arabesque is the production of a lifeline generated by energies within in response to energies without, the moving point of the walking stick pulled this way and that by its own vital impetus and by its response to external attractions. The resultant line is the graph of these constantly changing vector forces. It is unlike Hogarth's line only in being more wandering, reluctant, hesitant, given to turning back and looping over itself. It is unlike also in having no visible orientation or motivating goal.

Does it go from bottom to top or from top to bottom? Which way did Corporal Trim flourish his stick? There is no way to be sure.

Paradoxically, this wandering celibate line, which goes on producing itself only so long as it remains chaste, untied, has the power of generating progeny, sons and grandsons bound to their sire in duplicating family resemblance. One such child is Balzac's 'citation' of Corporal Trim's flourish as the epigraph to *La peau de chagrin*, about which there would be much to say. I shall limit myself here, however, to the lines of Friedrich Schlegel. Schlegel in the 'Letter on the Novel', from the *Dialogue on Poetry* (*Gespräch über die Poesie*) (1799–1800), puts the true novel (which includes for him Shakespeare and Ariosto, and is more or less identical with 'Romantic' poetry as such), under the double aegis of Sterne and of the Diderot of the Sterne-inspired *Jacques le fataliste*. The link here is the arabesque. Corporal Trim's flourish is generalized as the free, natural, and irregularly curving contours of the narrative line of a genuine novel, form par excellence of Romantic literature. Schlegel's arabesque, however, like Hogarth's line of beauty or even Corporal Trim's flourish, is not entirely unmotivated. It is determined even in its grotesque wanderings by its relation to an infinitely distant or absent center. This center creates the apparent disunities and wanton zigzags of a novel like *Tristram Shandy*. Such a novel breaks all the laws of dramatic unity, the Aristotlean unity of the 'letter', of the mimesis of an action, with beginning, middle, and end. At the same time the arabesque narrative sequence of the Romantic novel is secretly controlled by its concentration toward that infinite and invisible center. It has the unity of figurative language, of 'spirit' rather than 'letter'. The contrast with drama is a contrast between two kinds of unity, the unity of an immanent *logos* creating a direct and continuous *diegesis* (the letter), and, on the other hand, the arabesque unity of a relation to an infinitely distant or transcendent *logos* (the spirit):

A novel is a romantic book. You will pass that off as a meaningless tautology. But I want to draw your attention to the fact that when one thinks of a book, one thinks of a work, an existing whole (*ein für sich bestehendes Ganze*). There is then a very important contrast to drama, which is meant to be viewed; the novel, on the other hand, was from the oldest times for reading, and from this fact we can deduce almost all the differences in the manner of presentation of both forms. The drama should also be romantic, like all literature; but a novel is that only under certain limitations, an applied novel (*ein angewandter Roman*). On the contrary, the dramatic context (*der dramatische Zusammenhang*) of the story does not make the novel a whole, a work, if the whole composition is not related to a higher unity than that of the letter (*auf eine höhere Einheit, als jene Einheit des Buchstabens*) which it often does and should disregard; but it becomes a work through the bond of ideas through a spiritual central point (*durch das Band der Ideen, durch einen geistigen Zentralpunkt*).[6]

The contrast here is perhaps not entirely transparent at first sight. The wholeness of a drama, Schlegel is saying, is related to the fact that it is a visual form of art. This means that it must have the unity of the letter, that is of a literal representation, on the stage, of a continuous action. A novel, on the other hand, is for reading. It does not depend on being a continuous, literally represented spectacle. It can and should therefore have discontinuities and changes of register which could be represented on no stage. Its unity is the unity not of the letter but of the spirit, that is through an association of ideas relating each segment to the others by way of their common relation to a spiritual point which can never be represented as such, but only represented indirectly, in figure or in allegory. As Ludoviko, one of the characters in the dialogue, says, 'All beauty is allegory. One can express the highest exactly, since it is inexpressible, only allegorically (*Alle Schönheit ist Allegorie. Das Höcheste kann man eben, weil es unaussprechlich ist, nur allegorisch sagen*).'[7]

This idea or image (it is image as idea) of a line which is fragmented and at the same time controlled by its relation to an infinitely distant center is expressed in a remarkable passage from the second ending of the essay 'On Lessing': 'Is there a more beautiful symbol for the paradoxes of the philosophical life than some curved line which, drawn out with certain steadiness and lawfulness, can nevertheless always appear only as fragments, since a center for it lies at infinity (*Gibt es wohl ein schöneres Symbol für die Paradoxie des philosophischen Lebens, als jene krummen Linien, die mit sichtbarer Stetigkeit und Gesetzmässigkeit forteilend immer nur im Bruchstück erscheinen können, weil ihr eines Zentrum in der Unendlichkeit liegt*)?'[8] Hyperbole, tangent curve, parabola – these geometrical figures can be graphed, but never completely, and only in fragments, since one at least of their controlling points lies at an infinite distance, beyond the margin of any graph. A parabola, for example, is an ellipse with one focus at infinity, while an hyperbole is an ellipse inside out with two finite foci, and two more at opposite infinities, generating two lines moving doubly out toward infinity. The tangent curve, on the other hand, moves asymptotically toward an infinitely distant point, then reappears magically from minus infinity after a trajectory no eye, theory, or logic can follow rationally in the sense of seeing through it. Names of geometrical lines, these visible paradoxes are also names of figures of speech, figures in which in one way or another the incommensurability between the vehicle of expression and its meaning is particularly evident, as in the parables of Jesus in the New Testament or in the aphorisms of Friedrich

Schlegel himself. An aphorism is in fact another such figure. Etymologically, an aphorism is a definition established on the basis of a setting of boundaries. The word *horizon* has the same root.

The broken paradoxical line of Schlegel, ultimate permutation of the arabesque, is still a line, however. It would give still the model of a narrative line which might be graphed, at least in part. In this sense it is still a form of continuity or logic, however different this logic is from that of a line generated by a finite and visible center, the logic of the letter, of the mimetic representation of an action, as in Aristotle's definition of drama. Schlegel's theory of irony as 'permanent parabasis', however, suspends, interrupts, and pulverizes the narrative line altogether. It abolishes any conceivable center, finite or infinite, visible or invisible. Parabasis is the stepping forward of the chorus or an actor in a play to break the dramatic illusion and to speak directly to the audience, sometimes in the name of the author. If irony is parabasis, it is the one master trope which cannot be graphed as a line. Irony is the confounding, the point by point deconstruction, of any narrative order or determinable meaning. It does this by the abolishing of any identifiable controlling center, even at infinity. This explosion or powdering of the line can take place, however, only through the attempted production of the line. Irony is the basic trope of narrative fiction, for example in the perpetual discrepancy between author and narrator, or between narrator and character in 'indirect discourse'. All irony in narrative is one form or another of that doubling in the story-telling which makes its meaning undecidable, indecipherable, unreadable, unreadable even

All narrative is therefore the linear demonstration of the impossibility of linear coherence

as the 'allegory of unreadability'. All narrative is therefore the linear demonstration of the impossibility of linear coherence.

All fiction is in one way or another or in several ways at once a repetitive structure. Repetition is something occurring along the line which disintegrates the continuity of the line. This is true even though the series of repetitions may appear as the gradual covering over of a subversive implication, as the taming or organizing of irony back into a narrative sequence with beginning, middle, end, and immanent ground. Friedrich Schlegel himself was ultimately converted to Roman Catholicism and revised his earlier work, for example the *Gespräch über die Poesie*, in such a way as to make it less a putting in question of the certainties of Occidental metaphysics. The successive 'repetitions' of Schlegel in his modern interpreters have tended to reintegrate what he disarticulated in his earlier work. Schlegel's critics, even Soren Kierkegaard or Walter Benjamin, have tended to read him according to a Hegelian or Romantic paradigm of historical dialectics. The gunpowder remains along the line of repetitions, however, ready to explode again at any time, since irony is a power of demolition which does not spend its energy when it discharges.

I have followed here a brief historical line going from Hogarth through Sterne to Friedrich Schlegel. The sequence indicates various possible uses for the image of the line as a figure for narrative continuity or discontinuity, for all that part of the story in the middle, between start and finish. My line is itself a middle, since Hogarth is not by any means its beginning, nor Friedrich Schlegel its end, as I have indicated. The line stretches indefinitely before and after. Out of this truncated series I have made a little story line of my own, a line not much undermined, except retrospectively at the end, by irony. The sequence I have followed would need to be tested against many actual narratives in order to be confirmed or rejected as an adequate interpretative model giving a comprehensive range of possible middles. That remains to be done.

NOTES

1. Anchor ed., trans. David F. Swenson and Lillian Marvin Swenson (Garden City, NY: Doubleday, 1959), I, 35.
2. *An Autobiography*, Oxford Classics ed. (London: Oxford University Press, 1961), p. 204.
3. See Martin Price, 'The Irrelevant Detail and the Emergence of Form [in the novel]', *Literary Criticism: Idea and Act*, ed. W. K. Wimsatt (Berkeley, Los Angeles, CA and London: University of California Press, 1974), pp. 521–36; and Roland Barthes, 'L'Effet du réel,' *Communications*, No. 11 (1969), pp. 84–9.
4. I am following here Ronald Paulson, *Hogarth's Graphic Works*, revised ed., 2 vols (New Haven, CT and London: Yale University Press, 1970). The first plate of the *Analysis of Beauty* is plate 210 in Paulson; 'Tailpiece, or The Bathos' is plate 240, both in vol. II. The translations are given on I, 259.
5. Seeds of cucumber, pumpkin, gourd, thought to restrain passions and cool the blood.
6. Friedrich Schlegel, *Kritische Schriften* (München: Carl Hanser Verlag, 1964), p. 515, my trans. For the arabesque in Friedrich Schlegel, see Karl Konrad Polheim, *Die Arabesque: Ansichten und Ideen aus Friedrich Schlegels Poetik* (Paderborn, 1966), and Wolfgang Kaiser, *The Grotesque*. For the opposition between spirit and letter in

Friedrich Schlegel's theory of language, see Heinrich Nüsse, *Die Sprachtheorie Friedrich Schlegels* (Heidelberg: Carl Winter, Universitätsverlag, 1962), chs. 6–8, pp. 68–97.

7. *Kritische Schriften*, p. 505, my trans.
8. Ibid., p. 382, my trans.

CHAPTER TEN

'On Sterne's Page: Spatial Layout, Spatial Form, and Social Spaces in *Tristram Shandy*'*

CHRISTOPHER FANNING

Since the time of its first publication, readers of *Tristram Shandy* (1759–67) have struggled to account for its oddities of appearance and narrative method. Its lack of conventional novelistic form has caused critics to wonder whether *Tristram Shandy* is a 'novel' or rather some variety of philosophical commentary or anatomical satire. One answer to the problem of generic coherence has been to follow Tristram's own suggestion that he 'must go along with you to the end of the work'.[1] Following Wayne Booth's *The Rhetoric of Fiction*, one recurrent focus of criticism has been the sense of the narrator's presence as the unifying principle of the work. Part of what ultimately obviates the need for strict generic definitions is the way in which Tristram, as Booth phrases it, 'has ceased here to be distinguishable from what he relates'.[2] Sterne's unique integration of the sense of the narrator's presence into the formal structure of the narrative has had important implications for the history of narrative. Only recently, however, with renewed interest in the print culture of the era, has a further extension of this integration become apparent. A consideration of Sterne's attention to the physical material of the book in relation to questions of narrative presence in *Tristram Shandy* has become necessary.

This essay will inquire into Sterne's use of three different ideas of 'space' in *Tristram Shandy*: the space found in the fictional world, in fictional technique, and in printing. The first two ideas of space – the mimetic and the formal – are customary ways of considering 'fiction and

* Reprinted from *Eighteenth-Century Fiction*, 10 (July, 1998), 429–50.

space'. Both critical approaches employ space as a metaphor. One of the ways of interpreting a novel is to consider the mimetic spaces of fiction – the spaces of the fictional world that characters inhabit – as metaphors for its thematic concerns. In eighteenth-century fiction, obvious examples of this variety of space range from the enclosed, claustrophobic spaces of *Clarissa* to the freedom of the open road in *Tom Jones*, each having a metaphoric correlative in our ideas of the private and the public, the realms of thought and of action. A similar range is found in *Tristram Shandy*: the spatial separation of the men conversing in the parlour from Mrs Shandy and the midwife who are labouring over Tristram's birth in the bedroom above correlates with the separate spheres of male and female activity that are themselves figures for satiric distinctions between theory and practice; Tristram's journey through France in Volume VII is a spatially enacted metaphoric flight from death.

At the same time that mimetic space has metaphoric meaning in a work of fiction, the form of that work is often discussed in terms of a metaphor of abstract discursive 'space' that helps to articulate the manipulation of narrative sequence. This is a formal concern with the way in which the narrative is ordered. For example, when simultaneous events are placed into linear language, sequence is fragmented and narrative is said to have been 'spatialized'. Similarly, 'spatial form' is at work when motifs or images demand interconnections that thwart the supposedly sequential flow of language (syntax or narrative).[3] *Tristram Shandy* has long been recognized as a masterpiece of spatial form, especially in its representation of time.[4] Indeed, since the eighteenth century, most of the criticism interested in the odd form of Sterne's work has been an attempt to account for 'the whole narration always going backwards', as one eighteenth-century reader, Horace Walpole, put it.[5]

Although Sterne's fiction is remarkable for its combination of the formal and mimetic senses of space, neither the abstract conception of spatial form as a metaphoric representation of time nor the mimetic rendering of the spaces inhabited by the fictional characters shows the extent of his use of 'space' in *Tristram Shandy*, for he is deeply engaged in problematizing reading by means of the space literally upon and between the pages of his printed text: its *mise en page*, the spatial layout of the text.[6] Despite Sterne's expressed desire to read the newly completed Volume III of *Tristram Shandy* aloud,[7] oral readers of *Tristram Shandy* must encounter many moments at which they must either gloss over or describe inexpressible marks on the page, such as asterisks, dashes, and squiggles, or make a decision about what to read next: for example, either the Latin or the facing translation of Ernulphus's curse (III. XI: 202–11) or 'Slawkenburgius's Tale' (IV: 288–99). One wonders how Sterne intended to navigate the oddities of punctuation and layout found in the volume he wished to read aloud, especially the marbled page (III. XXXVI: 269–70). *Tristram Shandy* is a visual text that problematizes the conventions of oral delivery (a mode presupposing a temporal rather than a spatial orientation). Sterne's work draws attention to *mise en page*, a unique aspect of textuality that employs a notion of 'space' which differs from customary uses of that term in the criticism of fiction.

It has long been established that Sterne was very particular about the printed presentation of his work.[8] This is clear in Sterne's letter to the first publisher of *Tristram Shandy*, Robert Dodsley:

I propose . . . to print a lean edition, in two small volumes, of the size of Rasselas, and on the same paper and type. . . . The book shall be printed here, and the impression sent up to you; for as I live at York, and shall correct every proof myself, it shall go perfect into the world, and be printed in so creditable a way as to paper, type, &c., as to do no dishonour to you. (*Letters*, pp. 80–1)

Earlier that same year, in a jocoserious letter to the printer appended to *A Political Romance*, his first fictional work, Sterne makes clear the import-ance of the minutiae of the text: 'I have only to add . . . That, at your Peril, you do not presume to alter or transpose one Word, nor rectify one false Spelling, nor so much as add or diminish one Comma or Tittle, in or to my *Romance*' (*Letters*, p. 68).[9] This clear injunction to heed the minute particulars, the accidentals of the text, should concern readers as well as printers. In *Tristram Shandy*, such references to the printed appear-ance of the text intrude upon the narrative itself, reminding us that we are reading a printed artifact and that no simple translation from the text to an idealized oral communication is possible. Rather, we must read Sterne's print both as a text of mimetic verbal referents and as a non-verbal object that communicates by means of its manipulation of the space on the page. My particular interests here are to examine Sterne's use of space to represent not just this double imperative of written language, but also an aspect of communication that falls between these two poles, the most ambiguous non-verbal aspect of orality: silence.

*

The place to begin an examination of Sterne's treatment of silence is his work in a genre specifically designed for oral delivery, the sermon. Sterne's sermons also provide a relatively clear preliminary to the con-sideration of space in *Tristram Shandy*, for in the sermons the relationship between spatial layout and the silences of orality is uncomplicated by the narrative concerns of representing the topographical space in which characters exist. Of course, as with all things Sternean, such simplicity is accompanied by interesting problems. In the case of the sermons, we encounter a printed version which was *directly influenced* by the printed aesthetic of *Tristram Shandy*. Although Sterne's sermons represent twenty years of pulpit experience prior to the publication of *Tristram Shandy*, as far as their printed presentation is concerned, *Tristram Shandy* is as much an introduction to the sermons as the reverse, for Sterne revised his sermons and prepared them for the press in 1760 and 1766 *after* the publication of *Tristram Shandy*. The sermons in their printed form are remarkably – and intentionally – Shandean in appearance: *Tristram Shandy* and *The Sermons of Mr Yorick* share the same size and type, generously made spacious with a small number of lines per page, a double space between paragraphs, wide margins, and dashes of varying length.[10] The mutual influence of the *Sermons* and *Tristram Shandy* (the former written and orally delivered before the latter, yet laid out in print after) makes the sermons an interesting ground to explore the relationship of oral and visual.[11]

Sterne's sermons are by no means simple transcripts of his orations. In examining the role of space and the dash in the printed sermons and their relation to oral delivery, we are tracing Sterne's thematic interest in problems of communication: speech, silence, and graphological representation. Ultimately, we are inquiring into the meaning of the Shandean style. The sermon, as an oral genre, is in need of some kind of translation into its printed form – no mere transcript will convey the rhetorical impact of the preacher's presence. Having already begun to employ *mise en page* to the end of creating presence in *Tristram Shandy*, Sterne takes advantage of the same technique to supplement the preacher's absence with an architecture of the printed page that speaks eloquently not only as a translation of the oral delivery (now lost) but also as a statement in itself. Many of his sermons, such as 'Hezekiah and the Messengers' (sermon 17), are openly concerned with the problems of rhetoric, the lamentable need for a medium, such as the preacher himself, in order to communicate with God.[12] In sermon 17, Sterne laments his mediating role as a preacher and expresses a wish to be unnecessary, ultimately retreating into silence in the face of merely noisy rhetoric. Here it is not surprising to see the printed page enact some kind of non-verbal communication. In the first edition of this sermon, the final page has the appearance of an hourglass (see figure 1). The blocks of print visually enact the collapse of discourse there under discussion. The first paragraph offers five lines of text, the third, ten. The second paragraph is simultaneously more and less than a paragraph. It consists of one line, centred on the page, rather than merely indented:

——it is too late.

60   SERMON II.

virtuous man who did it, with infa-
my;——undo it all——I beseech you:
give him back his honour,——restore
the jewel you have taken from him,—
replace him in the eye of the world—

——it is too late.

It is painful to utter the reproaches
which should come in here.——I will
trust them with yourselves: in coming
from that quarter, they will more naturally produce such fruits as will not
set your teeth on edge——for they
will be the fruits of love and good
will, to the praise of GOD and the
happiness of the world, which I
wish.

SER-

FIGURE 1 *The Sermons of Mr Yorick* (1766), vol. 3, p. 60.

The line is not an independent sentence, but a fragment of the preceding paragraph, which concludes with a shorter dash. The ambiguous grammatical status of this line – it is simultaneously a sentence and a paragraph, but also neither – is foregrounded by its position on the page. Out of the ashes of rhetoric's collapse rises a new mode of communication: a silence which the preacher allows to envelop his words and which becomes visually represented by the white space surrounding the centre of this page.[13]

Elsewhere in the sermons, space, in conjunction with the dash, is explicitly associated with silence. In his sermon on 'Pride', the double space between paragraphs becomes itself a typographic paragraph of silence:

——Approach his bed of state——lift up the curtain——regard a moment with silence——

——are these cold hands and pale lips, all that is left of him who was canoniz'd by his own pride, or made a god of, by his flatterers?[14]

The role of the dash is here obviously dramatic or gestural, standing in for the actions described. Most effective here are the dashes at the end of the first paragraph of text and the beginning of the second. Just as the preceding actions are set off by dashes on either side, so is the silence granted textual status. In this sermon, this space is conveniently labelled 'silence'. In other sermons it is simply heard, often marked by the aposiopestic dash.[15]

Some sermons use white space (to some degree) and the dash (to a greater degree) in a more purely performative fashion, rather than as representations of performance. In such cases, they may not gesture at silence in itself, but rather at non-verbal actions. In 'National Mercies' (sermon 21), Sterne plays on the double space between paragraphs by eliminating it when two one-line paragraphs convey simultaneous events (see figure 2):

——The blessing was necessary,——
——and it was granted.——

In the fallen world, divine *fiat* – saying into being – is not only impossible, but unrepresentable. Nevertheless, Sterne's typographical collapse of the distinction between paragraphs attempts to collapse the distinction between (or rather, to reunite) word and deed in his representation of a miracle. This performative gesture conveys the original lost unity and simultaneously recognizes it as lost (by drawing attention to the fact that, if he had printed the two phrases over each other, both would be illegible). This is a spatialized rendering of what in oral delivery would be described as parataxis.

184 · SERMON VI.

If GOD then made us, as he did the Israelites, suck honey out of the flinty rock, and oil out of the flinty rock, how much more signal was his mercy in giving them to us without money, without price, in those good days which followed, when a long and a wise reign was as necessary to build up our church, as a short one was before to save it from ruins.——

——The blessing was necessary,——
——and it was granted.——

GOD having multiplied the years of that renowned princess to an uncommon number, giving her time, as well as a heart, to fix a wavering perse-
cuted

FIGURE 2 *The Sermons of Mr. Yorick*, vol. 3, p. 184.

[104]

it—'Tis a heavy tax upon that half of our fellow-creatures, brother *Shandy*, said my uncle *Toby*—'Tis a piteous burden upon 'em, continued he, shaking his head.—Yes, yes, 'tis a painful thing—said my father, shaking his head too—but certainly since shaking of heads came into fashion, never did two heads shake together, in concert, from two such different springs.

God bless } 'em all—said my uncle
Duce take } *Toby* and my father, each to himself.

CHAP. XIII.

HOLLA!—you chairman!—here's sixpence—do step into that bookseller's shop, and call me a *day-tall* critick. I am very willing to give any one

FIGURE 3 Laurence Sterne, *The Life and Opinions of Tristram Shandy, Gentleman* (London: R. and J. Dodsley, 1760–67), 9 vols, 4:104.

The very need to describe the technique using the terminology of sequence points out how the printed text attempts to transcend the sequentiality of oral reading. This has its parallel in a graphic device, which defies reading aloud, used in *Tristram Shandy* to represent simultaneous utterances of the Shandy brothers in Volume IV, chapter XII (see figure 3).[16]

This brief survey of Sterne's sermons has described his use of spatial layout to represent non-verbal aspects of orality, aspects dependent upon the presence of the preacher. In addition to a similar use of space to convey the non-verbal in *Tristram Shandy*, we encounter greater complexity as narrative issues bring formal and mimetic spaces to the fore. Early in the novel, this is notable in the deliberate association of the formal and the mimetic metaphors of space. In a single early chapter we are informed that Tristram intends to narrate his origins *ab ovo*, but also that what follows is not wholly relevant to his story, and the readers who 'do not choose to go so far back into these things' may 'skip over the remaining part of this Chapter'. Tristram here gives his readers a formal directive, pertaining to the order of his narration. This is accompanied, however, by a mimetic gesture, spoken to the 'curious and inquisitive' (I. IV: 5) readers who choose to remain for the extended deduction of the date of Tristram's conception, that evokes a shared intimate space:

—————Shut the door.—————

(I. IV: 6)

This gesture, linking the fragmentation of narrative sequence (spatial form) and the metaphoric intimacy of a private conversation (mimetic space), is a frequent one in Sterne's text. An interesting parallel occurs later in Volume I when Tristram addresses his female reader: 'How could you, Madam, be so inattentive in reading the last chapter?' (I. xx: 64). Here the intimacy of conversation is again marked by exclusion. However, rather than shutting the door, Tristram employs the formal, fictional space of the text: 'as a punishment for it [in-attentiveness], I do insist upon it, that you immediately turn back, that is, as soon as you get to the next full stop, and read the whole chapter over again' (I. xx: 64–5). While the female reader is engaged in a separate chapter – a different space – Tristram may converse confidentially with

While the female reader is engaged in a separate chapter – a different space – Tristram may converse confidentially with the male reader

the male reader. It is important to note that the varieties of space are so closely interwoven here that they cross over: textual distance becomes mimetic distance. This is an all-pervasive technique in *Tristram Shandy*, to the extent that the words of a narrator or character often carry both mimetic and diegetic implications, as when Tristram says of his mother, 'She listened . . . with composed intelligence, and would have done so to the end of the chapter' (V. xiii: 442): the reader cannot know whether this means 'to the natural conclusion of this activity (or the events represented)' or 'to the end of this chapter in the work known as *Tristram Shandy*' (see also Vol. I, chap. x, and Vol. VII, chap. xxii). Furthermore, Tristram draws the reader in by enunciating a notion of reading as spatial. His intimate conversation with the male reader concerns the (female) 'vicious taste' that cannot transcend a linear conception of 'reading straight forwards, more in quest of the adventures, than of the deep erudition and knowledge' (I. xx: 65). The spatial metaphor of depth contrasts the temporal sense of the 'straight forwards' sequence (although we should note that many such time references are only expressed through spatial metaphors).

Another instance of the conjunction of textual and mimetic space occurs in Volume III, this time placed outdoors in the intimacy of a country walk. Again, the mimetic space, this time not the static containment of the private room but the outdoor space through which the narrator and his friend Eugenius are travelling, is linked with the spatial form of fiction that (especially with the Shandean focus on the literal form) demands cross-referencing different pages and volumes:

> ———Here are two senses, cried *Eugenius*, as we walk'd along, pointing with the fore finger of his right hand to the word *Crevice*, in the fifty-second page of the second volume of this book of books,—here are two senses,———quoth he.———And here are two roads, replied I, turning short upon him,———a dirty and a clean one,———which shall we take? (III. xxxi: 258)

Interpretation takes place by means of spatializing the text – flipping through its pages in order to locate the place in the text to be considered – but it is also subject to the road metaphor derived from the geographical space in which the interpretation occurs.

The most extended mingling of *Tristram Shandy*'s mimetic time and place with textual time and place occurs in the travel metaphor of Volume VII. It is this volume that most strongly brings the applications of Shandyism into the world outside of textuality, into the human considerations of life and death in space and time, something beyond a bookish game. Volume VII begins with the metaphoric use of space ('DEATH himself knocked at my door'), interrupting another scene of intimate narration to Eugenius.

Thou hast had a narrow escape, Tristram, said Eugenius, taking hold of my hand as I finish'd my story——

But there is no *living*, Eugenius, replied I, at this rate; for as this *son of a whore* has found out my lodgings——(VII. I: 576)

What follows in Volume VII is an extended spatial metaphor asserting that life is found only in its participial form, living, which requires motion through space as opposed to lodgement, or stasis. As we have seen, such metaphoric uses of mimetic space are frequently linked to the spatial form of the work, as with, for example, Tristram's much-noted travels through Auxerre: 'I have been getting forwards in two different journies together, and with the same dash of the pen' (VII. XXVIII: 621). The insistence on the kinetic movement through space here supplies the moral framework underpinning the gestural nature of the spatial layout of both *Tristram Shandy* and *The Sermons of Mr Yorick* (as well as the spatial form of *Tristram Shandy*). Just as the success of Tristram's flight from Death is marked by the change from linear flight to the choreographed peasant dance at the end of Volume VII (accompanied by a denial of '*straight lines*' in the opening of Vol. VIII, chap. I, cross-referenced to Vol. VI, chap. XL), Sterne's page demands a lively eye that apprehends meaning not 'straight forwards', line by line from left to right, top to bottom, but in a dance that perceives the structure of the space, actively moving back and forth, in essence creating meaning by performing these actions.

We may trace the literal origins of this metaphoric dance by returning to the moment at which Tristram berates the 'straight forwards' reader. Here he not only asserts the spatial form of his work (by sending 'Madam' back to the previous chapter) as well as the intimate conversational space he shares with the male reader, but he also at this moment introduces a third variety of space into *Tristram Shandy*, one that shifts from the metaphoric uses of mimetic location and spatialized narrative to the performative space of the book as object. In wishing to demonstrate his 'deep erudition' (I. XX: 65), Tristram has recourse, for the first time in the work, to a traditional scholarly device, the footnote. The history of the footnote runs parallel to the history of printing, marking the spatial incorporation of what manuscript culture would call a marginal gloss, and oral culture a digression. As Hugh Kenner points out,

The footnote's relation to the passage from which it depends is established wholly by visual and typographic means, and will typically defeat all efforts of the speaking voice to clarify it without visual aid. Parentheses, like commas, tell the voice what to do: an asterisk tells the voice that it can do nothing. . . . The language has forsaken a vocal milieu, and a context of oral communication

between persons, and commenced to take advantage of the expressive possibilities of technological space.[17]

No stranger to digressions ('take them out of this book for instance, – you
might as well take the book along with them', I. xxii: 81), *Tristram
Shandy* recognizes the problem they present to narration which is conceived of in an oral fashion, requiring the repetition of the words from
which the digression began, as each digression returns to the subject,
having supposedly enriched our sense of it. The footnote asks us to
suspend the narration of the subject while supplementary information is
supplied, employing the space on the page to mark this process rather
than repetition in the text.[18] Sometimes, rather than supplying new
information, the footnote can also simply refer readers back to places
in previous volumes (for example, a note in Vol. III, chap. i, sends us back
to Vol. II, chap. xviii), drawing attention to what is known as 'spatial
form' (the cross-referenced fragmentation of sequence). In *Tristram Shandy*,
after the gesture of '——Shut the door——' and other metafictional
moments in which the reader finds himself or herself addressed in the
context of mimetic space, the extra-diegetic device of the footnote, so
clearly a function of the printed page, cannot occur without invoking the
intimate relationship of the author and reader which has been defined by
the metaphors of mimetic space. By this association, the printed text has
taken on a living presence of the kind formerly thought only available
within the intimate space of the lived world.

Footnotes may be called supplemental uses of space: at one level, that
of metaphoric spatial form, they fill in the gaps in the narrative, or
enlarge our sense of it. At the level of *mise en page*, printed in smaller type
and separated from the main text, they draw the eye to the bottom of the
page, providing, if one allows for the vertical orientation of the printed
page, at least a two-dimensional sense of the 'depth' for which Tristram
strives. This type of textual supplementarity, playing on the appearance
of scholarly apparatus, is characteristic of the dense textuality of
Scriblerian precursors of *Tristram Shandy* such as Swift's *A Tale of a Tub*
and especially Pope's *Dunciad Variorum* in which the weighty notes
dominate the space of the page. Sterne is clearly borrowing from this
tradition in his histrionic use of footnotes and asterisks. As we have
already seen in the sermons, however, the appearance of Sterne's page is
quite different from that of Scriblerian pages. The text of *Tristram Shandy*
is generously spaced (as figures 3–7 show). The celebrated dash has been
said to 'open up' the text rather than weigh it down.[19] What Sterne has
done is to take the Scriblerian models of textuality and sublimate them,
drawing in their sense of performativity, yet pointing it in a different

direction – not towards the opacity of language, but rather towards its ineffability. In the Scriblerian works the excessive presence of ink marks the performative text, whereas, for Sterne, with notable exceptions such as the marbled or black pages, it is the *absence* of excessive ink that enacts a performance. In other words, it is the unoccupied space on the page that produces many of the effects of *Tristram Shandy*.

it is the *absence* of excessive ink that enacts a performance. In other words, it is the unoccupied space on the page that produces many of the effects of *Tristram Shandy*

Let us examine what is perhaps the novel's most extended use of the space on the page. In the single chapter (Vol. VI, chap. XVIII) that relates the 'beds of justice' conversation between Mr and Mrs Shandy, the manipulation of spatial layout to convey passing time or silence, to create activity or stasis, and to explore the relationship of repetition and meaning, is combined with one of *Tristram Shandy*'s significant social spaces (see figures 4–7). This chapter, which returns us to the scene of the bedroom, is an important one for feminist critics concerned with the frequently silent or absent Mrs Shandy.[20] Here we witness the source of that silence and absence at work as Mrs Shandy displays her rhetorical skills in answering Mr Shandy. The question under consideration is whether or not young Tristram should be put into breeches early (to compensate for the mutilation of his genitals in the accident with the window sash). Mrs Shandy's technique, employed in Shandy Hall's most cathected space, is one that we have witnessed in connection with the spatialization of narrative: silence and repetition. And here Sterne's *mise en page* reinforces Mrs Shandy's non-discursive discourse (which so frustrates Mr Shandy's attempts at logocentric dialectic) through its third alternative of visual presentation.

In the 'beds of justice' chapter, Mrs Shandy is at her most rhetorical, simultaneously rejecting discourse and using it through subtle mutations – distorting echoes – of Mr Shandy's words. The mutations in Mrs Shandy's replies seem to demand an oral intonation for full effect, and, in many ways, this chapter can be read as a score annotated for performance. Let us first observe Mrs Shandy at work. As Walter strains to provoke a response with which he can engage his dialectic, she consistently fails to provide one. Instead, she mildly reduces both sense and syllables:

──I can not (making two syllables of it) imagine, quoth my father, who the duce he takes after.──

I cannot conceive, for my life,—said my mother.──

Or she potently concentrates:

I suppose, replied my father,—making some pause first,—he'll be exactly like other people's children.──

Exactly, said my mother.──

She amplifies (but subtly, only the first half of the sentence):

──And 'twill be lucky, if that's the worst on't, added my father.

It will be very lucky, answered my mother.

She anticipates Mr Shandy's conclusions:

──They should be of leather, said my father, turning him about again.— They will last him, said my mother, the longest. (VI. viii: 526–8)

Mrs Shandy's repetitious responses thwart linear progress. However, they also help create the atmosphere of a ritual, something from the realm of magic that has its own value outside of Walter's 'science'. Thus this is a chapter that Sterne could well read aloud, applying the lessons of translating the sermons into print in reverse, reading the space on the page in order to extend the chapter beyond itself into sound.

Every paragraph in the first edition of *Tristram Shandy* is separated by a double space. This spatial arrangement helps to establish a rhythm and a pace for the chapter. Because of the short paragraphs in Volume VI, chapter XVIII, there is extra white space on each page (the usual two and one-half first edition pages printed on a single page of a modern paperback edition become nearly three and one-half).[21] Treating the chapter as a score for performance, the question arises: should the pages be turned more quickly, because we are receiving 'less' information, or should the tempo of page turning be kept constant, and rests added to fill out the time of each page? The question is not so easily answered when one considers Sterne's careful pacing (and spacing) of his sermonic discourses. The white space on the page is given meaning if we account for the resonance of the preacher's voice. However, this chapter is not only a means to a performance: it is, in many ways, the performance itself, a ritualized space. For the visual reader, the sermons have suggested that this chapter, which consists mainly of short exchanges of uncommunicative dialogue, presents to the eye a visual silence, a series of discrete textual islands, unbridged, a spatial metaphor for the lack of communication. The critic sensitive to social spaces will also note how this chapter enacts the uncomfortable physical relationship of Mr and Mrs Shandy as they lie together in the same bed.

In the 'beds of justice' chapter, reading the white space as resonance is encouraged by the repetition in the passage – not only by Mrs Shandy, but by the text itself. Peter J. De Voogd has suggested (in the context of the arrangement of footnotes) that 'catchword-order' is worthy of serious consideration as one of Sterne's techniques in *Tristram Shandy*.[22] How far this should be taken is questionable, for, despite Sterne's intense interest in the printing of his work, his control over page division cannot be established. However, catchwords are an unavoidable aspect of all eighteenth-century texts, and one to which Sterne was quite sensitive: for the second edition of Volumes V and VI, it is possible that Sterne requested the catchword be omitted whenever it read 'CHAP'.[23] Although catchwords were mainly a device for the convenience of printers which readers were expected to ignore, Sterne's interests – both as a preacher and the author of *Tristram Shandy* – were in drawing attention to exactly such conventions. If we pay attention to them, catchwords serve to enhance the sense of repetition throughout the text.[24] In the 'beds of justice' chapter, the extra white space makes catchwords (and hence repetition) more frequent.[25] This causes a ritualizing incantatory feeling to settle over the chapter, slowing the reading. Walter's twice repeated 'Humph!' (VI. XVIII: 527) appears *three* times in the first edition – if the first 'Humph!', which is the catchword (figure 4), is pronounced. Is the fact that this word is the catchword accidental? Or is it the accidental of a musical score? After all, 'Humph' is an important argumentative technique in Shandy Hall, and it appears three times as Uncle Toby and Dr Slop argue over the 'Abuses of Conscience' sermon (II. XVII: 149–50).

Extra white space and more frequent catchwords are mutually supporting techniques for the creation of an incantatory tone in the 'beds of justice' chapter. Within the text of the chapter, Mrs Shandy's use of repetition confirms the tone conveyed by the extra-textual devices. Repetition is one of Mrs Shandy's two rhetorical techniques, the other of which is silence. Both techniques are a refusal to participate in discourse by disregarding the rules of dialectic either in the subtle mutations of what she repeats or in her failure to respond at all. That this is represented visually in the text of *Tristram Shandy* suggests that we may see this as a contribution to the debate between theory and practice which is the theme of the satire in *Tristram·Shandy*. As Walter Shandy's sterile words fall upon Mrs Shandy's frustrating silence, we are made aware that opinions unsupported by life are inadequate. Just as Tristram's race through France is a spatial affirmation of life, Mrs Shandy's room-bound debate with Walter draws support from the spatial architecture of the

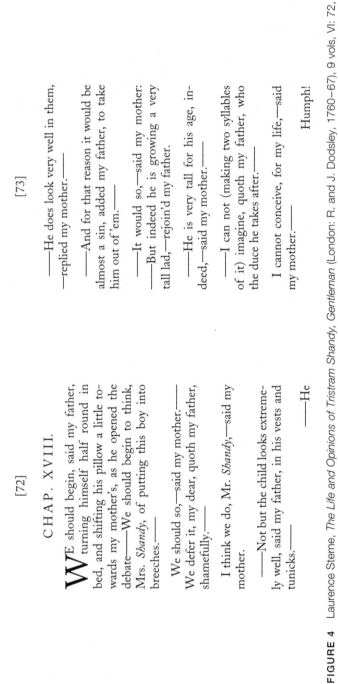

[72]

CHAP. XVIII.

WE should begin, said my father, turning himself half round in bed, and shifting his pillow a little towards my mother's, as he opened the debate——We should begin to think, Mrs. *Shandy*, of putting this boy into breeches.——

We should so,—said my mother.——
We defer it, my dear, quoth my father, shamefully.——

I think we do, Mr. *Shandy*,—said my mother.

——Not but the child looks extremely well, said my father, in his vests and tunicks.——

——He

[73]

——He does look very well in them,—replied my mother.——

——And for that reason it would be almost a sin, added my father, to take him out of 'em.——

——It would so,—said my mother:
——But indeed he is growing a very tall lad,—rejoin'd my father.

——He is very tall for his age, indeed,—said my mother.——

——I can not (making two syllables of it) imagine, quoth my father, who the duce he takes after.——

I cannot conceive, for my life,—said my mother.——

Humph!

FIGURE 4 Laurence Sterne, *The Life and Opinions of Tristram Shandy, Gentleman* (London: R. and J. Dodsley, 1760–67), 9 vols, VI: 72, 73. The remaining pages of chapter XVIII are reproduced in figures 5, 6, and 7.

[74]

Humph!——said my father.

(The dialogue ceased for a moment.)

——I am very short myself,——continued my father, gravely.

You are very short, Mr. *Shandy*,——said my mother.

Humph! quoth my father to himself, a second time: in muttering which, he plucked his pillow a little further from my mother's,——and turning about again, there was an end of the debate for three minutes and a half.

——When he gets these breeches made, cried my father in a higher tone, he'll look like a beast in 'em.

He

[75]

He will be very aukward in them at first, replied my mother.——

——And 'twill be lucky, if that's the worst on't, added my father.

It will be very lucky, answered my mother.

I suppose, replied my father,——making some pause first,——he'll be exactly like other people's children.——

Exactly, said my mother.——

——Though I should be sorry for that, added my father: and so the debate stopped again.

——They should be of leather, said my father, turning him about again.——

They

FIGURE 5

[76]

They will last him, said my mother, the longest.

But he can have no linings to 'em, replied my father.——

He cannot, said my mother.

'Twere better to have them of fustian, quoth my father.

Nothing can be better, quoth my mother.——

——Except dimity,—replied my father:——'Tis best of all,—replied my mother.

——One must not give him his death, however,—interrupted my father.

By no means, said my mother:—and so the dialogue stood still again.

I am

[77]

I am resolved, however, quoth my father, breaking silence the fourth time, he shall have no pockets in them.——

——There is no occasion for any, said my mother.——

I mean in his coat and waistcoat,—cried my father.

——I mean so too,—replied my mother.

——Though if he gets a gig or a top—Poor souls! it is a crown and a scepter to them,—they should have where to secure it.——

Order it as you please, Mr. *Shandy*, replied my mother.——

——But

FIGURE 6

[78]

——But don't you think it right? added my father, pressing the point home to her.

Perfectly, said my mother, if it pleases you, Mr. *Shandy.*——

——There's for you! cried my father, losing temper——Pleases me!——You never will distinguish, Mrs. *Shandy*, nor shall I ever teach you to do it, betwixt a point of pleasure and a point of con-venience.——This was on the *Sunday* night;——and further this chapter say-eth not.

CHAP. XIX.

AFTER my father had debated the af-fair of the breeches with my mother, —he consulted *Albertus Rubenius* upon it;

FIGURE 7

the very physical space on the page increases the impact of the satire, offering not just a score for performance, but a performance in itself, more subtle than the obvious typographical ploys for attention that force their presence upon the reader, because it acts by means of absence, empty space

'beds of justice' chapter, which draws upon the spatializing techniques of *Tristram Shandy* as a whole. The kinds of repetition that *Tristram Shandy* has employed elsewhere at the diegetic level as a function of digressions – the spatialized fragmentation of linear narrative – are employed by Mrs Shandy at the mimetic level to thwart Walter's linear dialectic.

This is a prime example of the integration of varieties of space in Sterne's fiction. Within a mimetic social space (which the reader has frequently encountered in moments of narrative self-reflexivity that draw attention to the spatial form of the work, such as the '——Shut the door.——' gesture or the 'two roads' debate discussed above) a character employs devices borrowed from the work's spatializing techniques. In addition, the very physical space on the page increases the impact of the satire, offering not just a score for performance but a performance in itself, more subtle than the obvious typographical ploys for attention that force their presence upon the reader, because it acts by means of absence, empty space.[26]

NOTES

1. Laurence Sterne, *The Life and Opinions of Tristram Shandy, Gentleman: The Text*, ed. Melvyn New and Joan New, 2 vols, Florida Edition of the Works of Laurence Sterne (Gainesville, FLA: University of Florida Press, 1978), VI. xx: 534. References are to the original volume and chapter numbers, followed by the page number in the Florida edition.

2. Wayne Booth, *The Rhetoric of Fiction* (Chicago, IL: University of Chicago Press, 1983), p. 223. According to Booth, the secret of *Tristram Shandy*'s 'coherence, its

form, seems to reside primarily in the role played by the teller, by Tristram, the dramatized narrator. He is himself in some way the central subject holding together materials which, were it not for his scatterbrained presence, would never have seemed to be separated in the first place' (p. 222).

3. The classic account is Joseph Frank, 'Spatial Form in Modern Literature' (1945), reprinted in *The Widening Gyre: Crisis and Mastery in Modern Literature* (Bloomington, IN: Indiana University Press, 1963), pp. 3–62.

4. See, for example, Jeffrey R. Smitten, '*Tristram Shandy* and Spatial Form', *Ariel* 8.4 (1977): 43–55; K. G. Simpson, 'At This Moment in Space: Time, Space and Values in *Tristram Shandy*', in *Laurence Sterne: Riddles and Mysteries*, ed. Valerie Grosvenor Myer (London: Vision; Totowa, NJ: Barnes and Noble, 1984), pp. 142–58; A. A. Mendilow, *Time and the Novel* (New York: Humanities Press, 1972), pp. 158–99; Jean-Jacques Mayoux, 'Variations on the Time-Sense in *Tristram Shandy*', in *The Winged Skull: Papers from the Laurence Sterne Bicentenary Conference*, ed. Arthur H. Cash and John M. Stedmond (Kent, OH: Kent State University Press, 1971), pp. 3–18; and William Freedman, *Laurence Sterne and the Origins of the Musical Novel* (Athens, GA: University of Georgia Press, 1978), pp. 52–86.

5. Horace Walpole, letter of 4 April 1760, quoted in *Sterne: The Critical Heritage*, ed. Alan B. Howes (London: Routledge & Kegan Paul, 1974), p. 55.

6. Walter J. Ong's *Orality and Literacy: The Technologizing of the Word* (Ithaca, NY: Cornell University Press, 1981), especially chap. 5, 'Print, Space and Closure', and chap. 6, 'Oral Memory, the Story Line and Characterization', provides a useful survey of the issues with which this essay is engaged. Peter J. De Voogd's '*Tristram Shandy* as Aesthetic Object', *Word and Image* 4: 1 (1988): 383–91, contains useful and suggestive comments, well illustrated, on the importance of the printed appearance of *Tristram Shandy* in the first editions.

7. 'I have just finished one volume of Shandy, and I want to read it to some one who I know can taste and rellish humour'. *Letters of Laurence Sterne*, ed. Lewis Perry Curtis (Oxford: Clarendon, 1935), 3 August 1760, p. 120. References are to this edition.

8. For a concise summary of Sterne's engagement with the printing process, see De Voogd, p. 383. Further work needs to be done on the relationships between Sterne's few surviving manuscripts and his printed text. My argument follows Gardner Stout's analysis of extant MSS of *A Sentimental Journey*, which concludes, cautiously, that Sterne's final intentions are represented in the *printed* version, which reflects substantive and accidental revisions made in proof. See *A Sentimental Journey Through France and Italy by Mr Yorick*, ed. Gardner D. Stout Jr (Berkeley, CA: University of California Press, 1967), pp. 49–57. Melvyn New's analysis of a MS (possibly in Sterne's hand) of the Le Fever episode stresses compositorial alterations accepted only tacitly by Sterne, suggesting that the MS has greater visual presence. See 'A Manuscript of the Le Fever Episode in *Tristram Shandy*', *Scriblerian* 23.2 (1991): 165–74. Unfortunately, the two extant sermon manuscripts correspond to sermons printed posthumously (numbers 28 and 37), and, therefore, cannot reveal Sterne's

intentions for print. On the one hand, a comparison of the MS for sermon 37 (Pierpont Morgan Library, MA 418) with its printed version reveals that many dashes were added by the printer according to a regularized Shandean style. On the other hand, it is worth noting that, unlike the sermons seen through the press by Sterne himself, in those posthumously published the dash lengths do not vary: surely an indication of Sterne's involvement at the printing stage consistent with the more famous printed features of *Tristram Shandy* such as the black and marbled pages, or the missing chapter.

9. Sterne's attention to minutiae did not diminish: there is evidence that, in 1767, he requested changes to the lengths of the dashes in Vols V and VI. See Melvyn New, Introduction, Florida Edition (pp. 835–7).

10. The evidence for sermons printed before *Tristram Shandy* is slender. Two of Sterne's sermons (numbers 5 and 27) were published individually in 1747 and 1750. These show intimations of the Shandean presentation with some use of varying dash lengths. The text of these early versions is on the whole less spacious than their later printings. Although there is double spacing between paragraphs, there are more lines per page (26 compared to 21 in 1760 and 19 in 1766) and less space within each line. A convenient comparison is Kenneth Monkman's facsimile of *A Political Romance* (Menston, England: Scolar, 1971), originally printed by Caesar Ward, printer of the two early sermons.

11. Appearances alone are not the only reason to consider the sermons as a way of understanding *Tristram Shandy*, for there is evidence to suggest that Sterne saw the sermons as dialogic companions to *Tristram Shandy*, designed to 'keep up a kind of balance, in my shandaic character' (*Letters*, p. 252).

12. See, for example, sermons 2, 3, and 23 for considerations of the preacher's own rhetoric, which I discuss in my article, 'Sermons on Sermonizing: The Pulpit Rhetoric of Swift and Sterne', forthcoming in *Philological Quarterly* 77: 4. Also, sermons 10, 26, and 42 discuss the rhetorical style of the scriptures.

13. Sterne's hand is apparent in the horizontal centring of the middle paragraph, although the vertical disposition of the text is likely the product of mere compositorial layout.

14. Laurence Sterne, *The Sermons*, ed. Melvyn New, vol. 4, Florida Edition of the Works of Laurence Sterne (Gainesville, FLA: University of Florida Press, 1996), sermon 24, p. 232. All references that do not appear in figures 1 and 2 are to this edition, cited by sermon and page number.

15. The best example is sermon 20, which employs the dash to represent the inadequacy of language to render the sentimental story of the prodigal son. It is also clear from the frequency with which the dash follows an exclamation that it represents a silent pause in which the exclamation may reverberate.

16. This device is used again to represent simultaneity in Vol. VII, chap. VIII and the syncopation of the abbess and novice of Andouillets in Vol. VII, chap. XXV.

17. Kenner's *aperçu* continues: 'The man who writes a marginal comment is conducting a dialogue with the text he is reading; but the man who composes a footnote, and

sends it to the printer along with his text, has discovered among the devices of printed language something analogous with counterpoint: a way of speaking in two voices at once, or of ballasting or modifying or even bombarding with exceptions his own discourse without interrupting it. It is a step in the direction of discontinuity: of organizing blocks of discourse simultaneously in space rather than consecutively in time.' Hugh Kenner, *The Stoic Comedians: Flaubert, Joyce, and Beckett* (Berkeley, CA: University of California Press, 1962), pp. 39–40.

18. Printing enhances our sense of both types of supplementary information: the footnote by means of economy of type, the digression or interruption by excessive expenditure of type through repetition – as with several examples involving Trim, including the narrative of 'The King of Bohemia and his Seven Castles' during the telling of which the title – formally centred on the page – is reprinted five times (VIII. XIX: 683–90). The narratological problem of attributing repetition to diegetic or mimetic levels in these and many other instances in *Tristram Shandy* needs further study.

19. There is critical disagreement about Sterne's dashes, centring around their meaning in either an oral/aural or visual context. For example, Michael Vande Berg notes that the English tradition of rhetorical pointing, which sees the visual as a script or score for the aural, was still current in Sterne's day. ' "Pictures of Pronunciation": Typographical Travels through *Tristram Shandy* and *Jacques le fataliste*', *Eighteenth-Century Studies* 21: 1 (1987): 23–4. On the other hand, Roger B. Moss argues that Sterne's punctuation forces a recognition of the disjunction of the aural and visual. 'Sterne's Punctuation', *Eighteenth-Century Studies* 15: 2 (1981–82): 180–1, and *passim*. Moss discusses the dash in similar terms, insisting on the unreadability of space in the novel (pp. 195–8). Yet, despite a declared interest in space, Moss discusses the dash as if its impact were identical in any context. Most critics argue that the dash opens up the text, but the nature of 'text' remains undefined – it is most often an abstraction rather than the printed object. Is the spatiality created by the dash maintained in the translation of the first edition into modern forms? Or do critics discuss their *idea* of the effect of the dash, conceived apart from the page?

20. Both John Traugott, *Tristram Shandy's World: Sterne's Philosophical Rhetoric* (Berkeley, CA: University of California Press, 1954), p. 115, and Helen Ostovich, 'Reader as Hobby-Horse in *Tristram Shandy*', *New Casebooks: The Life and Opinions of Tristram Shandy, Gentleman: Laurence Sterne*, ed. Melvyn New (London: Macmillan, 1992), 164–5, see Mrs Shandy's silence as an active rhetorical technique. Ostovich connects the 'beds of justice' conversation to Tristram's relationship with the female reader. Further references to feminist accounts of Mrs Shandy's silence appear in Ostovich's notes.

21. This is De Voogd's way of describing the difference between the first and modern editions (p. 385). The 'beds of justice' chapter averages approximately 81 words per page in contrast to about 125 per page in Vols I and II. Because the Florida Edition maintains the double space between paragraphs, the ratio of first edition pages to

Florida pages remains consistent with the other chapters: two to one. Many of this chapter's short paragraphs, however, appear as single lines in the Florida Edition.

22. De Voogd, p. 387.

23. This is the suggestion of Monkman in appendix 5 of the Florida Edition, pp. 929, 933.

24. In the dedication to Vol. I, for example, this repetition has the power to make 'one' appear three: the author shall think himself 'perhaps much happier than any [one] one (one only excepted).' I have supplied the catchword in square brackets.

25. Compare this chapter's ratio of 6 catchwords to its 563 words of text with, for example, the 4 catchwords and 630 words of text in Vol. II, chap. vi.

26. I wish to thank David Richter for comments on an earlier version of this essay.

Notes on Authors

CHRISTOPHER FANNING is Professor of English at Queen's University, Kingston, Ontario, Canada. His published writings in the areas of eighteenth-century poetry, prose, rhetoric and print culture include articles on Sterne's sermons, the pulpit rhetoric of Swift and Sterne, and Mary Barber.

CAROL HOULIHAN FLYNN is Professor of English at Tufts University, where she is also the Director of American Studies. Her scholarly works include *Samuel Richardson: A Man of Letters* (1982) and *The Body in Swift and Defoe* (1990). Her novel *Washed in the Blood* was published in 1983.

HEATHER JACKSON is Professor of English at the University of Toronto. Her main work has been in scholarly editing, especially as co-editor of two volumes of *Shorter Works and Fragments* (1995) and as editor of Volumes Three to Six of *Marginalia* (1992–2001) in the standard Bollingen Edition of the *Collected Works of Samuel Taylor Coleridge*. Her most recent publication has been the widely admired *Marginalia: Readers Writing in Books* (2001).

JONATHAN LAMB is Professor of English at the University of Princeton. He is the author of a number of articles on Sterne. His books include *Sterne's Fiction and the Double Principle* (1989), *The Rhetoric of Suffering: Reading The Book of Job in the Eighteenth Century* (1995) and, most recently, a study of eighteenth-century European exploration, *Preserving the Self in the South Seas, 1680–1840* (2001).

JULIET MCMASTER is Professor Emerita at the University of Alberta, Canada. She has written widely on eighteenth- and nineteenth-century literature. Her books include *Thackeray: The Major Novels* (1971), *Jane Austen on Love* (1978), *Trollope's Palliser Novels* (1978), *Dickens the Designer* (1987) and (with R. D. McMaster) *The Novel from Sterne to James* (1981).

J. HILLIS MILLER is Distinguished Professor of English and Comparative Literature in the University of California, Irvine. He previously was Professor at Johns Hopkins and Yale Universities. A key figure in American deconstruction, Professor Hillis Miller has published widely in the fields of nineteenth- and twentieth-century English and American literature, comparative literature and literary theory. His numerous books include *Fiction and Repetition* (1982); *The Ethics of Reading: Kant, de Man, Eliot, Trollope, James, and Benjamin* (1987); *Victorian Subjects* (1990); *Tropes, Parables, Performatives* (1990); *Theory*

Now and Then (1990); *Ariadne's Thread* (1992); *Illustration* (1992); *New Starts: Performative Topographies in Literature and Criticism* (1993); *Topographies* (1994); *Reading Narrative* (1998).

JOHN MULLAN, Senior Lecturer in English at University College London, is the author of *Sentiment and Sociability: The Language of Feeling in the Eighteenth Century* (1988). He has published on Defoe, Richardson and Sterne, and has recently edited Defoe for Oxford World's Classics (*Roxana* and *Memoirs of a Cavalier*). He is a regular reviewer and columnist in the *Guardian*.

MELVYN NEW is Professor of English at the University of Florida, and almost officially the doyen of Sterne studies. With Joan New, Richard A. Davies and W. G. Day he edited the Florida University Press *Tristram Shandy* (Text 1978, Notes 1986). His edition of Sterne's Sermons, volumes 4 and 5 of the Florida edition, appeared in 1996. His other publications on Sterne include numerous articles, the ground-breaking book *Laurence Sterne as Satirist* (1969) and the edited collections *Approaches to Teaching 'Tristram Shandy'* (1989), *Tristram Shandy: Contemporary Critical Essays* (1992) and *Critical Essays on Laurence Sterne* (1998).

RUTH PERRY is Professor of Literature at the Massachusetts Institute of Technology, and founder (in 1984) and first Director of the Women's Studies Programme there. Her books include *Women, Letters, and the Novel* (1981) and *The Celebrated Mary Astell* (1986). She is co-editor of a volume of essays on nurturing creativity, *Mothering the Mind* (1984).

EVE KOSOFSKY SEDGWICK is Distinguished Professor of English in the Graduate School of the City University of New York, and previously was Newman Ivey White Professor of English at Duke University. She is a poet, and a leading figure in gay and lesbian literatures, and queer theory. Her *Between Men: English Literature and Male Homosocial Desire* (1985) was a ground-breaking text in gender studies and men's studies. Her other major publications include *Epistemology of the Closet* (1990), *Tendencies* (1993) and *Dialogue on Love* (1999).

Further Reading

𝒵

EDITIONS

NEW, MELVYN and JOAN NEW (eds) *The Life and Opinions of Tristram Shandy, Gentleman: The Text* (Gainesville, FLA: University of Florida Press, 1978 (Volumes 1 and 2)). *The Notes*, ed. MELVYN NEW, with RICHARD A. DAVIES and W. G. DAY (Gainesville, FLA: University of Florida Press, 1984 (Volume 3)). The definitive scholarly edition, with authoritative and beautifully presented text, and explanatory notes of enormous fullness and scholarship. Indispensable.

NEW, MELVYN and JOAN NEW *The Life and Opinions of Tristram Shandy, Gentleman* (London: Penguin Books, 1997). With notes based on those of the Florida edition. Currently the best affordable edition.

STOUT, GARDNER D. (ed.) *A Sentimental Journey* (Berkeley, CA: University of California Press, 1967). The first scholarly edition of the *Journey*; the definitive Florida University Press edition of the *Journey* is imminent.

BIBLIOGRAPHIES

HARTLEY, LODWICK *Laurence Sterne in the Twentieth Century: An Essay and a Bibliography of Sternean Studies, 1900–1965* (Chapel Hill, NC: University of North Carolina Press, 1966).

HARTLEY, LODWICK *Laurence Sterne: An Annotated Bibliography, 1965–1977* (Boston, MA: G.K. Hall, 1978).

BIOGRAPHIES

CASH, ARTHUR H. *Laurence Sterne: The Early and Middle Years* (London: Methuen, 1975).

CASH, ARTHUR H. *Laurence Sterne: The Later Years* (London: Methuen, 1986).

CROSS, WILBUR L. *The Life and Times of Laurence Sterne* (New York: Macmillan, 1909; rev. edn New Haven, CT: Yale University Press, 1925, 1929).

ROSS, IAN CAMPBELL *Laurence Sterne: A Life* (Oxford: Oxford University Press, 2001).

BOOKS

HOLTZ, WILLIAM V. *Image and Immortality: a Study of Tristram Shandy* (Providence, RI: Brown University Press, 1970). In this learned and elegantly written book Holtz examines Sterne's interest in the visual arts, especially the works and writings of Hogarth, in relation to issues of realism and visual experience.

HOWES, ALAN B. *Sterne: the Critical Heritage* (London: Routledge, 1974). A full account, with extended extracts from criticism and commentary, of the reception of Sterne's novel from its publication onwards.

ISER, WOLFGANG *Laurence Sterne: Tristram Shandy* (Cambridge: Cambridge University Press, 1988). A reader-response analysis from this leading practitioner.

LAMB, JONATHAN *Sterne's Fiction and the Double Principle* (Cambridge: Cambridge University Press, 1989). The most challenging and ambitious full-length study of recent years, placing Sterne's rhetorical techniques of doubleness, suggestion, incompleteness and digression squarely within the intellectual context, especially the sceptical context, available to Sterne, in a discussion nonetheless everywhere deeply informed by modern principles and ideas, most notably from Derrida and Freud.

LOVERIDGE, MARK *Laurence Sterne and the Argument about Design* (London and New York: Macmillan and Barnes Noble, 1982). Sterne in the light of general Augustan and post-Augustan concepts of form and design. Perhaps most original and suggestive in its chapter on 'Sterne and the Scientific Study of Man'.

MOGLEN, HELENE *The Philosophical Irony of Laurence Sterne* (Gainesville, FLA: University Presses of Florida, 1975). The most thoroughgoing attempt to portray Sterne as a serious philosophic mind, a deep and creative reader of Locke, rather than merely a parodist and gadfly, and (by reason of that seriousness) a creator of the 'stream of consciousness' novel, and a forerunner of Bergson, James and Freud.

NEW, MELVYN *Laurence Sterne as Satirist: a Reading of Tristram Shandy* (Gainesville, FLA: University of Florida Press, 1969). An important and innovative book, arguing (in contrast with Moglen) that *Tristram* is not a psychological novel but a late Augustan satire, endorsing rationalist and Latitudinarian values, in which Yorick is a moral norm and satiric persona, while Tristram is the butt and target of satire, an ironized voice, riding his hobby-horse, resisting restraint and rule.

ROWSON, MARTIN *The Life and Opinions of Tristram Shandy, Gentleman* (London: Picador, 1996). A cartoon version of *Tristram*, in the light of modern ('Oliver Stone's *Tristram Shandy*', for instance) as well as eighteenth-century cultural issues, and as subtle and witty an account as the novel has received for a while. In its (negative) way a penetrating examination of the relation of *Tristram* and Theory. A remarkable and entirely unmissable creative and intellectual achievement.

TRAUGOTT, JOHN *Tristram Shandy's World: Sterne's Philosophical Rhetoric* (Berkeley, CA: University of California Press, 1954). A difficult and important book which argues that *Tristram* is a deliberate and powerful misreading of Locke, making space for a world not always rational, in which human beings may communicate by a private, often sentimental, often non-verbal rhetoric.

COLLECTIONS OF ESSAYS

BLOOM, HAROLD (ed.) *Laurence Sterne's Tristram Shandy*. Modern Critical Interpretations Series (New York: Chelsea House, 1987). Includes essays by van Ghent, Price, Paulson, Watt, Battestin, Alter and Max Byrd.

CASH, ARTHUR H. and JOHN M. STEDMOND (eds) *The Winged Skull: Papers from the Laurence Sterne Bicentenary Conference* (Kent, Ohio: Kent State University Press, 1971). Papers delivered at the University of York in 1968, by R. F. Brissenden, Jean-Jacques Mayoux, Denis Donoghue, Malcolm Bradbury, William Holtz, Helene Moglen, Clarence Tracy, Kenneth Monkman, Pat Rogers and others.

MYER, VALERIE GROSVENOR (ed.) *Laurence Sterne: Riddles and Mysteries* (London and Totowa, NJ: Vision and Barnes & Noble, 1984). Eleven informed and informative essays, divided into sections on 'Sex, Laughter and Death', 'The Intellectual Background' and 'Interpretation', with an 'Afterword' on Sterne and Austen.

NEW, MELVYN (ed.) *Approaches to Teaching Sterne's Tristram Shandy* (New York: MLA, 1989). Very much worth seeking out for its brief and lively essays by experienced and reflective scholars and teachers, all of them keenly aware of contemporary theoretical as well as pedagogical issues.

NEW, MELVYN (ed.) *Critical Essays on Laurence Sterne* (New York: G. K. Hall). Major collection for a scholarly audience of previously published and specially written new essays.

NEW, MELVYN (ed.) *New Casebooks: Tristram Shandy* (Basingstoke: Macmillan, 1992). Eight important essays published between 1951 and 1989.

PIERCE, DAVID and PETER DE VOOGD (eds) *Laurence Sterne in Modernism and Postmodernism* (Amsterdam: Rodopi, 1996). Adventurous essays on Sterne in the twentieth century, including comparisons with Proust, Joyce, Beckett, Nabokov, Kundera and Rushdie.

ARTICLES, CHAPTERS, ESSAYS

BENSTOCK, SHARI 'At the Margin of Discourse: Footnotes in the Fictional Text', *PMLA* 98 (1983): 204–25. A postmodern, deconstructive examination of the footnote as evidence of uncertain authority, as a rhetorical device which exposes authorial doubt even as it claims authority. Discusses *Tristram*, as well as *Tom Jones* and *Finnegan's Wake*. Does not, however, attempt to relate Sterne's procedures to practices of scholarly commentary in his own time or earlier.

BYRD, MAX 'Sterne and Swift: Augustan Continuities' in *Johnson and his Age*, ed. James Engell (Harvard English Studies, 12) (Cambridge, MA and London: Harvard University Press, 1984), pp. 509–29.

EHLERS, LEIGH A. 'Mrs Shandy's "Lint and Basilicon": the Importance of Women in *Tristram Shandy*', *South Atlantic Review* 46 (1981): 61–75. An important contribution to one of the most productive and active debates in recent Sterne criticism, whose other participants have included McMaster, Ostovich, Rabb, Loscocco, Perry.

FAIRER, DAVID 'Sentimental Translation in Mackenzie and Sterne', *Essays in Criticism* 49 (1999): 132–51. Sentimental understanding and exchange in two of the eighteenth century's key exponents of these themes.

FLORES, RALPH 'Changeling Fathering: *Tristram Shandy*' in Flores's *The Rhetoric of Doubtful Authority: Deconstructive Readings of Self-Questioning Narratives, St Augustine to Faulkner* (Ithaca, NY and London: Cornell

University Press, 1984). The last two sections of this chapter provide a detailed deconstructive rhetorical analysis of issues of identity, knowledge, paternity and authority in *Tristram*.

FRANK, JUDITH ' "A Man Who Laughs is Never Dangerous": Character and Class in Sterne's *A Sentimental Journey*', *ELH* 56 (1989): 97–124. A materialist consideration of class, sentiment and Sterne. Yorick is the bourgeois subject whose acts of imagination and characterization are seen as forms of social coercion and control.

HARRIES, ELIZABETH W. 'Sterne's Novels: Gathering up the Fragments', *ELH* 49 (1982): 35–49. Harries finds in Sterne's uses of fragments and the fragmentary not a pre-figuring of the modern but tendencies in Sterne's own intellectual world, themselves originating in Christ's injunction to the disciples to 'gather up the fragments that remain, that nothing be lost' (John 6: 12–13). Reprinted in New's 1992 collection.

HAWLEY, JUDITH '"Hints and Documents": A Bibliography for *Tristram Shandy*', a two-part essay published in *The Shandean* 3 (1991): 9–36; 4 (1992): 49–65. A thorough and valuable 'pseudo-bibliography' of books mentioned in *Tristram*, following a scholarly tradition initiated by Ferriar's *Illustrations of Sterne* (1798).

HAWLEY, JUDITH 'The Anatomy of *Tristram Shandy*' in Marie Mulvey Roberts and Roy Porter (eds), *Literature and Medicine during the Eighteenth Century* (London and New York: Routledge, 1993), pp. 84–100. An illuminating essay on the sources of Sterne's medical and obstetric knowledge, from Burton, Rabelais, Smellie, Chambers and others.

HUNTER, J. PAUL 'From Typology to Type: Agents of Change in Eighteenth-Century English Texts' in Margaret J. M. Ezell and Katherine O'Brien O'Keeffe, *Cultural Artifacts and the Production of Meaning: the Page, the Image, and the Body* (Ann Arbor, MI: University of Michigan Press, 1994), pp. 41–69. A ground-breaking contribution, for eighteenth-century studies, to our new concern with the materiality and social conditions of production of the literary (and non-literary) text, examining 'how broadly, how quickly, and how lastingly textual change is effected by technological moves', with reference to Pope's *Dunciad* and *Tristram Shandy*.

JEFFERSON, DOUGLAS '*Tristram Shandy* and the Tradition of Learned Wit', *Essays in Criticism* 1 (1951): 225–48. One of the most significant articles ever written on Sterne, discussing the relation of *Tristram* to scholastic and humanist wit, and especially to Rabelais, Cervantes, Montaigne and Swift. Reprinted in New's 1992 collection.

KAY, CAROL 'Sterne: Scenes of Play' in her *Political Constructions: Defoe, Richardson, and Sterne in Relation to Hobbes, Hume, and Burke* (Ithaca, NY: Cornell University Press, 1988), pp. 195–263. A witty and stimulating chapter devoted to *A Sentimental Journey* and (mostly) *Tristram*, considered in relation to Hobbesian ideas, including social 'compleasance'. Includes illuminating discussions of Whig and sexual politics.

KEYMER, THOMAS 'Narratives of Loss: *Tristram Shandy* and the *Poems of Ossian*' in Melvyn New (ed.), *Critical Essays on Laurence Sterne*, 1998, pp. 68–83. A remarkable work of critical insight, linking Macpherson's 'Fingal' poems and Sterne's great novel – two works apparently quite dissimilar – on the basis of their shared 'melancholy sense of the instability of language', and their vain attempt to recover a fugitive past.

KEYMER, THOMAS 'Dying by Numbers: *Tristram Shandy* and Serial Fiction', a two-part essay, published in *The Shandean* 8 (1996): 41–67; 9 (1997): 34–69. In this wide-ranging study Keymer deals with Samuel Richardson, Tobias Smollett and George Eliot as well as Sterne, and provides the best and fullest account of the context and implications of *Tristram*'s publication as an 'unstable, ongoing process, orchestrated as such by Sterne, recognized as such by his audience of the 1760s'.

LANDRY, DONNA and GERALD MACLEAN 'Of Forceps, Patents, and Paternity: *Tristram Shandy*', *Eighteenth-Century Studies* 23 (1989–90): 522–43. A highly theorized and densely scholarly analysis of Tristram's birth in relation to seventeenth- and eighteenth-century obstetrics and midwifery, which negotiates new historicist and materialist–feminist readings.

LOSCOCCO, PAULA 'Can't Live Without 'em: Walter Shandy and the Woman Within', *The Eighteenth Century* 32 (1991): 166–79. A response to (some have suggested, a refutation of) Ruth Perry's essay printed here. Argues that *Tristram* is not only a man's book but also, and deliberately, a failed book.

MCMASTER, JULIET 'Walter Shandy, Sterne, and Gender: a Feminist Foray', *English Studies in Canada* 15 (1989): 441–58.

MARKLEY, ROBERT 'Sentimentality as Performance: Shaftesbury, Sterne, and the Theatrics of Virtue' in Felicity Nussbaum and Laura Brown (eds), *The New Eighteenth Century: Theory, Politics, English Literature* (New York and London: Methuen, 1987). A historicist and Marxizing reading, locating sensibility in eighteenth-century historical circumstance. Tellingly relates Sterne's presentation of sensibility to the class implications of Shaftesbury's writings.

MARKLEY, ROBERT 'Tristram Shandy and "Narrative Middles": Hillis Miller and the Style of Deconstructive Criticism' in Robert Con Davis and Ronald Schleifer (eds), *Rhetoric and Form: Deconstruction at Yale* (Norman, OK: University of Oklahoma Press, 1985). A discussion, and exposition, of Miller's essay as a characteristically American exercise in rhetorical deconstruction, briefly considering *Tristram*.

MOSS, ROGER B. 'Sterne's Punctuation', *Eighteenth-Century Studies* 15 (1981–2): 179–200. An important study of Sterne's typography and its effect on reading.

NEW, MELVYN 'Sterne and the Narrative of Determinateness', *Eighteenth-Century Fiction* 4 (1992): 315–29. In response to Miller and Markley, and to Flores and Smyth, re-asserts that, for all Sterne's scepticism, his writing evinces the 'drive to order and comprehend'.

NEW, MELVYN 'Sterne, Warburton, and the Burden of Exuberant Wit', *Eighteenth-Century Studies* 15 (1982): 245–74. An essay specialized in theme but nevertheless broadly suggestive, discussing two opposite anxieties in Sterne: that he could only vainly aspire to the wit of his models Rabelais, Cervantes, Montaigne, Burton and Swift; and that his wit might itself give offence to Anglican seriousness and decency, as represented by the powerful and daunting figure of William Warburton, Bishop of Gloucester.

OSTOVICH, HELEN 'Reader as Hobby-Horse in *Tristram Shandy*', *Philological Quarterly* 68 (1989): 325–42. An account of Sterne's 'literary intercourse with the reader', more especially the female reader, drawing on reader-response and feminist theory. Reprinted in New's 1992 collection.

PARNELL, TIM 'Sterne and Kundera: The Novel of Variations and the "noisy foolishness of human certainty"', in David Pierce and David de Voogd (eds), *Laurence Sterne in Modernism and Postmodernism* (Amsterdam: Rodopi, 1993), pp. 147–55. Interrogates too-easy accommodations of Sterne to postmodern notions of narrative and semantic indeterminacy, and insists on the particularly contemporary nature of his scepticism.

PARNELL, TIM 'Swift, Sterne, and the Skeptical Tradition', *Studies in Eighteenth-Century Culture* 23 (1994): 221–42. A masterly and forceful article, elaborating Sterne's relation to the European Christian sceptical tradition of Erasmus, Rabelais and Montaigne, as well as Swift. Reprinted in Melvyn New's 1998 collection.

RABB, MELINDA ALLIKER 'Engendering Accounts in Sterne's *A Sentimental Journey*' in *Johnson and his Age*, ed. James Engell (Harvard English Studies, 12) (Cambridge, MA and London: Harvard University Press, 1984), pp. 531–58. On language and gender, the masculine nature of travel and the novel's exploration of metaphors of exchange, from a rigorous and subtle feminist perspective, and usefully one of a relatively small number of pieces which discuss the *Journey*.

ROGERS, PAT '*Tristram Shandy's* Polite Conversation', *Essays in Criticism* 32 (1982): 305–20. In the context of a debate about the methodology of annotation of English novels, discusses the use by Sterne of the kind of proverbial discourse to be found in Swift's 'Polite conversation'.

ROGERS, PAT 'Ziggerzagger Shandy: Sterne and the Aesthetics of the Crooked Line', *English* 42 (1993): 97–107. On the zig-zag line in Shandy, and elsewhere in the eighteenth century. Thematically commensurate with Hillis Miller's essay reprinted here, but in no way deconstructive in approach.

SMYTH, JOHN VIGNAUX 'Sterne: Rhetoric and Representation' and 'Philosophy of the Nose' in his *A Question of Eros: Irony in Sterne, Kierkegaard, and Barthes* (Tallahassee, FLA: Florida State University Press, 1986), pp. 13–98. An analysis of Sternean irony, rhetoric and semantic suggestion, with marked deconstructive tendencies.

SPACKS, PATRICIA M. 'The Beautiful Oblique: *Tristram Shandy*' in her *Imagining a Self: Autobiography and the Novel in Eighteenth-Century England* (Cambridge, MA: Harvard University Press, 1976), pp. 127–57. A significant essay in one of the major book-length studies of the interpenetrating relationship between the autobiographical and the fictional in Sterne's period.

SHKLOVSKY, VIKTOR 'A Parodying Novel: Sterne's *Tristram Shandy*' in John Traugott (ed.), *A Collection of Critical Essays* (Englewood Cliffs, NJ: Prentice Hall, 1968), pp. 66–89. Translated by W. George Isaak from Shklovsky's *O Teorii Prozy* (Moscow, 1929). A famous formalist essay which has been lastingly provocative and influential.

TUVESON, ERNEST 'Locke and Sterne' in J. A. Mazzeo (ed.), *Reason and Imagination: Studies in the History of Ideas, 1600–1800* (New York: Columbia University Press, 1962), pp. 255–77. An essential contribution to this debate, squaring one of the most obdurate circles in Sterne criticism. Tuveson parallels Sterne and Rabelais, to whom 'the new learning of the Renaissance provided a lever by which he could move the mass of dead ideas', and suggests that Sterne similarly found in Locke not only such principles of mental functioning as association, but an anti-scholastic and anti-metaphysical 'liberating force'.

WATTS, CAROL 'The Modernity of *Tristram Shandy*', *The Shandean* 6 (1994): 99–118. Watts acknowledges that *Tristram* 'appears to demonstrate many of the formal characteristics associated with postmodernist fiction', but advocates 'an understanding of modernity less in terms of its location as a specific historical period in which Tristram Shandy discovers himself than as what Michel Foucault calls an "attitude" to contemporary circumstance'. A revised version of this essay appears in the Pierce/De Voogd collection.

WEHRS, DONALD R. 'Sterne, Cervantes, Montaigne: Fideistic Skepticism and the Rhetoric of Desire', *Comparative Literature Studies* 25 (1988): 127–51. While invoking Bakhtin, Barthes and Lacan, Wehrs finds that the verbal doubleness of *Tristram*, and its persistent refusal of logical solutions and narrative closures, relates to Christian assimilations and adaptations, especially in Erasmus, Montaigne and Cervantes, of classical scepticism. Reprinted in New's 1992 collection.

ZIMMERMAN, EVERETT '*Tristram Shandy* and Narrative Representation', *The Eighteenth Century: Theory and Interpretation* 28 (1987): 127–47. Discusses *Tristram* both from the standpoint of modern textualism, and especially the Derridean questioning of presence, and with a view to the eighteenth-century debate about the status of history, the authority of documents and, above all, scriptural hermeneutics – a synthesis of approaches which intriguingly and suggestively echoes one trend in recent writing on Swift. Reprinted in New's 1992 collection.

Index